Broadcasting the Faith

Broadcasting the Faith

Protestant Religious Radio and Theology in America, 1920–50

MICHAEL E. POHLMAN

WIPF & STOCK · Eugene, Oregon

BROADCASTING THE FAITH
Protestant Religious Radio and Theology in America, 1920–50

Copyright © 2021 Michael E. Pohlman. All rights reserved. Except for brief quotations in critical publications or reviews, no part of this book may be reproduced in any manner without prior written permission from the publisher. Write: Permissions, Wipf and Stock Publishers, 199 W. 8th Ave., Suite 3, Eugene, OR 97401.

Wipf & Stock
An Imprint of Wipf and Stock Publishers
199 W. 8th Ave., Suite 3
Eugene, OR 97401

www.wipfandstock.com

PAPERBACK ISBN: 978-1-7252-9082-2
HARDCOVER ISBN: 978-1-7252-9083-9
EBOOK ISBN: 978-1-7252-9084-6

02/01/21

For Anna, a gift beyond measure and radiant example of how God has not dealt with me according to my sin.

Contents

Preface ix

1 Introduction 1

2 "Modernism's Moses" 16
  Harry Emerson Fosdick and Radio's *National Vespers*

3 Aimee Semple McPherson 41
  Radio Superstar of the Foursquare Gospel

4 Broadcasting Orthodoxy 77
  Walter Maier and the *Lutheran Hour*

5 "All We Do Is Toward Evangelism" 106
  Charles E. Fuller and the *Old Fashioned Revival Hour*

6 The Church in a Digital Age 139

Bibliography 143

Index 163

Preface

As this book goes to print the American church has endured nearly a year of COVID-19 resulting from a global pandemic. For long periods of time local churches had to shut their doors and resort to shepherding their people virtually. Churches great and small were forced to embrace technology like never before. Sunday morning corporate worship had to be streamed through Facebook or YouTube, sermons and Bible studies recorded and posted to websites and social media platforms, church apps rolled out, and Zoom calls and texting used in place of in-person meetings. Concerning to at least this observer is the seemingly uncritical embrace of technology by the church—as if theology in America is not at stake.

It would be naïve to think that the church's use of technology will not have long-term effects on what the church believes. Indeed, theology in America will be altered as a result of the faith being translated through various technologies with such ubiquity. To what extent theology is transformed will be seen over time.

Broadcasting the Faith is greatly relevant for our day as it studies a particular period in American religious history when the church uncritically embraced technology, specifically the technology of radio. It is, therefore, a cautionary tale with much to teach the contemporary church.

This book began in seed form in a PhD seminar on early twentieth century American evangelicalism. At this time my scholarly interests were in the field of American Puritan studies. But as I explored riveting subjects such as the fundamentalist-modernist controversy, its context and aftermath, and the fascinating cast of characters involved in this consequential event for American religious history, I began to experience an intellectual tug-of-war. You might say Perry Miller, Francis Bremer, Janice Knight, and David Hall lost this tug-of-war to George Marsden, Mark Noll, Nathan Hatch, and D. G. Hart.

Broadcasting the Faith could not have been completed without the generous support of many people. Professor Gregory Wills championed the idea from the beginning and helped me refine the thesis by challenging me to read widely and think critically. He pushed me to write tightly and labor to ensure that every sentence serves the purpose of advancing my argument. Where this does not happen, the fault lies only with me. Several other faculty members of The Southern Baptist Theological Seminary gave me invaluable academic training. These include David Puckett, Thomas Nettles, Gregg Allison, Shawn Wright, and Russell Moore. I owe a special debt of gratitude to R. Albert Mohler Jr. for the "seminars" he led me through over three years of serving as his executive producer. His unwavering standard of excellence has indelibly marked me.

My research was made more profitable than it otherwise would have been because of the expert help and patience of several archivists around the country. These include Ruth Tonkiss Cameron at Columbia University and Union Theological Seminary, Jackie Miller of the International Church of the Foursquare Gospel, Marvin Huggins at the Concordia Historical Institute, Nancy Gower at Fuller Seminary, and Steve Wejroch of the Archdiocese of Detroit.

No words can adequately express my gratitude for my in-laws Steve and Kathy Ovenell and their constant support. The same can be said of Cary and Barbara Young, for whom "friends" is far too weak a word. To my deep regret, my dad, Jerry, passed away before this book was complete. I owe him more than I could ever say. His memory continues to inspire me. Finally, I thank my wife and children. When I see them, I see the love and grace of God. On earth I have no greater treasure.

MICHAEL E. POHLMAN
Louisville, Kentucky
January 2021

1

Introduction

FROM THE EARLIEST DAYS of radio broadcasting, the zeal of religious Americans to use this medium of communication to propagate their faith also altered their faith. Historians have sometimes overlooked religion's presence in radio's infancy. However, the interrelationship between religion and radio was profoundly significant for both.

In the beginning of radio there was religion. Five years after 1901, when the Italian inventor Guglielmo Marconi successfully sent a radio signal across the Atlantic Ocean, the Canadian-born Reginald A. Fessenden conducted the first voice broadcast from Brant Rock, Massachusetts. The Christmas Eve broadcast, December 24, 1906, included "O Holy Night" on the violin and a reading from Luke 2. Church leaders recognized that radio presented an extraordinary opportunity to reach new audiences with the message of the gospel. By the early 1920s churches throughout America were broadcasting their message by radio. Although such important figures in the history of radio as Samuel Morse, Alexander Graham Bell, Heinrich Hertz, Guglielmo Marconi, Reginald Fessenden, and Lee DeForest are remembered, religion's role in the history of radio is neglected.

This book argues that religious radio in America sought to counter the secularization of American culture, but did so in a way that contributed to secularization by accelerating changes already evident in American religion, both conservative and liberal. Religious leaders sought to use radio to extend religious faith among the American people and to extend religious influence in American society. By some measures it succeeded admirably. The success, however, came at a cost. To reach the vast American audience, radio preachers transformed their sectarian messages into a religion more suitable to the masses. This was one of the unintended consequences of American religious radio. In seeking to preserve the influence of religion in American culture, religious broadcasters altered the religion they aimed to preserve.

"Modern broadcasting," observes Dennis Voskuil, "can be traced to 1912 when the United States Congress passed and President Taft signed the initial radio licensing law."[1] Eight years later, on November 1, 1920, Westinghouse Electric and Manufacturing Company established radio station KDKA in Pittsburgh, Pennsylvania. KDKA was the first station to feature nonexperimental broadcasts. It was also the first station to carry a regular radio broadcast of a church service:

> By January 2, 1921, KDKA was attempting a remote broadcast from the Pittsburgh Calvary Episcopal Church. Two Westinghouse engineers, one Jewish and one Catholic, were dressed in choir robes to handle the technical aspects of production, which involved three microphones. The Reverend Jan Van Etten felt all this symbolized the "universality of radio religion."[2]

From these humble beginnings the radio industry grew rapidly. By 1927 there were over seven hundred stations and over six million receiving sets. Erik Barnouw rightly compares the frenzy to embrace radio broadcasting to the Oklahoma land rush or the California gold rush.[3] Church leaders joined the radio rush. They embraced radio widely during the 1920s, though few church-owned stations survived the Great Depression. The Radio Act of 1927, an attempt by the federal government to bring order to the burgeoning radio industry, "led to the adoption of new technical standards (assigned frequencies, regular schedules, better equipment) for operating stations. Unable to afford the required equipment or personnel, religious stations sold off their licenses to private owners."[4]

This did not stop religion from making its way to the airwaves. Mainline Protestants were able to secure free time, also known as sustaining time, through cooperation with the Federal Council of Churches of Christ. Radio

---

1. Voskuil, "Reaching Out," 81.
2. Barnouw, *Tower of Babel*, 1:71.
3. Barnouw, *Tower of Babel*, 4.
4. Voskuil, "Reaching Out," 82.

networks such as the National Broadcasting Company (NBC) and the Columbia Broadcasting Company (CBS) were formed in the 1920s. These networks worked closely with the Federal Council (and local councils of churches such as the Greater New York Federation of Churches) to secure religious programming for their audiences.

Mainline Protestants dominated the most valuable airtime available to religious broadcasting, but they could not prevent other groups from crowding in. Fundamentalist Protestants produced programs that attracted significant radio audiences. In the 1920s fundamentalist radio preachers included Paul Radar in Chicago, John Roach Straton at Calvary Baptist Church in New York, Walter Maier and station KFUO in St. Louis, and Aimee Semple McPherson and station KFSG in Los Angeles. In 1928 Donald Grey Barnhouse became the first fundamentalist to have a regular program on a national network when CBS began broadcasting the Bible Study Hour weekly. The Bible Institute of Los Angeles (Biola) and Moody Bible Institute were fundamentalist schools that established their own radio stations. Biola began broadcasting from station KJS in 1922, and Moody opened WMBI in 1925. Mainline Protestant radio broadcasting declined in popularity in the 1930s and 1940s, but fundamentalist radio flourished, due in part to its remarkable ability to adapt programming to the marketplace. Fundamentalists in the 1930s and evangelicals in the 1940s accused the Federal Council of working with the networks to limit airtime to "nonestablishment" religious groups. To meet this threat, the National Association of Evangelicals was formed in 1942. In 1944 evangelical broadcasters established the National Religious Broadcasters to work in concert with the National Association of Evangelicals to further their radio interests.

The prominent radio preachers, both liberal and conservative, proclaimed rather diverse interpretations of the Christian message, and yet together they found millions of people receptive to their message. Radio religion may have accelerated the privatization of religion, but radio helped ensure that the voice of religion continued to shape the culture during some of the most tumultuous decades in our nation's history. This work will show that radio acted as what Peter Berger calls a "resistance movement"—a movement that sought to counter secularization in American culture.[5]

Broadcasting the faith, however, changed it. To make religion accessible to the masses, radio preachers accommodated their messages in ways suited to the medium of radio. Sectarianism and controversial polemics seemed ill suited to building audiences of sufficient size to answer radio's potential. All the prominent radio preachers made their peace with the

---

5. Berger, "From the Crisis" 16.

constraints of broadcast media and embraced a nonsectarian approach. The radio preachers who did not comply had to settle for reaching small audiences. However, the medium itself seemed ill spent on the few. It was a tool suited to reaching the many, a purpose inconsistent with sectarian preaching. Charles Fuller distanced himself from militant fundamentalism and achieved an enormous audience. Walter Maier forsook Lutheran particulars to bring "Christ to the nations" and gained a remarkable number of listeners throughout the nation and across denominational boundaries. Harry Emerson Fosdick preached simple virtues to a large, general Christian audience. Aimee Semple McPherson promoted a charismatic ecumenism and became one of the most recognized entertainers in the nation. The most influential voices of religious radio in the period from 1920 to 1950 eschewed substantive theological discourse. Although religious radio was intended to advance the influence of religion in American society, its lack of theological substance ironically promoted the secularization of the American church.

BACKGROUND

Radio studies have attracted some attention in academic circles.[6] Religious radio, however, has received scant attention. This neglect began with Erik Barnouw's three-volume *History of Broadcasting in the United States*, which was published between 1966 and 1970. Aside from a relatively brief section discussing Father Charles Coughlin's political sermons in volume 2, Barnouw neglects the role of religious radio in America. In *Listening In: Radio and the American Imagination*, Susan Douglas attempts to pick up the history where Barnouw left off, but she likewise gives little attention to the subject.[7] Nevertheless, some notable, broad overviews of religious broadcasting have been written.[8] Additionally, shorter studies by Tona Hangen, Quentin Schultze, Dennis Voskuil, and Joel Carpenter have provided helpful

---

6. Doherty, "Return with Us Now to Those Thrilling Days."

7. Douglas, *Listening In*, 52–54. In fact, the closest that Douglas comes to discussing religious radio is a section on "spiritualism" and radio in the early 1920s. Alfred Balk's otherwise helpful *The Rise of Radio* glosses over religious radio except for the expected reference to Father Charles Coughlin and his "anti-Semitic barbs" (224).

8. Hangen, *Redeeming the Dial*; Armstrong, *Electric Church*; Ward, *Air of Salvation*; Hill, *Airwaves to the Soul*.

scholarship on the issue.[9] Several critical biographies of prominent radio preachers have been written,[10] but much of the historiography is uncritical.[11]

SECULARIZATION THEORY

Secularization theory "contends that modernity is intrinsically and irreversibly antagonistic to religion. As a society becomes increasingly modernized, it inevitably becomes less religious."[12] As Steve Bruce argues, "modernization creates problems for religion."[13] Secularization theory does not merely posit a declining importance of religion at the "institutional" level, but also at the level of individual consciousness:

> Although the term "secularization theory" refers to works from the 1950s and 1960s, the key idea of the theory can indeed be traced to the Enlightenment. The idea is simple: Modernization necessarily leads to a decline of religion, both in society and in the minds of individuals.[14]

Likewise, Bruce defines secularization as the erosion of religion's significance at both levels:

> In brief, I see secularization as a social condition manifest in (a) the declining importance of religion for the operation of non-religious roles and institutions such as those of the state and the economy; (b) a decline in the social standing of religious roles and institutions; and (c) a decline in the extent to which people engage in religious practices, display beliefs of a religious kind, and conduct other aspects of their lives in a manner informed by such beliefs.[15]

With its roots in Enlightenment philosophy and seminal work by nineteenth-century social scientists such as Augustus Comte, Herbert Spencer,

---

9. Hangen, "Man of the Hour," 113–34; Schultze, "Evangelical Radio," 289–306; Voskuil, "Power of the Air," 69–95; Carpenter, *Revive Us Again*, 124–40.

10. Brinkley, *Voices of Protest*; Tull, *Father Coughlin and the New Deal*; Marcus, *Father Coughlin*; Warren, *Radio Priest*; Miller, *Harry Emerson Fosdick*; Epstein, *Sister McPherson*; Blumhofer, *Aimee Semple McPherson*; Sutton, *Aimee Semple McPherson*.

11. Maier, *Man Spoke*; Mugglebee, *Father Coughlin*; Smith, *Voice for God*; Daniel P. Fuller, *Give the Winds*.

12. Berger, "From the Crisis," 14.

13. Bruce, *God is Dead*, 2.

14. Berger, "Desecularization of the World," 2.

15. Bruce, *God is Dead*, 3.

Emile Durkheim, Max Weber, Karl Marx, Sigmund Freud, and Friedrich Nietzsche, the secularization thesis assumes that with modernization comes the death of God—or at least the utter insignificance of religion:

> In different ways, elements of that package [of modernization] cause religion to mutate so that it loses social significance.... The bottom line is this: individualism, diversity, and egalitarianism in the context of liberal democracy undermine the authority of religious beliefs.[16]

Furthermore, the theory of religion's irreversible decline has become "practically axiomatic among modern, sophisticated Westerners ... it is an idea that many urbane men and women no longer even think to question, so self-evident does it appear."[17]

Evidence suggests, however, that the "axiomatic" status of the secularization thesis warrants review. For example, even as they propose their own revision of the secularization thesis, Pipa Norris and Ronald Englehart observe that "during the last decade ... this thesis of the slow and steady death of religion has come under growing criticism; indeed, secularization theory is currently experiencing the most sustained challenge in its long history."[18]

The challenges have come from a host of scholars, not least of whom is Peter Berger, a former champion of the secularization thesis: "In recent decades historians, social scientists, and others have debated the validity of secularization theory ... the import of this debate is clear: Modernity may not be as antagonistic to religion as had previously been asserted."[19]

---

16. Bruce, *God is Dead*, 30.

17. Eberstadt, "How the West Really Lost God."

18. Norris and Inglehart, *Sacred and Secular*. The authors contend that "talk of burying the secularization theory is premature," but also that "there is no question that the traditional secularization thesis needs updating. It is obvious that religion has not disappeared from the world, nor does it seem likely to do so. Nevertheless, the concept of secularization captures an important part of what is going on" (4). The authors argue that where modernization has brought high levels of "existential security," secularization will be most measurable. In other words, religious demand is shaped by perceived security: "We predict that the strongest decline in religious participation will occur in affluent and secure nations, where the importance of religion has faded most. By contrast, where religious values remain a vital part of people's everyday lives, in poor agrarian societies, we also expect that people will be most active in worship and prayer" (21). Another modification of the secularization theory comes from Taylor, *Secular Age*. Taylor argues that secularization needs to be understood in terms of "conditions of belief." Secularization happens when a society moves from a condition in which "belief in God is unchallenged and indeed, unproblematic, to one in which it is understood to be one option among others, and frequently not the easiest to embrace." In other words, secularization occurs in a society when belief in God is an "embattled option" (3).

19. Berger, "From the Crisis," 14.

Berger explains, "Precisely to the extent that secularity and pluralism are phenomena of modernity, they are also the targets of miscellaneous countersecular and counterpluralistic 'resistance movements.'"[20] These resistance movements are evident, according to Berger, in "the upsurge of religious movements in the Third World." Such movements are particularly common in Iran. The revival of religion in the former Soviet Union and in the resurgence of evangelical Protestantism in the United States have also contributed to resistance movements.[21] Furthermore, Berger said,

> This interplay of secularizing and counter-secularizing forces is, I would contend, one of the most important topics for a sociology of contemporary religion. . . .
>
> Modernity, for fully understandable reasons, undermines all the old certainties; uncertainty is a condition that many people find very hard to bear; therefore, any movement (not only a religious one) that promises to provide or to renew certainty has a ready market.[22]

For Berger, these countersecular trends, or "resistance movements," are powerful enough to make the secularization thesis nonsensical: "My point is that the assumption that we live in a secularized world is false. The world today . . . is as furiously religious as it ever was, and in some places more so than ever."[23]

Rodney Stark and Roger Finke have led in the scholarly attempt to put the secularization thesis to rest. Unlike Norris and Inglehart, these sociologists of religion leave no room for a modified secularization paradigm: "There is no consistent relationship between religious participation and modernization. Indeed, the very few significant, long-term declines in religious participation to be seen anywhere in the world are greatly outnumbered by remarkable increases. What is needed is not a simple-minded theory of inevitable religious decline, but a theory to explain variation."[24]

---

20. Berger, "From the Crisis," 16.

21. Berger, "From the Crisis," 16–17. On the resurgence of evangelical Protestantism in the US, see Christian Smith, *American Evangelicalism*.

22. Berger, "Desecularization of the World," 7. See also Lester, "Oh Gods!" Lester makes a similar argument by invoking a form of Darwinian evolution to refer to how religion in the world has failed to "whither away on schedule." Relying heavily on the work of Rodney Stark, Lester contends, "Secularization of a sort certainly has occurred in the modern world—but religion seems to keep adapting to new social ecosystems, in a process one might refer to as 'supernatural selection.' It shows no sign of extinction, and 'theodiversity' is, if anything, on the rise."

23. Berger, "Desecularization of the World," 2.

24. Stark and Finke, *Acts of Faith*, 33.

Key to Stark and Finke's argument against secularization is that "change does not equate with decline."[25]

Religious-radio broadcasters countered secularization in the United States from 1920 to 1950, both by extending the reach of religion and by making religion more adaptable to modernization. Religious radio served as a resistance movement to the trends within modernization that threatened to marginalize religion in America. However, even as religious radio promoted religion, it reshaped it. This reshaped religion was a form of secularization, although not secularization in the sense of the inevitable decline of religion in the public and private spheres. Stark and Finke were right when they argued, "change does not equal decline." In terms of secularization, this book argues that while religious adherents may not have declined in America during the 1920–1950 period—in fact, they likely increased due to religious radio—adherents were embracing a more secularized version of religion than what existed in America prior to the advent of radio. Secularization, in this sense, helps explain not quantity of belief as much as the quality or content of belief.

RELIGIOUS TRANSFORMATION

Religious radio promoted the secularization of the American church by accelerating changes already evident in American religion, whether conservative or liberal. One of the changes already evident in American religion at the dawn of radio broadcasting was a movement away from a view of the Bible as definitive revelation from God. As Mark Noll has shown, with the rise of modern critical theories of the Bible in the final third of the nineteenth century, American thinking about the Bible became an "altered landscape."[26] Theological liberalism, popularized by Henry Ward Beecher in the late 1870s in New England, helped pave the way for Harry Emerson Fosdick who, like Beecher, was a theological liberal who "gloried in ambiguity and sentiment."[27] Theology in America in the late 1800s "was no longer viewed as a fixed body of eternally bound truths. It was seen rather as an evolutionary development that should adjust to the standards and needs of modern culture."[28] Radio exposure facilitated the spread of theological liberalism through popular preachers such as New York City pastor Dr. S.

---

25. Stark and Finke, *Acts of Faith*, 78.
26. Noll, *Between Faith and Criticism*.
27. Marsden, *Fundamentalism and American Culture*, 25.
28. Marsden, *Fundamentalism and American Culture*, 25.

Parkes Cadman, who, in 1923, began the *National Radio Pulpit*, and Harry Emerson Fosdick on *National Vespers*.

In responding to modernism, conservative radio preachers transformed American religion in ways consistent with what David Wells calls a "world cliché culture." By this, Wells means a culturally "thin" world where modernity flattens cultures with the weight of the generic, leaving no place for God:

> The sheer ubiquity of this public environment is what makes the naturalistic, materialistic, secular assumptions of everyday modern life seem so axiomatic, so completely beyond reproach. . . . The public sphere, dominated as it is by the omnipresence of bureaucracy, systems of manufacturing, the machinery of capitalism, and the audible confetti spewing out of the countless radios and televisions, makes it virtually impossible to think that in *this* world God has any meaningful place.[29]

Wells's "world cliché culture" is his application of Marshall McLuhan's concept of the "global village" outlined in his groundbreaking work, *Understanding Media*. McLuhan explains how electronic media, and radio in particular, serves to "retribalize mankind," transforming individualism into collectivism.[30] The argument in this work is that, by eschewing substantive theological content, religious radio contributed to a theological minimalism that, ironically, weakened the American church, leaving it more susceptible to the secularizing trends within modernism.

Another trend that religious radio supported was the movement toward religious sentimentalism. The success of McPherson's and Fuller's radio ministry, for example, can be explained in part by their unique ability to help their audiences feel a certain way about religion. Both figures masterfully evoked nostalgic religious feelings among their listeners—a longing for a religious experience free from the trappings of modernism, harkening back to a time when Protestant Christianity was united around the simple proclamation of the gospel.[31]

Religious radio accelerated a movement toward religious celebrity and democratization. American soil has always had its religious celebrities. From the founding of the Colonies, the impulse toward the democratization of religion has been strong. Consider Anne Hutchinson. Additionally,

---

29. Wells, *God in the Wasteland*, 10; emphasis original. Wells began this discussion in *No Place for Truth*, 53–92.

30. McLuhan, *Understanding Media*, 304.

31. Witham, *City upon a Hill*, 223. Witham emphasizes this point, especially as it relates to Fuller's *Old Fashioned Revival Hour*.

eighteenth-century evangelist George Whitefield "can be labeled Anglo-America's first modern celebrity, a preacher capable of commanding mass audiences (and offerings) across two continents, without any institutional support, through the sheer power of his personality."[32] However, as Nathan Hatch observes, this movement toward celebrity and democratization exploded in the wake of the American Revolution.[33] The radio preachers in this study are products of this populist impulse in American culture. The populist ethos in American culture helps account for the tremendous success that the fundamentalist radio preachers had in raising the necessary funds to stay on the air. With the rise of theological liberalism, McPherson, Maier, Fuller, and their peers represented the hope that religion would not be withheld from the rank and file. The democratization of religion in America also pushed radio preachers toward sensationalism to ensure that their programs stayed viable. This is best seen in the rise of McPherson, although Maier and Fuller were not immune to the temptation of sensationalism. As was the case in the decades following the American Revolution, the sovereign audience during the golden age of radio often flocked to "popularity rather than virtue."[34] Popularity was essential if one was to compete in the free marketplace of religion in America.[35]

Not only was popularity necessary, but religion itself needed to be framed in the language of commerce if it was to appeal to increasingly consumer-oriented listeners. Quentin Schultze is right to conclude that evangelicals "had a dynamic, market-sensitive message but little moral vision about the impact of the market on that message."[36] Radio contributed to the commoditization of the faith.[37]

---

32. Stout, *Divine Dramatist*, xiii.

33. Hatch, *Democratization of American Christianity*.

34. Hatch, *Democratization of American Christianity*, 135. Hatch's observation of several early American religious leaders could be said of McPherson as well: "As communicators, upstarts such as Elias Smith, Lorenzo Dow, William Miller, and Joseph Smith were all folk geniuses. They projected a presence that people found inviting, compelling, and authoritative" (134).

35. For a helpful treatment on how our "free marketplace of religion" came into existence, see Lambert, *Founding Fathers and the Place of Religion in America*. Lambert argues, "In deciding the place of religion in the new republic, the Founding Fathers, rather than designing a church-state framework of their own, endorsed the emerging free marketplace of religion" (8).

36. Schultze, *Christianity and the Mass Media*, 164.

37. Schultze, *Christianity and the Mass Media*, 164; see, also, Moore, *Selling God*; Prothero, *American Jesus*; Vaca, *Evangelicals Incorporated*.

METHODOLOGY

Broadcasting the Faith presents an intellectual and cultural history of the early years of religious radio. First, the study explains the ideas of each of four prominent radio preachers. Each radio personality had distinct doctrinal convictions that he or she brought to the microphone. The analyses include sermon manuscripts that were used on the air and audio recordings of radio sermons. Also, the radio preachers in this study published various works of theology, doctrine, and autobiography that illuminate what was being proclaimed over the air. Finally, extensive written correspondence reveals more completely what each radio preacher believed.

These radio preachers broadcast their doctrinal convictions, however, in a rapidly changing cultural landscape. Modernity brought challenges and opportunities to the church in America. Radio first became popular at the height of the fundamentalist-modernist controversy, a time when the contours of American Protestantism changed extensively. Radio amplified the controversy and hastened the division of fundamentalists and modernists. How radio preachers shaped the faith of millions of devout listeners during this era is an essential part of the story. Through an investigation of the correspondence to the various radio shows as well as the coverage of religious radio in the popular periodicals of the day, this work seeks to discover what was happening on the ground during this tumultuous era in American history.[38]

Conservative and liberal Protestants and Catholics flocked to the airwaves to offer their respective gospels to the masses. With few exceptions, the whole range of churches in America embraced radio technology. Recent scholarship on religious radio, however, tends to focus on either mainline liberal radio or revivalist fundamentalist radio.[39] *Broadcasting the Faith* aims to bring the two areas together and studies the rise and development of Protestant religious radio in the early twentieth century as one narrative. This helps explain why the particular individuals profiled in each chapter were selected. The radio preachers under investigation each gathered a massive radio audience. This fact increases the likelihood that the religion they proclaimed significantly impacted the religious landscape in America. Moreover, because each of the preachers profiled in this book represented

---

38. Longfield, *Presbyterian Controversy*. Longfield provides a helpful model for orienting cultural history around biographies. In telling the story of an institutional crisis (e.g., the Presbyterian Church [USA]), he investigates the stories of six men intimately involved in the controversy.

39. See, for example, Hangen, *Redeeming the Dial*; Voskuil, "Power of the Air," 69–95; Schultze, *Christianity and the Mass Media*, 139–74; Carpenter, *Revive Us Again*, 124–40.

different ecclesiastical constituencies, conclusions about religion as a whole are more credible. What was radio's impact on American religion? What findings are demonstrably true for Protestant religion as a whole, whether liberal or conservative? Treating the rise and development of Protestant religious radio as a whole affords a better analysis of these issues.[40]

Chapter 2 argues that Harry Emerson Fosdick's ministry accelerated a movement away from Protestant orthodoxy. Radio played an important role in Fosdick's successful effort to blaze a new theological trail for the modern era. In moving away from Protestant orthodoxy Fosdick preached simple virtues that focused on human self-interest. Foreshadowing his radio ministry, Fosdick, in a 1928 essay for *Harpers* magazine, outlined what should be the "main business" of every sermon: "Every sermon should have for its main business the solving of some problem—a vital, important problem, puzzling minds, burdening consciences, distracting lives." Fosdick continued, "There is nothing that people are so interested in as themselves, their own problems, and the way to solve them."[41] This audience-centered preaching left an indelible mark on the American church. Fosdick was the beneficiary, along with mainline Protestantism generally, of the favorable relationship between the newly established radio networks and the Federal Council of the Churches of Christ in America. Unlike his fundamentalist counterparts, Fosdick was given sustaining, or free, airtime. Through the broadcast of the *National Vespers Hour*, Fosdick was able to maintain a leading role in the fundamentalist-modernist controversy. Fosdick's childhood religion as well as his theological training at Colgate College and Union Seminary shaped his adult ministry in a direction that contrasted to the fundamentalism of his day.

Chapter 3 contends that Aimee Semple McPherson's ministry accelerated a movement toward an experiential religion with an ecumenical appeal for world evangelization. As one of the most celebrated Christian figures of the early twentieth century, McPherson's ministry helped make the American church more accepting of important aspects of secularization. McPherson was famous for her ministry and became one of the first religious-radio stars—an outcome that mirrored the Hollywood character

---

40. The African American church's relationship to radio is certainly an essential part of the story, and one that warrants more scholarly attention. While a fuller treatment is beyond the scope of this work, it is accurate to say that the themes of commercialization, commoditization, and celebrity, evident in varying degrees in each personality under investigation in this study, likewise run through the African American tradition in its more limited use of radio, but more obviously in its embrace of the phonograph. See, for example, Martin, *Preaching on Wax*.

41. Quoted in Witham, *City on a Hill*, 227.

of her southern California ministry and milieu. McPherson helped transform religion into entertainment by melding "Holy Spirit happiness with the giddy entertainment of the Roaring Twenties."[42] As Edith Blumhofer has shown,[43] McPherson's upbringing in rural Canada and exposure to the Salvation Army shaped her understanding of the faith in significant ways. It was during these childhood years, under the tutelage of charismatic preachers and teachers, that McPherson learned techniques such as drama and storytelling to communicate the faith. Coupled with the force of her personality and the available medium of radio, these techniques helped her create a ministry empire.

Chapter 4 argues that Walter Maier's ministry accelerated a movement toward a simple orthodoxy. Maier was fully convinced of the confessional Lutheranism in which he was raised and trained. For Maier, Lutheranism was orthodoxy. However, the message he broadcast eschewed Lutheran particulars for the bold proclamation of the basic convictions shared by fundamentalists generally. Maier's ascension to radio fame appears surprising given that it coincided with the ascendancy of modernism and theological liberalism. The story of Maier and the *Lutheran Hour* illustrates that the basics of orthodoxy were by no means dead at the popular level. Maier's life was a paradox: a devout Lutheran and first-rate scholar (he earned his PhD from Harvard) who preached simple orthodoxy to the masses. Maier's upbringing, theological training, and ecclesiological home helped shape in him a longing for learning and people. These factors help explain his early embrace of radio technology. Maier is rightly understood as a fundamentalist, but not in the vein of McPherson. Maier's religion was not an experiential ecumenism, nor did he set out to attain celebrity status or a ministry empire. Maier did share with McPherson a willingness to decry certain aspects of modernity, such as Darwinism, atheism, and communism. Maier stands alone in his emphasis on strengthening families. Broadcasts abound with Maier's effort to protect the institution of marriage and child-rearing from the broader moral collapse he perceived in modern America. Maier is rightly compared to Fuller, as he too showed a commitment to a simple orthodoxy and higher education.

Chapter 5 argues that Charles Fuller's ministry contributed to the transformation of American religion by defining it primarily in terms of evangelism. His success uncovered a particular mood in America: one tired of the militant fundamentalism of the early decades of the century but not ready to abandon the fundamentals of the faith for theological liberalism.

---

42. Witham, *City on a Hill*, 233.
43. Blumhofer, *Aimee Semple McPherson*.

Fuller epitomized the new evangelicalism that would eventually dominate the airwaves. By defining evangelical Protestantism in terms of evangelism, Fuller's radio program became a unifying force within the broader evangelical movement. Fuller's childhood and the influence of his parents shaped his faith by nurturing in him a longing for world evangelization. In particular, Fuller's father was a significant factor in developing his understanding of foreign missions, which drove Fuller to take full advantage of radio's global reach. Also, during the *Old Fashioned Revival Hour*'s peak years, Fuller broadcast the program live each week before thousands of audience members at the Long Beach Municipal Auditorium (1943–58). For many, these performances became their church, thus accelerating a move away from a robust ecclesiology in American evangelicalism. Fuller was a movement leader. He played the key role in the formation of the National Association of Evangelicals in 1942 and the National Religious Broadcasters in 1944. The *Old Fashioned Revival Hour* was also known for the popularity of its music. The songs were theologically accessible and musically simple, intended to evoke nostalgic religious feelings. The songs accelerated a move away from substantive theological thought toward sentimentalism.[44] Fuller's particular brand of evangelical faith contrasted with Fosdick's social gospel and had much more in common with Maier's *Lutheran Hour*. Fuller's use of entertainment and marketing mirrored in many ways that of McPherson's. Neither hesitated to take full advantage of modern means of promotion.

In chapter 6 religious radio is considered against the backdrop of the emergence of television as the dominant communication medium in America. By the late 1940s, radio's golden age had come to a close, and it was up to the church in America to reconsider its message in an increasingly image-oriented culture. Surprisingly, given the church's nearly universal rush to radio technology, conservative religion in America has not been nearly as ubiquitous on television as it once was on radio. American evangelicals can learn from religion's experience on radio as the faith moves increasingly to the internet.

In each of these chapters the recurring theme is that religious radio in America sought to counter the secularization of American culture, but

---

44. Referring to Paul Rader's Chicago Tabernacle radio broadcasts in the 1930s, Carpenter, *Revive Us Again*, observes, "Tabernacle music became radio-tailored as well. Gospel songs had to have a message that was simple and patently obvious, a lively tempo, or a stirring melody, and they had to do their work within one or two verses. . . . Like radio jingles, the gospel choruses being composed by the Tabernacle musicians had to be easy to memorize, with catchy melodies and rhythms that almost sang themselves, so that people would find themselves humming and singing them again and again" (128). Charles Fuller and Rudy Atwood would use this same successful formula on broadcasts of the *Old Fashioned Revival Hour*.

did so in a way that contributed significantly to it. In seeking to preserve the influence of religion in American culture, it altered the religion it aimed to preserve and made the American church more accepting of important aspects of secularization. This was an unintended consequence of American religious radio.

2

"Modernism's Moses"

Harry Emerson Fosdick and Radio's *National Vespers*

IN TELLING THE STORY of Harry Emerson Fosdick and *National Vespers*, I argue that his radio ministry countered the secularization of American culture, but at the same time contributed to secularization by facilitating a movement away from Protestant orthodoxy in America.[1] Fosdick saw radio as a powerful tool to serve mankind—to bring healing and hope to America during a time of tremendous national challenge. In addition, Fosdick used radio to continue what he began as a student at Colgate University and

---

1. Miller, *Harry Emerson Fosdick*, 3, 7, 9. Miller outlines three ways to view the life of Harry Emerson Fosdick. First, Fosdick's life may be viewed as a commitment to service. Second, his life may be viewed as "a revolt against the Calvinist ethos, that historic, powerful Protestant force suffused with convictions of the depravity of man, the awful precariousness of human existence, and the pitiless judgment of a wrathful deity." Third, Fosdick's life may be viewed "as a rebellion against creedal sectarianism, his admirers employing such descriptions as 'Fighting Rebel' and his enemies dubbing him 'the Jesse James of the theological world.'" In this chapter I argue that Fosdick thought he was best serving mankind by abandoning Protestant orthodoxy for a new theological system better suited for the modern era. This included his revolt against Calvinism and any form of creedal sectarianism. Fosdick's radio career on *National Vespers* is part of the dramatic story of the rise of religious radio. Summaries of this story can be found in Hangen, *Redeeming the Dial*, 21–36; Carpenter, *Revive Us Again*, 124–40; Voskuil, "Reaching Out," 81–86; Voskuil, "Power of the Air," 69–92.

Union Theological Seminary, namely a relentless assault on the orthodoxy he inherited as a child. It is this aspect of Fosdick's ministry that sets him at odds with the other radio preachers in this study. For McPherson, Maier, and Fuller, radio was a means of reaffirming the old-time religion. In this sense all three are rightly seen as fundamentalists. Fosdick, in contrast, was determined to move away from Protestant orthodoxy by creating a new religious direction for the modern era. Fosdick succeeded remarkably, and radio was an important medium in that success.

THE FUNDAMENTALIST-MODERNIST CONTROVERSY

The fundamentalist-modernist controversy had its origin in the American Presbyterian Church but with far-reaching implications for Protestant religion in America generally. The controversy was over not only theology, but also Christianity's relationship with modernity. Beginning in the early 1920s, the controversy ended in 1936 when J. Gresham Machen and many other conservatives left the Presbyterian Church to form the Orthodox Presbyterian Church in America.[2]

Fosdick's role in the fundamentalist-modernist controversy anticipated his use of radio to stimulate a movement away from Protestant orthodoxy in America. The fundamentalist-modernist controversy gave Fosdick a national platform that made his radio career possible. Indeed, without the fundamentalist-modernist controversy, it is likely that Fosdick may never have had such a significant role in radio.

Fosdick's famous May 1922 sermon, "Shall the Fundamentalists Win?" helped him earn the title, *Modernism's Moses*. A Baptist, Fosdick declared from New York City's First Presbyterian Church that belief in the virgin birth of the Lord and belief in his substitutionary death were unnecessary. He also preached that belief in the doctrine of inerrancy was "a positive peril to the spiritual life" and that belief in the literal second coming of Christ was a folly.[3]

Fosdick described the address as "a plea for tolerance."[4] The Fundamentalist response was swift and relentless.[5] For example, John Roach

2. For helpful works on the fundamentalist-modernist controversy, see especially Marsden, *Fundamentalism and American Culture*; Longfield, *Presbyterian Controversy*; Hart, *Defending the Faith*; Miller, *Harry Emerson Fosdick*; Larson, *Summer for the Gods*.

3. Pultz, *Preaching Ministry*, 192, 196, 199.

4. Fosdick, *Living of These Days*, 2.

5. Miller, *Harry Emerson Fosdick*, vividly describes the state of the United States Presbyterian Church in the early twentieth century: "No major denomination was more desperately driven by controversy in the 1920s than the Presbyterian Church,

Straton, pastor of New York City's Calvary Baptist Church, protested that "in his sermon against Fundamentalists, he [Fosdick] takes up four great doctrines of Christianity: the virgin birth, the inspiration of the Scriptures, the atonement of Jesus and the second coming of our Lord. He rejects the Bible teaching on all of these great doctrines."[6] Within five months of Fosdick's sermon the Presbytery of Philadelphia sent a formal protest to the General Assembly of the Presbyterian Church of New York. Led by Clarence E. Macartney, the protest was based "primarily on a sermon preached by Dr. Fosdick last May on 'Shall the Fundamentalists Win?'"[7] The controversy over Fosdick raged through the Presbyterian General Assembly meetings of 1923 and 1924, resulting in an invitation by the Assembly for Fosdick to become a Presbyterian minister under the authority of the denomination. Fosdick declined the invitation, seeing in it a cleverly disguised attempt by conservatives within the denomination to try him for heresy. "Once within the regular ranks of the Presbyterian ministry," Fosdick remarked, "I could be tried for heresy the first time I uttered a liberal conviction, and obviously many irritated and watchful men were itching for the chance."[8] Fosdick knew he could never constrain himself to any form of creedal Christianity. In the letter he wrote to the Presbytery of New York declining the invitation of the General Assembly, he acknowledged that becoming a Presbyterian meant "a definite creedal subscription, a solemn assumption of theological vows in terms of the Westminster Confession."[9] This he could not do. Fosdick resigned from his pastoral duties at the First Presbyterian Church

---

U.S.A. Boasting almost two million communicants, ten thousand ministers, and ten thousand churches, these adherents to the Westminster Confession of Faith had social prestige, political power, economic influence, and a rich intellectual tradition. The liberal wing was strong and growing as the twentieth century opened and deepened, but conservative strength was also formidable and aggressive under the leadership of such champions as the reverend layman William Jennings Bryan; the respected Princeton theologian, J. Gresham Machen; the popular revivalist William A. (Billy) Sunday; the wealthy, pious merchant John Wanamaker; and a galaxy of pulpit giants from Clarence Edward Macartney in Philadelphia to Mark A. Matthews in Seattle" (112).

6. Straton, in "Pulpit Assails Dr. Fosdick."

7. "Presbyterians Move against Dr. Fosdick." Fosdick never expressed regret for preaching 'Shall the Fundamentalists Win?' On the contrary, he viewed it as one of his most significant contributions to the church: "Not once in his private or public correspondence at the time or later did Fosdick express regret for preaching the sermon. As he wrote to a Presbyterian leader, 'I am profoundly sorry that the sermon has been misinterpreted; I am profoundly sorry that it has caused a disturbance; but I cannot honestly be sorry at all that I preached the sermon. When I get to heaven I expect it to be one of the stars in my crown.'" Miller, *Harry Emerson Fosdick*, 117.

8. Fosdick, *Living of These Days*, 171.

9. Fosdick, *Living of These Days*, 172.

and gave his farewell sermon on March 1, 1925. After five-and-a-half years at First Presbyterian, much of it filled with controversy, Fosdick had established himself as one of theological liberalism's leading lights.

Fosdick experienced controversy in one form or another most of his life. In his biography of Fosdick, Robert Moats Miller remarked, "It was not in Fosdick's nature to walk away from a fight. Nor was it in his character to remain an uncommitted spectator above the raging of great events."[10] For Fosdick, the "raging of great events" was the clash between fundamentalists and modernists, and his life was witness to the fact that he was not an "uncommitted spectator." As an author, pastor, counselor, lecturer, and preacher, Fosdick strove against the fundamentalists while propagating a modernist faith. Miller's succinct description was that "nonconformity was in Fosdick's blood."[11] Fosdick's nonconformity brought him to the forefront of the fundamentalist-modernist controversy, and the controversy launched him into a public role that made his radio career possible.

THE MAKING OF A MODERNIST

Fosdick's religious upbringing and theological training at Colgate College and Union Theological Seminary shaped his adult ministry in profound ways. These formative influences help explain Fosdick's efforts, particularly through radio, to depart from Protestant orthodoxy.

Fosdick lived during a time of frenetic change in America. He believed that traditional orthodoxy was not sufficient to meet the challenges of modernity. Fosdick was born on May 24, 1878, in Buffalo, New York, and died on October 5, 1969, in Bronxville, New York. His life spanned some of the most momentous events in American history. Fosdick lived through the close of the Victorian era and saw the rise and development of modernity, including Darwinism and historical criticism. He experienced the Great Depression and witnessed two World Wars. Fosdick watched rural America yield to urbanization with its powerful economic and technological innovations. Fosdick lived during a time when immigration was drastically changing the face of America and fueling industrialization. Bradley Longfield reports that during the last forty years of the nineteenth century, "Approximately fourteen million Europeans came to America's shores . . . so that in 1900 immigrants and their children made up over one-third of America's population."[12] Fosdick believed that a person could not truly un-

10. Miller, *Harry Emerson Fosdick*, 78.
11. Miller, *Harry Emerson Fosdick*, 9.
12. Longfield, *Presbyterian Controversy*, 16.

derstand America without reckoning with the impact of immigration and the families that marked the nation: "This restless, ambitious, forward-looking America which I knew in my boyhood had been created by plain people, by families of common folk, often by 'dispossessed persons' from foreign lands, and one cannot understand that America without looking at it from the family angle."[13] This outlook contributed to Fosdick's rejection of the old orthodoxy and fueled his efforts to reform Christianity in the modern era.

The changes thrust upon America during the early twentieth century not only influenced Fosdick's theological outlook, but also his childhood religious experience. Fosdick was born to Frank Sheldon and Amie Weaver Fosdick. There is ample evidence that Fosdick was deeply grateful for his parents: "On a hundred instances the mature Harry Emerson Fosdick recalled his parents in admiration and affection; not a single extant public or private expression carries a hint of disrespect or criticism."[14] Fosdick remembered with great fondness his childhood home: "At home the basic security of love and loyalty was so taken for granted, that no other possibility was thought of, and whatever problems and tragedies came, the stability and happiness of the family were unquestionable."[15] This stable home included a Baptist heritage that Fosdick cherished. However, not all of the Christian examples of his childhood were remembered with equal fondness. Fosdick recalled his abhorrence of the "pettiness and obscurantism" of his childhood religion and the "miserable legalism" that came with the old orthodoxy:

> The main source of unhappiness for me in early school days was my religion. I took it desperately in earnest. I judge that from the beginning I was predestined to religion as my predominant interest and major vocation, for from the time I overrode all objections and joined the church when I was seven, I was always struggling with it. The happy aspects of it I found in my family, where Christianity was the natural, practical, livable spirit of the home. But some of the most wretched hours of my boyhood were caused by the pettiness and obscurantism, the miserable legalism and terrifying appeals to fear that were associated with the religion of the churches.[16]

Such was Fosdick's negative experience of religion from the churches of his youth that, at age eight, "the thought of God became a horror."[17] Fos-

13. Fosdick, *Living of These Days*, 3.
14. Miller, *Harry Emerson Fosdick*, 15.
15. Fosdick, *Living of These Days*, 31.
16. Fosdick, *Living of These Days*, 33.
17. Fosdick, *Living of These Days*, 34.

dick's radio ministry wanted to help people avoid the agony over religion he experienced as a child. For example, Fosdick recalled the terror over hell he felt as a nine-year-old:

> I was a sensitive boy, deeply religious, and, as I see it now, morbidly conscientious, and the effect upon me of hell-fire-and-brimstone preaching was deplorable. I vividly recall weeping at night for fear of going to hell, with my mystified and baffled mother trying to comfort me. Once, when I was nine years old, my father found me so pale that he thought me ill. The fact was that I was in agony for fear that I had committed the unpardonable sin, and reading that day in the book of Revelation about the horrors of hell, I was sick with terror.[18]

Fosdick experienced these "onsets of morbidity" sporadically. "To picture them as overshadowing my childhood," Fosdick warned, "would be absurd." However, the influence on his ministry in later years would be permanent: "But it still is true that in those early days the iron entered my soul and the scene was set for rebellion against the puerility and debasement of a legalistic and terrifying religion."[19] Radio became an instrument of his rebellion.

Fosdick's adult ministry cannot be understood apart from his childhood religious experiences. His relentless efforts to reject Protestant orthodoxy were a reaction to the "hell-fire-and brimstone preaching" he heard as a child and found "deplorable." Radio became for Fosdick a medium of communication that he could use in his crusade against sectarianism.

Fosdick's radio ministry benefited greatly from his years of higher education. College and seminary training equipped Fosdick with the intellectual foundation necessary to effectively reject Protestant orthodoxy.

In September 1895, eighteen-year-old Fosdick began his freshman year at Colgate University, "a small Baptist school numbering (exclusive of the Academy and Seminary) approximately 150 students and fifteen faculty."[20] The significance of the five years Fosdick spent in Hamilton, New York (four years at Colgate plus one year at the seminary), cannot be overstated. It was during these years that Fosdick resolved to abandon his orthodox heritage and become a champion of the "new theology"—the liberal, progressive Christianity that had been emerging since the 1870s.[21] For Fosdick, these

18. Fosdick, *Living of These Days*, 36.
19. Fosdick, *Living of These Days*, 35–36.
20. Miller, *Harry Emerson Fosdick*, 29.
21. Hudson, *American Protestantism*, 135. Hudson describes the state of Protestantism as Fosdick entered his years of higher education: "Apart from its busyness, the

years included a "struggle for a credible faith"—the intense effort on his part to be both intelligent and a Christian. "My real struggle," Fosdick admitted, "concerned the intellectual credibility of Christian faith."[22] Looking back on his time at Colgate, Fosdick explained his break with orthodoxy as "stunning" and "revolutionary." It produced an ecstasy for one who had been liberated from great bondage:

> Just when the first crack in the old structure began I am not sure, but it concerned the stories of the Hebrew strong man, Samson. So childishly my religious doubts commenced. Why, I argued with myself, should I feel under duress to believe the Samson stories, while feeling under no similar coercion to believe tales about the Greek strong man, Hercules? Answering that naïve question—as after some inner tussling I did, by acknowledging that there was no more reason to believe Hebrew than Greek folklore—the conclusion was plain: I did not have to believe anything simply because it was in the Bible. How stunning that conclusion was, it is not easy now for an educated mind to understand. For me, as for many others in my time, it was revolutionary. The old basis of authority was gone. Truth was an open field to be explored. What one believed had to be discovered. Nothing could be settled by a text.[23]

This revolutionary discovery by Fosdick that he did not have to believe everything in the Bible determined the theology he took to the air during his radio career. Fosdick's theological liberalism led him to eschew doctrinal preaching and to substitute simple virtues in its place.

In the summer of 1897, after his freshman year at Colgate, the "old structure" of orthodoxy was not merely cracked for Fosdick, but destroyed: "I no longer believed the old stuff I had been taught. Moreover, I no longer merely doubted it. I rose in indignant revolt against it."[24] Fosdick broke with orthodoxy comprehensively:

---

most conspicuous feature of American Protestantism as it moved toward the close of the nineteenth century had been its loss of identity. The theological erosion of earlier decades had dismantled its historic intellectual defenses, and the way was open to a rather complete assimilation of Protestantism to the model of the world. As a result, by the end of the century, American Protestantism had become more the creature of American culture than its creator." This context helps explain why it was so easy for Fosdick and countless others to abandon orthodoxy and embrace the "new theology."

22. Fosdick, *Living of These Days*, 53, 56.
23. Fosdick, *Living of These Days*, 52.
24. Fosdick, *Living of These Days*, 52.

> When my religion was disturbed, I was disturbed from the ground up. Others might pass through this phase of questioning and doubt and take it easily. I took it hard. All my sophomore year I thought fast and furiously. I do not mean that I did nothing else except struggle over religion. I had a good time. But behind the scenes I was vehemently rebelling against the kind of bibliolatry and theology I had been taught.[25]

Consistent with Fosdick's self-proclaimed rebellion against orthodoxy, he said to his mother upon leaving for his junior year at Colgate, "I'll behave as though there is a God, but mentally I'm going to clear God out of the universe and start all over to see what I can find."[26] What Fosdick found was theological liberalism—the system of theology he would later preach on the airwaves as he grew a new antiorthodox following.

William Newton Clarke, as the most influential professor in Fosdick's life, helped equip Fosdick for his public ministry of rebellion. Fosdick's effectiveness in moving theology in America away from the old orthodoxy has much to do with Clarke's influence on Fosdick's life and thinking. In Fosdick's quest for a credible faith, Clarke was preeminent: "Most of all Professor William Newton Clarke, of the Theological Seminary, helped me." Clarke proved that the new progressive Christianity could produce a genuine piety. "Long before I knew him as a loyal personal friend," Fosdick wrote, "he was a powerful influence in my life. He was an honest man, saying what he really thought, defying the obscurantism of old opinions and daring to phrase the Christian faith in the categories of modern thinking. Every time he walked across campus he was a living argument that it could be done." Fosdick's tribute to Clarke demonstrates his importance in shaping the experiential religion that became the hallmark of Fosdick's ministry and helped accelerate religious change in America:

> The major effect which William Newton Clarke had upon me at first was to outflank my intellectual difficulties. He went back behind the forms of doctrine to the basic and abiding experiences of which they were the attempted expression and interpretation. He made essential religion live again for me, real and vital, and let the mental formulations trail along afterward as a matter to be taken up at the mind's leisure. To use his own comparison, he was sure the stars were there, though we had to change our astronomy, and the flowers real, though botany might alter its explanations. He himself was one of the most inspiring teachers

25. Fosdick, *Living of These Days*, 53.
26. Fosdick, *Living of These Days*, 54.

> I ever sat under. I recall more than once leaving his classroom to seek solitude, that I might gradually come down from the heights to the mundane earth again.[27]

To Fosdick, Clarke was a "door" into the new landscape of undogmatic experiential religion. In his autobiography, Fosdick noted, "All the best meanings of personal religion could be mine again without the crucifixion of the intellect—this assurance he brought me and it was music to my ears."[28] Perhaps Fosdick's greatest compliment to Clarke was crediting him for his entering the Christian ministry: "Had it not been for him [Clarke], I suspect that I should never have been a Christian minister."[29] While at Colgate, Fosdick sensed an undeniable call to vocational ministry. He recalled entering his senior year set in his rejection of orthodoxy and committed to ministerial work:

> Thus I headed for the ministry with very little that could presage a welcome by the church. I was through with orthodox dogma. I had not the faintest interest in any sect or denomination. I could not have told clearly what I believed about any major Christian doctrine. I did not see how any denomination could ever accept me as its minister. But I did not care. I wanted to make a contribution to the spiritual life of my generation. I said that to myself again and again. That was all I felt sure about. If I prepared myself to make a spiritual contribution to my generation, somewhere a door would open—with that faith I headed toward the ministry.[30]

Colgate was the venue where Fosdick's desire to help people—to "make a spiritual contribution" to his generation—merged with his rebellion against "orthodox dogma."

---

27. Fosdick, *Living of These Days*, 65.

28. Fosdick, *Living of These Days*, 66. Fosdick credited Clarke and his liberalism with stopping countless like-minded individuals from abandoning Christianity: "What present day critics of liberalism often fail to see is its absolute necessity to multitudes of us who would not have been Christians at all unless we could thus have escaped the bondage of the then reigning orthodoxy . . . it offered to a generation of earnest youth the only chance they had to be honest while being Christian. As for men such as Dr. Clarke, their revolt, like that of Jesus against the orthodoxy of his time, was in the interest of a deeper, more vital, more transforming Christian experience than literalism, legalism and authoritarianism could supply. The result for many of us was not alone a new theology but a new spiritual life."

29. Fosdick, *Living of These Days*, 65.

30. Fosdick, *Living of These Days*, 57.

After graduation Fosdick spent another year studying theology at Colgate. However, he craved a greater intellectual challenge and enrolled at Union Theological Seminary in New York City. Over the next three years (1901–1904) Union's faculty guided Fosdick's theological development. Due to the inerrancy controversies in the late 1890s involving Charles Briggs and Arthur Cushman McGiffert, by 1901 Union had officially severed ties with the US Presbyterian Church, "becoming interdenominational in both leadership and outlook."[31] As a theological institution, Union had undergone the same break with orthodoxy that Fosdick had encountered at Colgate. Union Seminary, like William Newton Clarke, made a deep impression on his life and ministry:

> It would be useless here to try and undertake an adequate appraisal of what Union Seminary meant to me. It offered a kind of intellectual liberty in the study of religion of which I had dreamed. . . . My generation desperately needed emancipation from the old, hidebound orthodoxies, and Union made this possible for us, without loss of Christian vitality and devotion. . . . Men who came from ampler university backgrounds and freer church associations might take Union's attitude for granted; to me it meant the liberation of my mind and at the same time the retention of my Christianity.[32]

In taking classes from eminent liberal professors such as "Francis Brown in Old Testament Hebrew, Arthur Cushman McGiffert in church history, George William Knox in the philosophy of religion, and James Everett Frame in New Testament Greek," Fosdick declared, "one's mind was stretched."[33]

The most pronounced mark that Union Seminary left on Fosdick, and one that would influence his later ministry, was the experiential approach to religion. Fosdick recalled how, at the dawn of the twentieth century as he was entering seminary, "the old foundations of Biblical authority were shaken and, consciously or not, a direct appeal to Christian experience became more and more the factual basis for theology."[34] Arthur McGiffert, Adolf von Harnack's loyal disciple, fostered in Fosdick an emphasis on the experiential aspects of religion: "Both Harnack and McGiffert stressed, as Fosdick was to do, the moral much more than the doctrinal and emphasized the infinite

---

31. Miller, *Harry Emerson Fosdick*, 50. On the character of Union Theological Seminary, see especially Handy, *History of Union Theological Seminary*.

32. Fosdick, *Living of These Days*, 76–77.

33. Fosdick, *Living of These Days*, 77.

34. Fosdick, *Living of These Days*, 64.

value of the human soul and the claims of human brotherhood."[35] Fosdick confessed, "Another factor in my struggle for a convinced faith has been emphasis on direct, immediate personal experience as the solid ground for assurance. . . . Christian thinking, like all thinking, starts with experience which outlives all changes in doctrine about it, and constitutes the ever-recurrent test and criterion of truth, and the ultimate basis of religious certainty."[36] Miller captures the indebtedness that Fosdick felt to Union Seminary: "A half-century after graduating from Union, on the occasion of the endowment of a chair in his name, Fosdick truthfully declared: 'This seminary made my ministry possible. Over fifty years ago, I came here a confused and hungry student, wishing above all else to teach and preach the Christian gospel, but wondering how I could do it with intellectual integrity and self-respect. And here the doors were opened.'"[37]

Upon graduating from Union Theological Seminary, Fosdick's formal training ceased. The "making of a modernist" was complete. What remained for Fosdick was to take his aspiration to help people and his crusade against orthodoxy to other venues. These venues would include various churches, dozens of books, colleges and universities worldwide, and, of course, radio.

National Vespers

Radio was one of Fosdick's primary tools in transforming Protestant orthodoxy in America and around the world. This emerging technology served Fosdick's campaign against fundamentalism and helped him leave an indelible mark on theology in America.

The National Broadcasting Company (NBC) was formed in 1926. On October 2, 1927, the new network began the *National Vespers Hour* as a public service, featuring Fosdick. Not wanting to adversely affect "small churches, especially those in the country . . . when their parishioners stayed at home and heard sermons over the radio,"[38] NBC envisioned an afternoon program. In 1931 *National Vespers* was cut to a half hour.

Fosdick was the beneficiary of the favorable relationship between the newly established radio networks and the Federal Council of the Churches of Christ in America. Unlike his fundamentalist counterparts, Fosdick was given sustaining (i.e., free) airtime. To maintain his independence, Fosdick never accepted compensation for his radio work.

35. Miller, *Harry Emerson Fosdick*, 51.
36. Fosdick, *Living of These Days*, 234–35.
37. Fosdick, *Living of These Days*, 53.
38. *New York Times*, (no article title), October 1, 1927.

Under Fosdick's preaching the program grew rapidly in popularity and influence. In 1944 Frank C. Goodman, executive secretary of the Department of National Religious Radio for the Federal Council of Churches of Christ in America, offered a brief history of the first seventeen years of *National Vespers*. Goodman included the October 2, 1927, start date and the modest beginning of sixteen stations. He proceeded to record the phenomenal growth of the program with its peak of 125 stations and an estimated audience of twenty-five million people. During this time over one million letters were sent to Dr. Fosdick.[39] In recording her own history of *National Vespers*, Betty Gough, one of Fosdick's personal secretaries at Riverside Church, featured the staggering amount of letters—8,248—received in response to the sermon "A Time to Stress Unity" delivered on March 12, 1944. In addition, Gough chronicled the season with the greatest number of letters—134,827—for the period from October 1944 through May 1945.[40] Given these figures, it is fitting that Fosdick became known as "the dean of all ministers of the air."[41] Miller argued that "Fosdick's national influence cannot be understood without reference to *National Vespers*."[42] Moreover, radio played a vital role in Fosdick's efforts to make a "contribution to the spiritual life" of his generation and aided his crusade against orthodoxy.

National Vespers was not Fosdick's first episode in radio. From October 12, 1924, until March 22, 1925, Fosdick preached fourteen sermons on station WJZ in New York City. Also, beginning October 3, 1926, and continuing through the spring of 1927, WJZ regularly broadcast the morning service of Fosdick's Park Avenue Baptist Church.[43] Having tasted the power of broadcasting, Fosdick seized the opportunity presented to him in October 1927 to become the featured speaker on NBC's *National Vespers*. For the next nineteen years Fosdick helped advance Protestant religious broadcasting and became one of the most recognized voices in America.

Fosdick saw that radio preaching was here to stay. One of the primary motives for Fosdick's involvement in radio was to prevent the fundamentalists from monopolizing the airwaves: "Sunday mornings the air will be full of sermons in any case," Fosdick predicted. "The query is only whose sermons will be on the air. It is needless to name those representing a type

---

39. Frank Goodman, "History of National Vespers," 1939, Harry Emerson Fosdick Collection.
40. Betty Gough, Notes on *National Vespers*, Harry Emerson Fosdick Collection.
41. Miller, *Harry Emerson Fosdick*, 379.
42. Miller, *Harry Emerson Fosdick*, 380.
43. Miller, *Harry Emerson Fosdick*, 382.

of Christianity which you and I do not believe in. Ought we to leave the air to their monopoly? I do not believe we should."[44]

Fosdick's war against the old orthodoxy included preemptive action. Radio also afforded him the chance to speak directly to fundamentalists in the hope of persuading them of the error of their ways:

> One opportunity which came with radio preaching I especially welcomed: it gave me the chance to speak directly to my fundamentalist brethren in their homes. I did not by any means persuade all of them—there are plenty left—but the radio ministry helped, as in the case of one listener who wrote: "I had always thought you were a devil with horns and a tail, but I have been listening to you over the air recently, and what you say seems to be Christian."[45]

Another fundamentalist expressed similar sentiments:

> I tell you all this to try to convey to you, if possible, my state of mind when listening to you yesterday—or, to be more exact, when I started to listen to you, for sitting there in the gathering twilight I experienced a complete reversal of sentiment and I can't tell you when I have started to work on a Monday morning feeling so much at peace with all the world as I do today. No, I don't think I am a modernist, I am still a fundamentalist, but, Oh! What a load has been lifted from my mind—the responsibility of convincing all my friends that everything in the Bible *must* [emphasis original] be taken literally and anyone teaching anything else is simply subverting the truth.[46]

Part of Fosdick's strategy to transform traditional orthodoxy in America was to use radio to change minds. It worked.

Fosdick was determined to broadcast messages contrary to the orthodoxy of the day. "Nothing narrow, sectarian, exclusive and merely partisan will do," stated Fosdick. The radio preacher "must strike a universal note and deal with elemental human problems."[47] Fosdick did not hesitate to express his disdain for the old-time religion. The following summary of Fosdick's inaugural *National Vespers* sermon, "The Use and Misuse of Religion," preached on October 2, 1927, set the tone for future broadcasts:

---

44. Miller, *Harry Emerson Fosdick*, 384.

45. Fosdick, *Living of These Days*, 225.

46. Letter from a self-proclaimed 'fundamentalist,' Harry Emerson Fosdick Collection.

47. Fosdick, *Living of These Days*, 226.

> Religion is a very powerful force but on that account it is very dangerous. It can do immense damage as well as immense good. Obviously a great deal of our popular religion goes wrong, and leaves ruin behind it, like the Mississippi when it bursts its banks. We all need to face honestly, therefore, a searching question: "What is our religion doing to our characters?" Dr. Fosdick does not ask his auditors to change their religions, but he does ask them to face up to this question of the effect of their religion on their character.[48]

For Fosdick, traditional orthodoxy had left ruin in its wake, and it was time to abandon it in favor of an experiential religion more compatible with modernity.

Fosdick's ministry facilitated a movement toward religion as character formation. In doing so, Fosdick did not merely speak against fundamentalism. He also sought to advance his modernism through a positive presentation of his convictions. Fosdick believed that the best way to help people was to focus on the "elemental human problems" of this world. If he could help his listeners get along better in this life, Fosdick believed, then his ministry was effective and the old orthodoxy thwarted. Therefore, rather than doctrinal discourses, sermons emphasized personal morality and the character traits that should mark the Christian. For example, NBC published the following summary of Fosdick's May 6, 1928, broadcast: "Dr. Fosdick thinks that the Christian life is marked, when it is genuine, not so much by familiar institutional associations as by a superior quality of character. Jesus' question to his disciples, 'What do ye more than others?' is the kind of question that he would ask of his disciples in every generation. And unless Christianity can produce this superior type of living above the average, it is failing at its central task."[49] For Fosdick, the essence of Christianity was not only experiencing God, but displaying "a superior quality of character." A "superior type of living" was Christianity's "central task." This superior character, Fosdick was eager to say, came from God. For Fosdick, the thought of goodness without God was the difference between common decency and true virtue. For example, on his broadcast on October 16, 1938, Fosdick criticized those who were arguing for morality without God:

> And now, in our time, the slogan rises, Goodness without God, as if to say that this no-God idea does not matter. Believe me, it does matter! It may not matter to your minor moralities, but

---

48. Harry Emerson Fosdick Collection. Fosdick preached every sermon from a full manuscript. The broadcast summaries are taken from these manuscripts.

49. "What Do Ye More Than Others?" Harry Emerson Fosdick Collection.

it does matter to your morale. You can get many a common decency without conscious recognition of God but you cannot get Christ—not by a long sea-mile—not his character, not his stamina, doing what he did, standing for what he stood, loving as he loved, facing Gethsemane and the Cross as he faced them. You cannot get that. When character reaches great dimensions, it takes God. It no longer is merely from the teeth out, or individual volition. It is like a river that flows not so much from us as through us, and the voice of its many waters is not, Goodness without God, but a vaster matter: "Not by might, nor by power, but by my Spirit, saith the Lord of hosts."[50]

Fosdick transformed religion toward an experiential moralism that is inspired and empowered by the example of Christ. Fosdick's central message was virtuous living, but not a moralism void of God. Another example further illustrates the point. With the end of World War II near, Fosdick recognized that many people's Christian faith was being challenged through "emotional disillusionment." Fosdick offered help by pointing to Jesus Christ as the ultimate example of how to live and be saved:

> The world needs salvation. That word comes to life again in a crisis such as this. If ever mankind needed to be saved, we do; and only from the kind of faith and character that Christ revealed, can our salvation come. Every other road we take, choosing Antichrist instead, leads to the chasm of an earthly hell. We ought to see that clearly. In Christ's basic faiths about God and man, his principles of justice and good will, workout in human relationships with patience and determination, lies our hope.[51]

Fosdick retained central roles for Jesus Christ and the need for salvation in his moralistic version of Christianity; this proved effective in motivating people toward his new vision.

Another method by which Fosdick nudged people his way was by emphasizing the here and now. Fosdick was determined to help people live "victoriously" in this life. Very little attention, therefore, is given in Fosdick's radio broadcasts to the "heavenly hope" that the fundamentalists emphasized. Fosdick's emphasis on the here and now is seen in the official summary of Fosdick's radio sermon on October 28, 1928, "Almost":

> Dr. Fosdick points out that life is largely made up of *almosts*. A high ideal almost reached is better than a low one, yet we often just fail to reach a good we know and could reach if would.

50. "How Fares Goodness without God?" Harry Emerson Fosdick Collection.
51. "What an Armistice Day!" November 11, 1945, Harry Emerson Fosdick Collection.

Perhaps we are prevented by the "almost" of fear, dreading a new way of living, or the almost of doubt, disbelieving in our own possibilities. In Bernina Pass are two small lakes hardly 100 feet apart. One flows into the Adriatic, the other into the Black Sea. So in life Dr. Fosdick sees tremendous issues of destiny dependent on hairbreadth escapes. Safety lies in coming completely over into the good we know, not almost but altogether.[52]

Never doubting the potential of "our own possibilities," Fosdick pressed people into believing that they could attain a better life if they only "would." For Fosdick, the power to overcome the *almosts* of life was "religion's central gift": "Dr. Fosdick reminds us that many folks regard religion as primarily an endeavor to explain the world, forgetting that Jesus did not say, 'I have explained the world,' but 'I have overcome the world.' This power of overcoming the world is religion's central gift. It makes a man transcendent over trouble and begets in him a victorious life. It cannot always furnish explanations, but it can always furnish power to overcome."[53] Fosdick's preaching transformed traditional orthodoxy's emphasis on the hereafter to an emphasis on the here and now.

Fosdick combined his effort to undermine orthodoxy—what he called "closed religion"—with an emphasis on human achievement:

> You see, there are, as Bergson said, two kinds of religion, the closed and the open. I wish more young people would see that. If they did, they would not be so ready to give up religion. Two kinds of religion, the closed and the open! Closed religion is the kind that imposes on people, from without, set creeds and negative commandments, and so constricts and freezes life. Open religion is the kind that puts inside a man something good, true, beautiful, around which life becomes organized and to which it is his glory to be loyal. Closed religion can be one of the most damning curses in human life. Open religion is the supreme builder of personal character. When a man gets the right kind of compass inside him and takes it in earnest, then begins the day of great sailing.[54]

With Fosdick we see religion transform from an emphasis on God to an emphasis on man and his efforts to fare better in this life. What Fosdick

---

52. "*National Vespers* Radio Bulletin," National Broadcasting Company, Harry Emerson Fosdick Collection.

53. "Overcoming The World," *National Vesper* Radio Bulletin, National Broadcasting Company, Harry Emerson Fosdick Collection.

54. "Life's Central Demand: Be a Real Person," December 4, 1938, Harry Emerson Fosdick Collection.

wanted to give the modern world was an approach to religious belief that was better able to build personal character—something, he believed, that creedal Christianity could never do.

Fosdick shifted the popular religious discussion away from substantive theological discourse by warning of traditional orthodoxy's tendency to become overly technical and therefore divorced from real life. For example, in the radio address, "Putting Religion into the Thick of Daily Life," Fosdick again sought to advance his modernism against the backdrop of the reigning orthodoxy of his day:

> No greater disaster can befall religion than to become separated from real life, and that is what's happening all the time. Religion displays a fatal tendency to become technical—theologically technical, so that doctrine grows sophisticated; ecclesiastically technical, so that the theory of the church becomes complicated; ritualistically technical, with rites and ceremonies endlessly multiplied. So at last a highly specialized religious realm is created, with its complex ideologies, its abstruse symbolisms, its conventional vocabularies. Then into the church comes some youth untrained in all this technicality, facing, it may be, a deep personal need, and like a stranger in a foreign land he looks on this intricate religious realm and cries, What has that to do with life?[55]

For Fosdick, the fundamentalists had buried true religion under the weight of "technicalities," and this gave no help to people in their daily lives. Fosdick was convinced that Jesus offered a better way than the "technical religionists":

> The deep difference between conventional religion on the one side and Jesus on the other was due to his idea not only of what sacredness meant, but of what truth meant. Technical religionists habitually discuss the truth about religion—refining their religious definitions, debating their religious distinctions, often splitting hairs over their religious conclusions—and then, into the midst of this technical debate about what is true in religion, a soul like Jesus comes, and everybody feels the difference. When you analyze that difference, much of it lies here—Jesus does not start with religion and inquire the truth about that; he starts with life itself and inquires the truth about that. Into the midst of the

---

55. "Putting Religion into the Thick of Daily Life," February 14, 1940, Harry Emerson Fosdick Collection.

technical debates of the religionists he projects his tremendous question, What is the everlasting truth about life itself?[56]

Fosdick also believed that religion was not about propositional truth statements or technical debates about religion—it was about living. Fosdick was determined to move religion in America away from theological discussion and toward virtuous living. This, according to Fosdick, is the all-important example that Jesus brought humankind.

Consistent with Fosdick's radio efforts to advance his modernist agenda, Fosdick used *National Vespers* to broadcast his pacifism. Fosdick's forays into politics over the air contributed to religion's transformation by using traditional religious language to advance a particular political agenda.[57] For example, having been a staunch supporter of America's involvement in World War I, Fosdick changed his position on war and sought to persuade others through radio. After noting his generation's "about-face" on the meaning of war, Fosdick confessed,

> I shared with my generation this revolutionary change of opinion, but as a Christian my revolt went deeper and raised issues with which the Christian conscience today everywhere is struggling. In the first world conflict I saw war at firsthand, and went through the disillusionment of its aftermath, confronting with increasing agony the anti-Christian nature of war's causes, processes and results. I could not dodge my conscience: I must never again put my Christian ministry at the nation's disposal for the sanction and backing of war. So I became a pacifist.[58]

The clearest statement of Fosdick's antiwar position came in his February 21, 1937, broadcast. Fosdick's sermon, "Five Sectors of the Peace Movement," had five points, each detailing what must be included in the peace movement if wars were to cease.[59]

In Fosdick's first point he called on his listeners to hate war emotionally while reminding them that this, in itself, is not sufficient: "The greatest

---

56. "Putting Religion into the Thick of Daily Life," February 14, 1940, Harry Emerson Fosdick Collection.

57. The influence of political rhetoric on religion in America is dramatically seen in one of Fosdick's contemporaries the Roman Catholic Father Charles Coughlin. For his role in the history of religious radio in America, see Brinkley, *Voices of Protest*; Marcus, *Father Coughlin*; Tull, *Father Coughlin and the New Deal*; Kazin, *Populist Persuasion*, 110–33.

58. Fosdick, *Living of These Days*, 293.

59. All quotes from this sermon are found in "Five Sectors of the Peace Movement," Harry Emerson Fosdick Collection.

single enemy of democracy today is neither communism nor fascism but war. If, then, we still have loyalty left to the finest traditions of our American heritage, we had better hate war. But emotionally hating war is not enough." Fosdick called for more than emotion: action against war and creating viable alternatives to war were necessary to achieve peace. In his second point, Fosdick outlined the importance of pacifism to the Christian:

> The individual refusal to participate in war, is, I think of first-rate significance, but it is not enough. What pacifism really does is to sit in judgment on war. It says, This whole war business is so hideous in its processes and disastrous in its results that we will take any punishment society may mete out rather than participate in it. We may not be able to stop war in our generation but one thing we can do, bear our witness against it as irremediably, everlastingly wrong. And to die saying that, we think, is better than to have condoned, excused, or shared this hideous evil.

For Fosdick, an antiwar sentiment had reached what appears to be a level of primary importance in religion. This emphasis contributed to the transformation of religion by elevating personal moral virtue—pacifism—above political concerns and even above the national interest.

Fosdick continued to signal a change in emphasis from religion to politics in his third point, in which he tried to demonstrate the futility of war by showing the irony of Europe's antagonist:

> For what nation in Europe today peculiarly disturbs our hopes of peace? Germany under Hitler. But I thought it was Germany we lately fought a great war against? It was. I thought we conquered Germany. We did. I thought we did to Germany what modern war knows how to do to a beaten enemy and then followed it with one of the most oppressive, not to say outrageous, peace treaties in all history. We did. And now, a few years afterwards, Germany, armed to the teeth again, is on the march. That is just how efficient war is. It cannot do even this first, simple, obvious thing it is supposed to do—really conquer a powerful modern nation. Do you say that Hitler makes war? I say war made Hitler.

By depicting Hitler as a product of a war culture Fosdick moved into a discussion far removed from the core doctrines of Protestant orthodoxy.

In his fourth point Fosdick emphasized the economic reconstruction that he believed had to take place if war was to cease:

> Any way one looks at the war question, one finds economics in the foreground. We cannot have economic war with tariffs

and monetary policies and still expect peace. We cannot have predatory economic imperialism such as the Western world practiced on Africa for a long and terrible century, and of which Ethiopia was only the latest episode, and still expect peace. We cannot have an economic order overwhelmingly motivated by the acquisitive desire for profits, first for individuals, second for corporate aggregates of individuals, and still expect peace. Those who say that the economic preconditions of peace are fundamental are right. Peace will cost profound economic reconstruction.

In contrast to the intense American nationalism Fosdick displayed leading up to and through World War I,[60] by 1937 he did not hesitate to condemn what he perceived as the Western world's "predatory economic imperialism." With this emphasis Fosdick sounded much like his Roman Catholic contemporary and radio broadcast colleague, Father Charles Coughlin. This in itself accelerated a diminishing of theological distinctions between Protestants and Catholics because two of radio's most recognized voices were not divided by theology as a matter of first importance, but were united by personal ethical theories.

In his fifth point, Fosdick called for "international collective security" as a necessary prerequisite to peace. What is significant about this idea is how peace is discussed in terms of peace among nations. No longer was peace being discussed with any explicit reference to the Protestant gospel:

> For we know how to get peace. We have already achieved peace. Within nations, where constituent states and provinces have surrendered to a central authority their right to use violence against one another, we have already achieved peace. That is the secret of the American union. Once Vermont, New Hampshire and New York nearly went to war. Once there was a great war between the North and South. Now, however, we are confident that a true union exists, in which the constituent states have surrendered to a central authority not all their sovereignty but one item in it, the right to use violence one against another. The world can have peace whenever the world wants it enough to fulfill this condition. The major precondition of war, that makes it almost inevitable, is sixty-odd national states refusing to surrender to a central court and administration this one item of their sovereignty.

---

60. See Miller, *Harry Emerson Fosdick*, 74–92.

The old orthodoxy with its emphasis on how a sinner can have peace with God through Jesus Christ was being displaced by a "gospel" of political peace.

Fosdick saved his most forceful words for the closing, invoking traditional religious language to make his point:

> In the meantime, I beg of you, work on all these five fronts. Let us stop being bigots in the peace movement! Let us cease excommunicating one another! All these five sectors are indispensable in the work for peace. Find the place where you can make your best contribution. For it surely is hypocrisy to call Christ "Lord, Lord" and not take our stand against this accursed thing, this anti-Christ.

War, for Fosdick, was nothing less than an "accursed thing," an "anti-Christ," and it was the Christian's duty to labor against it. Consistent with the Bible, traditional orthodoxy viewed false gospels as "accursed" and false teachers as "anti-Christs." Fosdick used these terms as references to political realities. He also exhorted his listeners to "cease excommunicating one another." With the word *excommunication*, Fosdick transformed a word that had typically been used to speak of church discipline to appeal for cooperation in the peace movement.[61] Fosdick's adaptation of religious language to describe political realities was a clear example of the secularization of religion in America.

One of the clearest expressions of a radio program's reach and influence is an examination of the letters that are written in response. Fosdick's rebellion against orthodoxy, practical advice for spiritual living, and antiwar sentiments won him a massive following. By examining this following we can better understand the extent to which Fosdick influenced American religion.

The Federal Council of Churches, the sponsoring agent of *National Vespers*, was routinely flooded with letters expressing gratitude to Dr.

---

61. Harry Emerson Fosdick Collection. Fosdick would broadcast a similar message on November 8, 1942, entitled, "Peace, Peace, When There Is No Peace." His antiwar sentiment is clear: "This Armistice Day we are sober. The achievement of peace is plainly the most difficult task mankind ever undertook. If we ever get it, it will be, as it were, a miracle, the obstacles to it are so terrific and the cost of it so immense. It is not enough to hate war, to call it mankind's major curse from which all other curses spawn, to renounce it or decide to stay out of it. It is not enough to love peace, desire it and sing its praises. The only way to escape war is to create realistic political substitutes for it. The only way to win peace is to pay its enormous price. In such a sober spirit this week we celebrate Armistice Day."

Fosdick and his radio ministry. Betty Gough, Fosdick's secretary for decades, catalogued some of the mail statistics:

> In 1947 someone asked the question, What was the largest number of letters received as a result of one sermon, and the answer was the sermon of March 12, 1944, for the sermon "A Time to Stress Unity." 8,248 letters came in about it. The season when the greatest number of letters came in was the one beginning in October 1944 and running through May 1945, with 34 weeks, and 27 broadcasts by Dr. Fosdick. The number received was 134,827.[62]

A listener from a "small town" in 1928 wrote, "One feels every day the urge to express gratitude in some way for the richness that you are adding to our lives. A few years ago I was able to get into New York for a weekend, I counted it a rare treat if I could stand in line for an hour on Sunday morning and possibly secure a seat to hear Dr. Fosdick speak and now, thanks to you, I sit in my own easy chair and what a feast of good things I enjoy."[63] A retired school teacher took the time to write, "I wish very much to tell you that I enjoy the Sunday vespers exceedingly—the organ, quartet, familiar hymns and, best of all, the sermon. It is meat and drink to my soul. I hunger for just such sermons. At 5:30 p.m. I lock my doors, put out the lights, so that no one may interrupt me, and then listen in. The hour is all too short."[64] One enthusiastic listener could not hold back his appreciation:

> I beg to express my appreciation of the National Radio Vespers. I consider this the finest thing that comes to us over the radio. As for Dr. Fosdick you have found just the right man. His personality travels over the radio, which is a most remarkable thing, as we usually think we have to see a man to feel his personality. I doubt if there is another preacher in the U.S. who is such an inspiration as Dr. Fosdick is. He appeals powerfully to all kinds of people, whether they have any religion or not. He is *Everyman's* preacher.[65]

Another letter gave the picture of several people huddled around the radio, captured by Fosdick's words: "We have a radio in the home and for weeks have been getting the Radio Vespers and you! That hour is the most helpful and enjoyable of the whole week and that is saying much, since we

---

62. Harry Emerson Fosdick Collection.
63. Harry Emerson Fosdick Collection.
64. Harry Emerson Fosdick Collection.
65. Harry Emerson Fosdick Collection, emphasis original.

get many fine programs. Nearly always there are friends and neighbors who join us to listen in."⁶⁶ Fosdick's radio program even captured the imagination of at least one self-professed non-Christian for the simple reason that Fosdick was not a fundamentalist:

> I have listened to your Sunday afternoon discussions for two years or more and have long wanted to write and tell you how highly I appreciate your broad and tolerant views on the question of religion. My neglect so far in doing this comes from the fact that *I am not a Christian* and hence am somewhat reluctant in expressing my feelings to one who is a confessed Christian. You see Doctor, I have had my [—-]ings with Christians before and I am somewhat gun shy. However, after listening to your radio talk today I decided to take the plunge. . . . Frankly I am still a free thinker, agnostic, skeptic or whatever the right name happens to be, and do not accept a great deal of what you say in your talks. However, the point I want to get at is this: that of all the radio preachers I listen to, and I listen to quite a few, you are positively the only one who interests me. Your tolerance is not only broad it is light, and what is more important, intelligent. And so even though I cannot always follow your line of reasoning still at the end of your discussions I find myself in a content [———] mood and not irritated or plain mad as I usually am after listening to some of the so-called Christian lights of our day. Do not think I intend to flatter you for there is no reason why I should. I only want to convey my sincere thanks and appreciation to one who seems to have a sympathetic understanding of the feelings and viewpoints of those who like myself are regarded by the majority of Christendom as "infidels" and therefore fit subjects for the "Fiery Pit."⁶⁷

The hundreds of thousands of letters that streamed into the program demonstrated the wide influence of Fosdick's ideas. "Modernism's Moses" was leading multitudes of people out of arid and stultifying orthodoxy and into the more reasonable and practical piety of theological liberalism.

When Fosdick retired from Riverside Church and as a professor at Union Seminary, he also walked away from the microphone. The *New York Times* announced his departure on November 21, 1946:

> The Rev. Dr. John Sutherland Bonnell, pastor of the Fifth Avenue Presbyterian Church, has been appointed to succeed the Rev. Dr. Harry Emerson Fosdick on the weekly 'National

66. Harry Emerson Fosdick Collection.
67. Harry Emerson Fosdick Collection, emphasis added.

Vespers' radio program, it was announced yesterday. The program is broadcast each Sunday by the American Broadcasting Company. The appointment was made by the Radio Committee of the Federal Council of Churches in America.

When Dr. Fosdick recently retired as pastor of the Riverside Church and as Professor of Homiletics in Union Theological Seminary he decided also to give up the weekly half-hour radio program he had founded and conducted for almost a score of years.... It has been estimated that Dr. Fosdick preached weekly to radio audiences of 2,500,000 to 3,000,000 persons.[68]

By preaching over the air to as many as three million people each week, Fosdick's radio ministry left an indelible mark on the American church and the direction of Protestantism for years to come.

Harry Emerson Fosdick died of a heart attack on October 5, 1969, at the age of 91. In his obituary in the *New York Times*, Edward Fiske referred to Fosdick as "an apostle of theological liberalism" who spent much of his ministry career in the throes of the modernist-fundamentalist conflict. Fiske continued, "In this polarized and tension-filled situation, Dr. Fosdick clearly stood with the iconoclasts. He rejected the worldview of the Fundamentalists and paid little attention to the doctrines that they regarded as the tests of orthodoxy."[69] The obituary reveals something important about Fosdick that, ironically, made him more like the fundamentalists than he would ever dare admit:

> In the mid-thirties he preached a famous sermon entitled, "The Church Must Go Beyond Modernism." In it he declared that the battle against Fundamentalism had been won and urged modernists to abandon the polemics of the past and confidently move on to the new task of criticizing culture. "We cannot harmonize Christ with culture," he declared. "What Christ does to modern culture is to challenge it."[70]

With fundamentalism severely weakened in the mid-1930s, Fosdick was looking for another fight. Fosdick's positive talk about peace, victorious living, and unity required doing battle against the enemies of the modernist gospel. If the fundamentalists had been defeated, then it was time to battle the materialism and selfishness of modern secularism. Compared to the old orthodox religion, however, Fosdick's liberal Christianity had already conceded the chief ground to secularism.

68. Harry Emerson Fosdick Collection.
69. Fiske, "Harry Emerson Fosdick Dies."
70. Fiske, "Harry Emerson Fosdick Dies."

CONCLUSION

Harry Emerson Fosdick's ministry career was marked by a commitment to practical spiritual living as well as a relentless rebellion against the theological orthodoxy of his youth. Radio was a major instrument that Fosdick employed to transform American religion from traditional orthodoxy to a theological system more compatible with the modern spirit. *National Vespers* aired at a time when radio was quickly becoming a dominant form of media in America. Fosdick rode the wave known as radio's Golden Age. As early as 1941 the record shows Fosdick receiving letters from supporters thanking him for his television ministry. At the height of his influence, Fosdick's radio ministry was being augmented by his television ministry. In telling the story of Harry Emerson Fosdick and *National Vespers*, this chapter argued that Fosdick's radio ministry was a driving force in a growing movement away from Protestant orthodoxy in America. Fosdick saw radio as a powerful tool to serve mankind—to bring healing and hope to America during a time of tremendous national challenge—and one way to do that was to motivate people toward a new approach to their faith. This movement is the aspect of Fosdick's ministry that sets him at odds with the other radio preachers in this study. For McPherson, Maier, and Fuller, radio was a means of reaffirming the old-time religion. In this sense, all three are rightly seen as fundamentalists. Fosdick, in contrast, was determined to move away from Protestant orthodoxy by blazing a new theological trail for the modern era. He persuaded large numbers of people to follow him into a liberal faith, a faith that in many respects was designed as a compromise with modern secular commitments. Radio played an important role in that success.

# 3

Aimee Semple McPherson

Radio Superstar of the Foursquare Gospel

AIMEE SEMPLE MCPHERSON'S MINISTRY accelerated a movement in America toward an experiential religion with an ecumenical appeal for world evangelization. As one of the most celebrated Christian figures of the early twentieth century, McPherson's ministry helped make the American church more accepting of important aspects of secularization. McPherson eschewed substantive theological content in favor of a doctrinal minimalism capable of crossing denominational lines. Simply put, McPherson's ministry transformed religion in America. Radio played a major role in this transformation.[1]

McPherson used the December 1923 issue of her newsletter, the *Bridal Call Foursquare*, to announce her ambitious radio intentions, clearly indicating that, from the earliest days of her career in Los Angeles, radio was to play a key role in her ministry:

> An almost unbelievable miracle has happened to the modern preacher! It has become possible to stand in the pulpit and, speaking in a normal voice, reach hundreds of thousands of listeners. Imagine being seated comfortably in your own home

---

1. On the life and ministry career of Aimee Semple McPherson, see especially Sutton, *Aimee Semple McPherson*; Epstein, *Sister McPherson*; Blumhofer, *Aimee Semple McPherson*; Hangen, *Redeeming the Dial*, 57–79.

and hearing a whole church service being rendered 4,000 miles away! As pastor of Angelus Temple, the writer thinks so highly of the possibilities of winning souls by speaking through the air that she has arranged for a powerful 500 watt Class A broadcasting station to be installed at the earliest possible date.[2]

When it came to radio, McPherson did what she always did: she strove to outdo the competition. It was not enough for this nationally recognized itinerant preacher from rural Canada to simply have a radio show. She wanted an entire station dedicated to Christian programming. In a worldwide fundraising blitz that lasted about a year, Sister McPherson raised the necessary $25,000 for equipment and oversaw the installation of two massive radio towers perched atop the dome of the 5,300-seat Angelus Temple in Los Angeles.[3] On February 6, 1924, Kall Foursquare Gospel (KFSG) went on the air, making it "the first totally religious station, owned by a church, in the nation" and making McPherson the "first woman to receive a license from the United States of America for a radio station."[4] The Foursquare Gospel was ready to be broadcast over the airwaves. Radio was the primary means of mass communication that McPherson harnessed to transform American religion.

---

2. Cited in Duarte, "History of Radio Station KFSG."

3. Duarte, "History of Radio Station KFSG," 8. In addition to the cost of equipment, station KFSG initially cost about $10,000 annually to operate (5). McPherson acknowledged the substantial start-up costs but remained determined to proceed: "This did rather nonplus us for the moment, having so many other lines of activity that also demand large outlays for the Master's service. Nevertheless, the Lord had said, 'Go ye into all the world and preach the gospel to every creature,' and where in all the world could we find a method which so completely fulfill the Master's desire and command as the preaching over radio; for wherever a tiny cottage or desert shack or millionaire's residence up-flung its antennae, wherever the rich man roamed, or wherever the sick man turned feverishly upon is cot and turned on his radio receiving set, there he could hear the story of Jesus and His love" (5). McPherson's primary means of raising funds for KFSG was through her magazine, *Bridal Call Foursquare*. In *Redeeming the Dial*, Hangen notes the importance of the revivalist networks and print media for the success of evangelical radio: "Sister McPherson's magazine campaign for funds to establish KFSG underscored the key role that the medium of print, and the experience gained in itinerant tent revivalism, played in launching the medium of radio within the evangelical subculture. Both revival and print networks paved the way for radio to unify the national community of like-minded Christians by creating and strengthening what we might today call 'virtual communities': people sharing common interests and goals but physically separated over long distances. What radio would add to this already vibrant evangelical world—and what Sister McPherson found so exciting to contemplate—was simultaneity of experience" (66).

4. Duarte, "History of Radio Station KFSG," 5.

McPherson's relatively brief ministry career was successful in advancing the influence of religion in American culture. McPherson's ministry, however, changed religion in America. In doing so, McPherson contributed to the secularization of the American church. This was an unintended consequence of McPherson's ministry.

McPherson's life and ministry is filled with ironies. She was born in a small rural town in eastern Canada (Ingersoll, Ontario) but became famous in one of the fastest growing cities in America in the 1920s and 1930s (Los Angeles). McPherson was a preacher who decried worldliness and encouraged piety but employed many of the methods of Hollywood and the broader secular world to garner publicity. Moreover, although McPherson was the author of the "Foursquare Gospel"—an attempt to summarize simply the centrality of Jesus and the work of the Holy Spirit in the life of the Christian—McPherson herself, more often than not, was the center of attention in her life and ministry.

McPherson's use of radio in particular was ironic. On the one hand, it served to promote the old-time religion that was being marginalized in an increasingly secular nation. The hundreds of thousands of people who tuned in to KFSG on a daily or weekly basis were encouraged by what Matthew Sutton calls "a hybrid pentecostal-fundamentalist theology."[5] On the other hand, radio also facilitated the fame of McPherson that, intentionally or not, took attention away from substantive theological content on the airwaves. As Edith Blumhofer observes, "Sister herself was what the crowds really craved."[6] McPherson became a cultural phenomenon by eschewing doctrine and theology—"She disdained formal philosophy and theology"[7]—instead promoting an experiential religion with an ecumenical appeal for world evangelization. As one of the most celebrated Christian figures of the early twentieth century, McPherson unwittingly contributed to the subversion of theology in America.

THE MAKING OF A CHRISTIAN SUPERSTAR

McPherson's adult ministry was shaped by her childhood in profound ways. For example, in her autobiography, *This Is That,* McPherson presented her birth as the answer to her mother's earnest prayer for a daughter. This daughter, her mother hoped, would fulfill the ministry given to one who had been "caught in the devil's net" of domesticity:

5. Sutton, *Aimee Semple McPherson*, 53.
6. Blumhofer, *Aimee Semple McPherson*, 230.
7. Blumhofer, *Aimee Semple McPherson*, 19.

One day, after reading over and over the story of Hannah, she went to her room, and closing the door, kneeled by her bed, and prayed unto the Lord, and vowed a vow, saying—

"Oh, Lord, You called me to preach the Gospel, but somehow I have failed You and cannot go, but if You will only hear my prayer, as you heard Hannah's prayer of old, and give me a little baby girl, I will give her unreservedly into Your service, that she may preach the word I should have preached, fill the place I should have filled, and live the life I should have lived in Thy service. O Lord, hear and answer me; give me the witness that Thou hast heard me, O Lord, for Thine own Name's sake. Amen."

Turning toward the window, she swept back the curtains and gazed wistfully up at the dark clouds shrouding the face of the sky and shutting out the sunshine beyond.

Suddenly there came a rift in the clouds, and a ray of sunlight illumined yonder hilltop, moved quickly down the slope of the hill, reached the valley, the orchard, the house itself, and fell upon the white, anxious face with its tear-reddened eyes, framed in the window, lighting it with divine radiance, hope and courage, and swept on into the room, flooding it with golden glory.[8]

In telling her birth narrative, two themes that marked McPherson's life and ministry stand out: her self-conscious exceptionalism[9] and her emphasis on subjective religious experience. McPherson was the "chosen one" to carry out her mother's unfulfilled ministry. Moreover, the confirmation of McPherson's birth came through an experience of the divine—a ray of light piercing through the clouds and into the room of a praying mother. These themes came back again and again in McPherson's ministry and helped create the larger-than-life persona that would help change American religion.

McPherson's childhood exposure to the Salvation Army and Methodism helped shape her adult ministry. She was born to James and Mildred "Minnie" Kennedy in rural Salford, Ontario, on October 9, 1890. McPherson was the only child born into a family that farmed one hundred acres, including three orchards. James was a devout Methodist and Minnie a devoted member of the Salvation Army. Edith Blumhofer explained how both Methodism and the Salvation Army deeply influenced McPherson:

---

8. McPherson, *This Is That*, 16.

9. Biographers have made much of the theme of American exceptionalism in McPherson's preaching, but McPherson's conviction that she was set apart for sacred purposes was, perhaps, the more dominant theme in her ministry. Indeed, McPherson was convinced that *she* was exceptional.

> Both the proprieties of the Protestantism of the broader culture and the fervor of the Salvation Army formed little McPherson's religious impressions. In her home, they were typified by the contrasting religious styles of James and Minnie. Outside the home, they were reinforced by the relative magnificence of Salford's new Methodist Church and by Ingersoll's starkly utilitarian Salvation Army barracks. In the hushed surroundings of the former, reverence found expression in decorous worship. In the simple setting of the latter, commitment expressed itself in the noise of battle and impromptu shouts of victory.[10]

McPherson's adult ministry shared many of the qualities of the Salvation Army, including her penchant for publicity and the fact that she, like an army, "never arrived anywhere quietly."[11] McPherson wrote of the profound influence that her mother had on her religious development from an early age and throughout most of her adult life and ministry:

> If anyone should ask me which of my childhood memories I hold most dear, I should skip over the beloved wee lambies, the big Newfoundland dog, the bossies, the colts, the downy little goslings and chickens, my white doves, and numerous other childish treasures of my heart, and should tell of that hallowed twilight hour when, clasped tightly in my Mother's arms, we rocked to and fro in the big old comfy rocker, as she told me the most wonderful Bible stories and sang hymns of the Saviour's love.[12]

During McPherson's childhood years her mother served as Junior Sergeant-Major in the Salvation Army, a position that gave her responsibility for the spiritual care of "a great flock of young people."[13] "Very proud was I of my Mother's imposing title," remembered McPherson. She continued, "It seemed very grand and important to me, and not satisfied to await the next meeting at the barracks, I would often convert the big bedroom upstairs into a meeting house."[14] With this McPherson proceeded to conduct

---

10. Blumhofer, *Aimee Semple McPherson*, 45–46. For a detailed discussion of the Salvation Army in Ontario during McPherson's childhood, see 33–52.

11. Blumhofer, *Aimee Semple McPherson*, 35.

12. McPherson, *This Is That*, 22–27. In this autobiography, there is almost no mention of her father in the chapter on McPherson's childhood days. McPherson appears to give essentially all the credit for her early exposure to Christianity to her mother. McPherson's mother played a vital role in her adult ministry until the early 1930s when they had a falling out over finances.

13. McPherson, *This Is That*, 26.

14. McPherson, *This Is That*, 26.

her own Salvation Army meetings, doing her best imitation of the local Sergeant-Major. This included reciting an opening prayer, singing a solo, giving a testimony, and reading the Bible before closing the pretend meeting in prayer.[15] McPherson saw all of this through the lens of her exceptionalism: "As you can see God has His hand upon me, and the desires of my heart, and the aspirations of my mind in these early days."[16] These experiences were the training ground for McPherson's adult ministry.

Even in the relatively wholesome surroundings of rural Canada in the early twentieth century, McPherson was exposed to aspects of modernity that challenged her budding Christian faith. For example, as a young teenager, McPherson began experimenting with the entertainment arts in her local Methodist church. McPherson had a natural presence on stage and quickly became a hit doing mostly comedic skits and plays before Christian audiences.[17] "The praise and applause of the people," McPherson recalled, "was very alluring to some of us younger ones, and we often talked together of going on the stage, arguing that the church was giving us a good training on this line and that anyway there was not much difference whether a play or a concert was given in the church or at the theatre."[18] These dramatic rehearsals would become one of the hallmarks of McPherson's adult ministry with Sunday church services at Angelus Temple becoming famous for dramatic gospel presentations. McPherson's love for applause as a young person continued as an adult. Other temptations at this time included novels, motion pictures, and McPherson's first "college ball"—a formal dance that her mother agreed to let McPherson attend only after much "pleading and coaxing."[19] McPherson recalled that during these adolescent days her "heart was growing cold and far from God."[20]

The biggest challenge for McPherson at this time, however, was her confrontation with evolutionary biology. This struggle helped shape her later opposition to Darwinism—a belief system she opposed vigorously as an adult. After being introduced to Darwin and his theory of evolution in high school, McPherson admitted, "How these theories or teachings impressed other students I cannot say, but they had a remarkable effect upon me."[21] To try and find a resolution to her growing crisis of faith, McPherson sought

15. McPherson, *This Is That*, 26.
16. McPherson, *This Is That*, 26.
17. McPherson, *This Is That*, 28.
18. McPherson, *This Is That*, 28.
19. McPherson, *This Is That*, 29.
20. McPherson, *Lost and Restored*, 122.
21. McPherson, *This Is That*, 30.

counsel from area pastors about the relationship between faith and science. McPherson remained unsettled. Matthew Sutton explains what McPherson did next:

> Receiving no satisfactory answers, she sent a letter to the Family Herald and Weekly Star, a Canadian national paper, asking why taxpayers supported schools that obviously undermined Christianity. Its publication provided Aimee with her first exposure to fame: the letter provoked responses from all over North America.[22]

This episode helps explain McPherson's swift adoption of mass media, including radio, during her adult ministry and the way she was able to contribute to the transformation of American religion. For McPherson, mass media, including print, radio, and film, played a vital role in her efforts to promote her particular brand of old-time religion.

As for the problems posed by Darwinism, a seventeen-year-old McPherson concluded that belief in the Bible and in evolutionary theory could not be harmonized. If human beings were merely a result of a process of evolution, McPherson reasoned, then the Bible was not truthful when it claimed that God created mankind. McPherson began to think sympathetically of the modernist preachers who said there were errors and mistakes in the Bible. McPherson let these arguments play out to their logical conclusion:

> Well, then, if the Bible is mistaken in one place it is very apt to be mistaken in others. Its information is not reliable, and I guess there's no God at all, and that's why Christians act so pious in church on Sundays and do as they please through the week. No, I guess there *is* no God.[23]

Before long, however, McPherson abandoned her atheism in an abrupt conversion. Never again would evolutionary biology be a stumbling block for McPherson. In fact, opposition to Darwinism became one of the marks of her ministry to reclaim the old-time religion for the modern era. It happened during the Christmas season of 1907.[24] The Ingersoll Pentecostal

---

22. Sutton, *Aimee Semple McPherson*, 10.

23. Sutton, *Aimee Semple McPherson*, 30, emphasis original.

24. Sutton, *Aimee Semple McPherson*, 34–40; Epstein, *Sister McPherson*, 473. Epstein estimates that McPherson's conversion took place in February 1908. This, however, is to ignore McPherson's own testimony and misunderstand the pentecostal teaching of a post-conversion baptism in the Holy Spirit. Although it is true that McPherson believed her baptism in the Holy Spirit to be in February 1908, she understood her conversion to be in December 1907. For the correct sequence of McPherson's conversion and baptism in the Holy Spirit, see Blumhofer, *Aimee Semple McPherson*, 60–66.

Mission was hosting a "Holy Ghost Revival" led by the itinerant preacher Robert Semple. McPherson had been driving down Main Street when a sign advertising "Pentecostal Power" and "meetings every night and all day Sunday" caught her eye. With her father's approval McPherson made plans to attend the next day's meeting. Upon arriving at the meeting McPherson noted that there was "something strange about these people, they seemed to be so earnest." She also appears to have been immediately smitten with Robert Semple:

> Then a tall young man, six feet two inches in height, rose to his feet on the platform and taking his Bible in his hand opened it and began to read. His was a frank, kindly face, with Irish blue eyes that had the light of heaven in them, chestnut brown hair, with one rebellious brown curl which would insist in falling down close to his eye no matter how often he brushed it back.[25]

But Semple's looks were not the only thing that captured McPherson's heart. His words pierced "like an arrow through my heart, for he was preaching under divine inspiration and in power and demonstration of the Holy Spirit." She continued,

> He really spoke as though he believed there was a Jesus and a Holy Spirit, not some vague, mythical, intangible shadow, something away off yonder in the clouds, but a real, living, vital, tangible, moving reality dwelling in our hearts and lives—making us His temple—causing us to walk in Godliness, holiness and adoration in His presence.... It was just God, God, God from one end to the other, and his words seemed to rain down upon me, and every one of them hurt some particular part of my spirit and life until I could not tell where I hurt the worst.[26]

---

25. Sutton, *Aimee Semple McPherson*, 35. Robert Semple was instructed in pentecostal theology and practice in Chicago by William Durham, a participant in 1907 in the Azusa Street revivals in Los Angeles. See Sutton, *Aimee Semple McPherson*, 39. Durham became very controversial as he abandoned the traditional pentecostal (and Wesleyan) understanding of a "second blessing" in favor of his own doctrine of "The Finished Work" that "assigned sanctification to the moment of conversion." See Synan, *Holiness-Pentecostal Tradition*, 149–52. Probably due to the early influence of Semple, McPherson adopted the "finished work" view of sanctification for much of her ministry career. This put her at odds with many Pentecostals, but also opened doors for evangelistic cooperation that she may not have experienced otherwise. In 1936 until her death it appears that McPherson made a conscious effort to return to classic Pentecostalism by advocating a "second blessing" in the Holy Spirit evidenced by speaking in tongues. See Sutton, *Aimee Semple McPherson*, 200–201.

26. Sutton, *Aimee Semple McPherson*, 36.

Semple had taken as his text the second chapter of Acts with its exhortation of repentance and faith in Jesus Christ. True to the pentecostal tradition, Semple authenticated his message by speaking in tongues, which McPherson interpreted as a word from God to her: "To me it was the voice of God thundering into my soul awful words of conviction and condemnation, and though the message was spoken in tongues it seemed as though God had said to me—'YOU are a poor, lost, miserable, hell-deserving sinner!'"[27] McPherson left the meeting that night under deep conviction, convinced that if she were to die, she was not ready to meet the Lord. For days McPherson struggled with an inner turmoil that she believed "few [had] known."[28] The breakthrough came on the third day:

> At the end of the third day, while driving home from school, I could stand it no longer. The lowering skies above, the trees, the fields, the very road beneath me seemed to look down upon me with displeasure, and I could see written everywhere—"Poor, lost, miserable, hell-deserving sinner!" Utterly at the end of myself—not stopping to think what preachers or entertainment committees or anyone else would think—I threw up my hands, and all alone in that country road, I screamed aloud toward the heavens: "Oh, Lord God, be merciful to me, a sinner!" Immediately the most wonderful change took place in my soul. Darkness passed away and light entered. The sky was filled with brightness, the trees, the fields, and the little snowbirds flitting to and fro were praising the Lord and smiling upon me.[29]

McPherson's conversion was not merely the experience of throwing up her hands and screaming to the heavens or sensing darkness pass away and light break in. In McPherson's mind she experienced the blood of Christ in a way that led to tears and song:

> So conscious was I of the pardoning blood of Jesus that I seemed to feel it flowing over me. I discovered that my face was bathed in tears, which dropped on my hands as I held the reins. And without effort or apparent thought on my part I was singing that old familiar hymn: "Take my life and let it be consecrated, Lord, to Thee; take my moments and my days, let them flow in ceaseless praise."[30]

---

27. Sutton, *Aimee Semple McPherson*, 37.
28. McPherson, *Lost and Restored*, 125.
29. McPherson, *This is That*, 39.
30. McPherson, *This is That*, 39.

McPherson had experienced salvation. The rest of McPherson's days would be spent, as the title of another of her autobiographies reads, "in the service of the King," laboring to give others this same experience of God. McPherson's conversion experience explains in part the experiential religion she brought to the masses through her radio ministry. Rather than precise doctrinal formulations or polemical theology, this charismatic experience was paramount in McPherson's ministry and contributed to the transformation of American religion.

McPherson not only came away from the revival service of 1907 with an awakened faith, but also with love for a man, the Irish Pentecostal evangelist Robert Semple, who became the first of her three husbands. Semple's influence on McPherson shaped her ministry for life. They were married in August 1908, and in 1910 they set off to convert China. Just a few weeks after their arrival in the country, both McPherson and Robert contracted dysentery and malaria, landing them in a Hong Kong hospital built for missionaries. Only McPherson departed China alive. As part of her personal testimony, McPherson told the story publicly many times. Through it all, McPherson emphasized her powerful experience of the "Blessed Holy Spirit, the Comforter":

> Then, as I stood by his bed, and saw that, unconscious as he was, the light of the glory world illuminated his face, I sank down in a heap at the side of the bed and clung to his cold hand. Then, at that moment, when all the world seemed to be crumbling and slipping from beneath my feet, the Comforter, the Blessed Holy Spirit, whom Jesus had sent, rose up within me and revealed Jesus in such a precious way, made the will of God so sweet, showed the prepared mansions so real, that there, by the death-bed of Robert Semple, from whom I had never dreamed of parting, the Blessed Holy Spirit, the Comforter, enabled me to say, "Glory to Jesus! The Lord gave and the Lord taketh away. Blessed be the name of the Lord!"[31]

McPherson, not yet twenty years old, was a widow, sick, and eight-months pregnant living in a foreign country with no family to support her. Her relationship with Robert Semple, however, left an indelible mark on McPherson, and, consequently, Semple's experiential religion continued to have influence on multitudes of people through McPherson's ministry.

---

31. McPherson, *Lost and Restored*, 134-35.

THE CALL TO FULL-TIME ITINERATE MINISTRY

McPherson's sense of call to full-time evangelistic ministry came to her through an experiential "crisis" that further demonstrates what would become her hallmark emphasis on religious experience over the air. Within two years, Aimee, then in New York living with her daughter and mother who had taken a job at the Manhattan headquarters of the Salvation Army, met and married Harold McPherson, a grocery store salesman.[32] Aimee wondered if she would be able to forfeit the life of vocational ministry that she had envisioned with her first husband Robert Semple for the domestic life Harold desired for her. She could not. Aimee equated her efforts to abandon her call to evangelistic work with the disobedience of Jonah in the Old Testament:

> It was at this time that I married and settled down to furnish a comfortable home. I was like Jonah running away from Nineveh, and enjoyed about as rough a passage when I tried to get out of the evangelistic work and settle down to domestic life. In the flesh, I was weary of having no home or abiding city. We engaged a modern flat, and I settled down to enjoy a comfortable passage from Joppa to Tarshish. All the time I heard the call, clear and distinct as Jonah did, "Preach the Word."[33]

Only after undergoing two surgeries, battling depression, and enduring a nervous breakdown, did McPherson, on her deathbed, yield to the Lord and agree to reenter vocational ministry:

> Just before losing consciousness, as I hovered between life and death, came the voice of my Lord, so loud that it startled me: "NOW WILL YOU GO?" And I knew that it was "Go," one way or the other: that if I did not go into the work as a soul-winner and get back into the will of God, Jesus would take me to Himself before He would permit me to go on without Him and be lost. . . . With my little remaining strength, I managed to gasp: "Yes Lord I'll go." And go I did![34]

Within two weeks, "to the amazement of everyone," McPherson was up and well and resolved to not allow anything to hinder her call back to full-time gospel ministry. This included her marriage to Harold, who tried to take up the life of an itinerant evangelist in the hope of keeping his

---

32. Blumhofer, *Aimee Semple McPherson*, 109–30.
33. Blumhofer, *Aimee Semple McPherson*, 135.
34. McPherson, *This Is That*, 78.

marriage intact. The effort failed. In June 1915, Aimee left Harold and, with her two children (she and Harold had a son, Rolf), recommitted herself to the life of an itinerant preacher. Her marriage to Harold was a casualty of Aimee's Jonah-like "fleeing to Tarshish":

> When McPherson told her life story, she always glossed over her relationship with Harold as if it had never held any charm or significance. Using a pointed biblical analogy, in one of her autobiographies she called the period of her marriage to Harold "From Nineveh to Tarshish and Back." In her mind, what had happened was clear: like the prophet Jonah in the Old Testament, she had attempted to run from God, and Harold had been part of that running.[35]

McPherson's justification for leaving her husband is instructive. It shows how religion in America could now make room for doing something that at one time would be considered sinful behavior, namely, leaving a spouse for reasons related to one's career. Not only did McPherson's experientialist faith permit her to leave Harold given her sense of call to vocational ministry, it demanded that she do so.

For the next several years McPherson traveled throughout eastern Canada, New England, and Florida, honing her evangelistic skills at various pentecostal camp meetings. McPherson moved from one revival meeting to the next in her "Gospel Car"—a 1912 Packard with evangelistic slogans emblazoned on the sides, such as "Where will you spend eternity?" and "Judgment Day is coming: Get right with God."[36] This use of a car to "advertise" the faith demonstrates McPherson's willingness to use mass marketing tools in the service of religion. This impulse found many outlets during her later ministry in Los Angeles. Tona Hangen summarizes these itinerant years while giving insight into McPherson's indefatigable spirit and outreach to rural and urban folks alike:

> She preached to black and white migrant workers in Florida cotton and tobacco fields, among poor and working classes in large cities and mountain towns along the route, following an emerging Pentecostal grassroots network. During these years she lived meeting to meeting, never more than a few dollars ahead. She camped under her car, fished for dinner, and relied on the charity of others to feed herself and her family.[37]

---

35. Blumhofer, *Aimee Semple McPherson*, 131. For the reference to "From Nineveh to Tarshish and Back" see McPherson, *This Is That*, 71–81.

36. Foursquare Heritage Center.

37. Hangen, *Redeeming the Dial*, 60–61.

These and other similar experiences shaped McPherson's ecumenism. McPherson's Pentecostalism, with its doctrinal minimalism, was perfectly suited to mass radio appeal.

McPherson first arrived in Los Angeles toward the end of 1918. She had travelled the country with her mother and two small children.[38] McPherson was in Los Angeles for a series of revival meetings taking place at the Pentecostal Mission known as Victoria Hall, a downtown mission that seated approximately one thousand people.[39] McPherson was an instant success:

> As she had in the east, McPherson quickly gathered a following, and her children—who were often seen in the services and talked about in the sermons—won their hearts. As McPherson told it, one Sunday night a woman stood to announce that God had instructed her to give Mrs. McPherson a lot on which to build a home for the children. The offer of land sparked a chain reaction in which people volunteered everything necessary from construction oversight to furniture to landscaping. A builder in the audience volunteered his services, and just three months later the house McPherson would always fondly call "the house that God built" was ready for occupancy. It stood near Culver City, across from a public school, and McPherson marveled that God had paid such close attention to all her needs. In the autobiography written soon after, she concluded her description of the house with the words: "Let everybody that reads say 'Glory'!" The family moved in, with a housekeeper who cared for the children, leaving McPherson and her mother free for itinerant evangelism.[40]

This event demonstrates how McPherson's ministry accelerated a trend in American religion toward celebrity. Through her dynamic personality, McPherson was able to win over the masses.

McPherson's appeal on the revival circuit was not only her abilities as a performer. Her appeal relied on her preaching the "old-time gospel" in an idiom that promoted "old-time experience." In other words, McPherson held out the promise of an experience with God as people decided to embrace old-fashioned Bible Christianity. Miraculous healing played a prominent role in McPherson's ministry, but it was not paramount. One of her biographers explained, "People always clamored for more healing,

---

38. Blumhofer, *Aimee Semple McPherson*, 135.
39. Blumhofer, *Aimee Semple McPherson*, 141.
40. Blumhofer, *Aimee Semple McPherson*, 142.

and sometimes, touched by their desperation, she acquiesced. But for the most part, she focused her energies on the call to decision about the gospel that had deep roots in the revival tradition."[41] Indeed, what drew the masses to McPherson was her "experience-oriented, dynamic packaging of the Christian gospel: something happened to them, just as it had happened to her and, as she promised, would happen to anyone who dared to believe."[42] McPherson's "dynamic packaging of the Christian gospel" in terms of "experience" minimized any need for substantive theological discourse in her ministry. This "experience-oriented" approach to religion contributed to the transformation of theology in America and helped leave the American church ill equipped to repel some of the secularizing trends within modernity.

THE FOUNDATION FOR A RELIGIOUS EMPIRE: ANGELUS TEMPLE

By the early 1920s the years of itinerant preaching had begun to take a toll on McPherson. She decided to put down roots in Los Angeles, at first thinking she would build a modest tabernacle for her evangelistic headquarters. Modesty, however, was not her strong suit. McPherson began planning an elaborate gospel temple to be erected on a plot of land she and her mother had purchased in the Echo Park area of Los Angeles:

> When McPherson initially decided to build in Los Angeles, she had a relatively simple plan in mind. She hoped to erect a wooden "tabernacle" that might hold twenty-five hundred people. But as her popularity grew, she began dreaming of a larger edifice. By the end of 1921, her contractor wrote "that it would never do to erect a building on that parcel of land to accommodate so small a congregation." McPherson agreed. She no longer envisioned a temporary, inexpensive, mobile shelter, a "tabernacle" in the tradition of the Hebrews' wanderings in the wilderness, but a new "temple" to rival King Solomon's in all its splendor and glory. Los Angeles would have a class A, modern, fireproof church that could seat fifty-three hundred people.[43]

The burgeoning city of Los Angeles in the 1920s seemed the perfect place for McPherson to establish her evangelistic work. "In Los Angeles, she

---

41. Blumhofer, *Aimee Semple McPherson*, 152.

42. Blumhofer, *Aimee Semple McPherson*, 202. More will be said on this when McPherson's broadcast sermons are analyzed.

43. Sutton, *Aimee Semple McPherson*, 15.

managed to corral the energy of local boosters, the theology of fundamentalism, and the show biz style of Hollywood into a single religious movement, which surged across the nation and ultimately around the world."[44] What made Los Angeles such a ripe city for someone with McPherson's religious charisma and ambition? One historian of Los Angeles suggested that McPherson, as a "classic nonconformist," was successful because she was surrounded by a whole city bursting with nonconformists in the 1920s and 1930s. This unique milieu of southern California gave McPherson the ideal audience for her particular brand of Christianity:

> Just why southern California and especially Los Angeles should be such a magnet for the offbeat and the eccentric has been a fascinating puzzle. The credit had been laid to climate, geography, and growing pains. The early arrival of health faddists and faith healers is chiefly explained by the prevalence of desperate invalids who were attracted by the climate. To this same group of unfortunates, who believed themselves poised on the edge of eternity, may also be attributed much of the success of salvationists. But this does not account for the Golden Age of Crackpotism in the 1920's and 1930's, when the sick and the old were no longer the chief immigrants.
>
> The larger explanation is that Los Angeles is perennially refreshing itself with newcomers who have left behind them the pressures for conformity. Established and little changing communities, with their patterns of behavior rutted by long practice, have been put far behind. The influence of church, neighborhood, and home are beyond reach; one finds oneself in a city of strangers, for whose opinions and judgments one cares very little. The human personality, whose chief enemy is timidity, finds in the Los Angeles milieu far less to fear. This is the state of mind that has been the city's opportunity for greatness. Too often, however, this opportunity has been frittered away in pursuit of the shallow, the bizarre, and the absurd.[45]

McPherson's personality was given free range in the wide-open religious culture of Los Angeles in the early twentieth century. Her ministry, with its particular brand of charismatic faith, spurred a shift away from established norms of religion and of society.

Another author, and a contemporary of McPherson, described Los Angeles in the 1920s and early 1930s as a hotbed for the "bizarre"—a category that included McPherson:

44. Sutton, *Aimee Semple McPherson*, 8.
45. Nadeau, *Los Angeles*, 228.

> The city is internationally known for its metaphysical versatility, and each year erstwhile Christians in alarming numbers desert the orthodox evangelical churches for temples more bizarre. It is largely, perhaps, a climatic phenomenon. After the frozen folk of Vermont and Wisconsin have been exposed to the melting atmosphere of southern California for ninety days, a subtle change comes over them. Thereafter they demand something more exotic, if not more erotic, than the frigid stuff to which they have been accustomed. This accounts for all the theological love-cults and spiritual schools of sex aberration. Briefly, it may be set down that any geomancer, soothsayer, holy jumper, herb doctor, whirling dervish, snake-charmer, medicaster, table turner, or Evil Eye—practicing any form of black magic, demonology, joint-jerking, witchcraft, thaumaturgy, spirit-rapping, back-rubbing, physical torture, or dietical novelty—any such will find assured success and prosperity in Los Angeles despite fierce competition. All kinds of quacks, therefore, have poured into Los Angeles and southern California for the last twenty years.
>
> The greatest of these, one of the most remarkable women on earth, was, and is, the Reverend Aimee Semple McPherson.[46]

McPherson's experience-oriented, traditional religion helped accelerate a trend away from the old orthodoxy that the masses in the eastern and middle part of the country had fled.

McPherson's ministry must be viewed in the context of the Azusa Street Revival of 1906–1909. This "Pentecostal revolution which occurred in the holiness movement,"[47] paved the way for McPherson's ministry. The event, as reported in the *Los Angeles Times*, included innovative doctrine and religious zeal:

> Meetings are held in a tumble-down shack on Azusa Street, near San Pedro Street, and the devotees of the weird doctrine practice the most fanatical rites, preach the wildest theories, and work themselves into a state of mad excitement in their peculiar zeal. Colored people and a sprinkling of whites compose the congregation, and night is made hideous in the neighborhood by the howlings of the worshippers, who spend hours swaying forth and back in a nerve-racking attitude of prayer and supplication.

---

46. Mayo, *Los Angeles*, 69–70.
47. Synan, *The Holiness-Pentecostal Tradition*, 84.

They claim to have the "gift of tongues" and to be able to comprehend the babel.[48]

William J. Seymour, an African American disciple of Charles F. Parham, led the revival marking the advent of the modern pentecostal movement in America. Seymour advocated the central tenets of the holiness movement, including the "second blessing" of the Holy Spirit for full sanctification. What Seymour (and Parham) popularized was the teaching that this second blessing was evidenced by speaking in tongues. When Seymour first came to Los Angeles from Houston in February 1906, his preaching and prayer meetings were sparsely attended. However, by September of that year, as many as 1,500 people could be seen gathering at the renovated church building at 312 Azusa Street. The revival was getting national attention:

> As the Azusa revival continued, hundreds and later thousands of people began to flock to the mission, both the curious and the serious. Every day trains unloaded visitors from all over the continent. News accounts of the meeting spread across the nation in both the secular and religious press.[49]

The Azusa Street Revival and spread of Pentecostalism in America at this time helps explain McPherson's success. Her ministry entered into a major movement in American religion toward Pentecostalism and other charismatic expressions of the faith identified not primarily by doctrine, but by experience.

McPherson's success in southern California can also be understood apart from the unique circumstances of Los Angeles in the early twentieth century. As Edith Blumhofer explains,

> [McPherson] tapped into a deep reservoir of popular piety in mainstream Protestant denominations and convinced ordinary people of many religious affiliations that she spoke to their needs in their language.... For years, science, psychology, and progressive education had mocked the simple, tough, enduring gospel faith that stood at the core of the revival tradition. The response everywhere seemed to vindicate Sister's insistence that North Americans were spiritually starved. Their churches had succumbed to modern pressures. Movies, radios, and automobiles had transformed American life and had introduced a new set of heroes that were not so convincing as their predecessors had been. Sister seemed to offer something that filled the void:

---

48. Synan, *The Holiness-Pentecostal Tradition*, 84–85.
49. Synan, *The Holiness-Pentecostal Tradition*, 98.

she reassured people that, despite the assaults of modern theories, the ridicule of sophisticates, the disenchantment of intellectuals, and the revisionism of the new scholarship, the "tried and true" gospel that had sustained Americans in the past remained valid in the present and stood as the only hope for the future.[50]

More than an innovator, McPherson was a great popularizer. She applied her considerable talents to fanning the winds of change that were whipping through the American religious landscape.

McPherson accelerated a movement in American religion toward a charismatic ecumenism during a time when modernity threatened to make religion a thing of the past. McPherson helped preserve American religion by tapping into the populist impulse in American culture. However, McPherson's aversion to robust theology and doctrine, while successfully advancing religion, also changed it, making the American church more vulnerable to some of the secularizing trends within modernity.

With the completion of the $1.5-million Angelus Temple in January 1923, McPherson laid the foundation for her religious empire that eventually included a state-of-the-art radio station and Bible school for training evangelists. The radio station and training center allowed McPherson to always think beyond the walls of Angelus Temple. Her longing was to see her influence and fame spread throughout the globe.[51] In this, McPherson was greatly successful. Her success helped transform American religion.

THE FOURSQUARE GOSPEL

To accomplish her goal of a worldwide ministry, McPherson developed the idea of a "Foursquare Gospel." During a sermon in Oakland, California, in October 1922, she proclaimed, "It came to me by inspiration. A perfect Gospel! A complete Gospel for body, for soul, for spirit, and for eternity. . . . In

50. Blumhofer, *Aimee Semple McPherson*, 17, 152–53.

51. "The Great Temple Is Dedicated." McPherson's self-conscious exceptionalism is demonstrated in her comments to a *Los Angeles Times* reporter on the day of the new temple's dedication: "Today is the happiest day of my life. I can hardly believe yet that this great temple has been built for me—that so much of my work has been accomplished. I heard the call to God's work, and left my home on a Canadian farm when I was 17 years old. Since then I have been preaching constantly. Winter found me in the South, summer found me in the North—always conducting evangelistic services. I spent a few years in China in missionary work. Four years ago I came to California. I loved the country and resolved to stay. Something within me told me I must. I arrived here with only $10. At no time have I had any backing or a board of directors, yet today I am holding dedication services in this wonderful temple, built entirely by the contributions of friends from every country of the world. I have never been so happy."

my soul was born a harmony that was struck and sustained upon four, full, quivering strings, and from it were plucked words that sprang and leaped into being—the Foursquare Gospel."[52] By 1922 McPherson had "stripped the Pentecostalism of her youth down to its core" and "shap[ed] it into a less controversial, more ecumenical form of revivalist evangelicalism."[53] What was the content of this "perfect Gospel" that came, according to McPherson, by inspiration of God and was preached weekly to thousands at Angelus Temple and to tens of thousands over the airwaves? It may be that McPherson's "appeal was not ideological or theological but better described in domestic terms. People perceived McPherson as motherly, warm, caring, kind, real."[54] Still, without question, McPherson advanced an identifiable theological system, and the evidence indicates that her "simple gospel of individual salvation" and affirmation of "religious experience and emotional outlet" allowed her to forge relationships across denominational lines with a doctrinal system that "did not in itself alienate," but was actually "unitive."[55]

The hallmarks of McPherson's theology consisted of four "major facets," each designed to give picture to "Jesus Christ in the full four phases of His ministry":[56] a "Savior to a sin-cursed, Satan-deceived world"; a "Baptizer with the Holy Ghost and fire to a timid, weak-kneed Church"; a "great Physician to a sick and dying humanity"; and a "Coming King of Peace to a world tired of war, strife, greed, hate and suffering."[57] McPherson claimed that the Foursquare Gospel was revealed to her while preaching through the Old Testament book of Ezekiel:

> At a meeting in Oakland, California, the Spirit of God was manifested to a wonderful degree. The great tent, which seated 8,000, was packed, and multitudes were standing around its borders. Many had pilgrimaged from afar. Every heart seemed hungry. The subject was "The Vision of Ezekiel" (1:1–28). My soul was awed! My heart athrill! The blazing glory of that heavenly vision seemed to fill not only the tabernacle but the whole earth. In the clouds of heaven—which folded and infolded in fiery glory—Ezekiel had beheld the Being whose glory no mortal can describe. As he gazed upon that marvelous revelation of the Omnipotent One, he perceived four faces. The faces—those of

52. Cited in Sutton, *Aimee Semple McPherson*, 44.
53. Sutton, *Aimee Semple McPherson*, 37.
54. Blumhofer, *Aimee Semple McPherson*, 18.
55. Sutton, *Aimee Semple McPherson*, 37; Blumhofer, *Aimee Semple McPherson*, 17, 18.
56. McPherson, *Foursquare Gospel*, 13.
57. McPherson, *Foursquare Gospel*, 14, emphasis original.

a man, a lion, an ox, and an eagle. These four faces were likened unto the four phases of the Gospel of Jesus Christ.[58]

McPherson frequently faced criticism that she was being novel or innovative with the gospel. For example, she was often asked how she could have insight into a gospel system that had apparently eluded the Christian church for nearly two millennia. Not surprisingly, McPherson's answer was rooted in her self-conscious exceptionalism:

> You may say, "Angelus Temple, Church of the Foursquare Gospel, is only a few years old!" True. True also that the Foursquare Gospel in title is comparatively new; but God has in His Divine Providence chosen to emphasize in these latter days, the four important phases of His Son's Ministry. I have stated that the Foursquare message existed from eternity in type and shadow but for the last few years of time God has seemingly saved this special definition of His Word. The Foursquare Gospel is entirely based on the Word of God and proclaims to a needy world the message of Jesus; the Savior, Baptizer, Healer and Coming King.[59]

McPherson considered herself God's chosen instrument in "the last few years of time" to herald to a needy world the most important aspects of Jesus's ministry. Blumhofer adds, "Sister's worldview was emphatically apocalyptic. The absolute certainty that Jesus was coming soon gave urgency and direction to the restlessness many radical evangelicals felt. Time was short; opportunity beckoned now."[60] McPherson considered herself a key figure in Pentecostalism's "restoration of New Testament power and practice to the church, the 'latter rain' that marked the full recovery of the church's pristine message."[61] "The restoration came as revival, quickening, and empowerment for the church, but it was far more than an ordinary revival: the revival was itself a sign—a 'sign of the times.' Pentecostalism was God's voice 'thundering forth His last appeal.'"[62]

---

58. McPherson, *Foursquare Gospel*, 21–22.
59. McPherson, *Foursquare Gospel*, 21.
60. Blumhofer, *Aimee Semple McPherson*, 205.
61. Blumhofer, *Aimee Semple McPherson*, 206.
62. Blumhofer, *Aimee Semple McPherson*, 207. But Pentecostalism proved too restrictive for McPherson. Blumhofer, *Aimee Semple McPherson*, notes, "Pentecostalism shaped her worldview, but both her inclination and her experiences caused her to adapt its idiom and modify some of its features so that her efforts took on an ecumenical evangelical flavor."

McPherson's theological system, in fact, found its home in the older Pentecostalism of the Wesleyan-Holiness tradition, a point she was at pains to make by the mid-1930s. This tradition includes a set of beliefs and practices traceable to the Methodist movement of the late eighteenth century in England founded by John Wesley. Wesley's teaching on Christian perfection or sanctification inspired a movement that stretched across the Atlantic Ocean. Christian perfection in the Wesleyan-Holiness tradition teaches that Christians can attain holiness (i.e., freedom from voluntary sin) through a distinct second work of grace or baptism in the Holy Spirit. This teaching was systematized and popularized in Wesley's "Plain Account of Christian Perfection." The teaching was propagated in America through preachers such as Francis Asbury, whom Wesley himself put in charge of overseeing the American branch of Methodism.[63] In the 1920s and 1930s McPherson added her own nuances to the tradition in the form of her "Foursquare Gospel" further transforming American religion along charismatic lines.

Another key biblical text for McPherson's theological system was Hebrews 13:8: "Jesus Christ is the same yesterday, and today and forever."[64] The simple premise that McPherson sought to communicate—consistent with her Pentecostalism—was that what was true for the first-century church was true for the contemporary church. In other words, based on the immanence of Jesus Christ, today's Christian can expect to experience the power of the gospel in the same ways that first-century Christians experienced the gospel as demonstrated in the New Testament. For McPherson it was quite simple: if Jesus Christ is the same yesterday, today, and forever, then he remained a savior, baptizer, healer, and coming king for modern Americans.[65] This elementary message of divine power countered the hell fire and brimstone that marked much of the revivalism of McPherson's day. One of McPherson's biographers, Matthew Sutton, explained that "instead of the retributive deity of many revivalists, McPherson promoted a loving, benevolent, and immanent God who worked with humans in the twentieth century exactly as he had in the first to save souls."[66] Indeed, "Sister simply

---

63. For a helpful discussion of Wesley, Christian perfectionism, and the spread of Methodism in America see especially Synan, *Holiness-Pentecostal Tradition*, 8–21.

64. Blumhofer, *Aimee Semple McPherson*, 214, argues that this text "facilitated her appeal to a broad constituency."

65. In *Foursquare Gospel*, McPherson's most exhaustive defense of her theology, she does not offer detailed exegesis of particular biblical texts for her assertions. Rather, her method is to simply quote various verses that appear to support her doctrine.

66. Sutton, *Aimee Semple McPherson*, 47. Likewise, Blumhofer, *Aimee Semple McPherson*, 212, argues, "Using the labels 'Biblical Christianity' or 'Full Gospel Evangelism,' she validated her views by appealing to the New Testament—especially to examples of experience in the Gospels and Acts of the Apostles. If it had happened then,

took the Gospels at face value and promised people that God would meet their needs. The mood was upbeat, confident, friendly, and affirming."[67] This "mood" found fertile soil in which to grow in 1920s and 1930s America and helped transform religion. McPherson's ministry accelerated a movement toward thinking of Christianity in terms of a "mood" or "feeling." Subjective emotion was displacing objective doctrine.

It is not hard to understand how this simple, fourfold gospel message found a receptive audience in the turbulent decades of the 1920s and 1930s. Theological modernism, with its critical methods of biblical interpretation, seemed to make Christianity less accessible to the common man. Additionally, as urbanization continued to radically alter the cultural landscape of the country, people longed for what was tried and true. "Just give me that old-time religion" was the cry of the day for thousands of Americans bewildered by the rapid rate of change and beset by collapsing moral standards and economic distress. Perhaps the most significant cause for McPherson's appeal was that she sought to transcend the fundamentalist-modernist controversy, which had been heating up significantly since 1910. McPherson's message didn't come with a fight. By emphasizing Christ-centered experience rather than doctrinal distinctives, McPherson was able to reach far beyond traditional Pentecostal circles. Edith Blumhofer makes this point by noting the denominational composition of Angelus Temple:

> Angelus Temple was explicitly interdenominational from the start. That, Sister insisted, was the "key" to the "whole wonderful outpouring" that seemed to manifest itself wherever she turned. Sister did not present the Temple as a Pentecostal church but rather as a church that stood for the "whole gospel," or "full gospel evangelism." . . . The Temple was neutral turf where Methodists, Lutherans, Baptists, Presbyterians, Pentecostals, and others met as one, their differences forgotten in their devotion to Christ and their pursuit of common goals.[68]

McPherson had her finger on the pulse of the times and knew what the people wanted. McPherson's challenge was to capitalize on all of the ways that her creative genius conceived of bringing the Foursquare Gospel to the masses. As Providence would have it, one of those ways was radio. In seeking to preserve the influence of religion in American culture, McPherson's ministry helped popularize an experiential Christianity suited for the masses.

---

it could happen now: human need was the same, and Christ was, too."
    67. Blumhofer, *Aimee Semple McPherson*, 212.
    68. Blumhofer, *Aimee Semple McPherson*, 250.

RADIO STATION KFSG (KALL FOUR SQUARE GOSPEL)

Radio was ideally suited for the charismatic ecumenism that McPherson preached. By broadcasting the Foursquare Gospel, McPherson was not only preserving religion in America, but transforming it as well.

For the June 1924 edition of the *Bridal Call Foursquare*, Sister McPherson wrote a poem exalting the medium of radio. The last three stanzas of "The Cathedral of the Air" demonstrate radio's biggest draw for the evangelist—its global reach:

> The Cathedral of the Air am I—,
> The church with no boundary line.
> A marvel to all, a sign of the times.
> I stand at this latter day, ready to speak,
> Ready to preach, the Gospel everywhere,
> Affording possibilities hitherto unknown.
>
> Of scattering the gospel seed
> Throughout the earth—wind blown.
> Ready to pierce the darkness,
> To penetrate each wall, with the message of life,
> And a message of hope
> That heralds the Coming King.
>
> The Cathedral of the Air am I—,
> the voice with a million tongues.
> But knowing no better name for me,
> They call me—RADIO.[69]

McPherson saw radio as the perfect technology to expand her reach beyond the walls of the Angelus Temple. Radio offered the promise of "a million tongues"—the opportunity to be God's special agent of gospel proclamation on a global scale. Given McPherson's conviction that she was set apart in these "latter days" for this very purpose, it only made sense to embrace radio broadcasting as a ministry tool. "In the midst of this great revival and outpouring of the Holy Spirit," wrote KFSG's official historian, "Aimee Semple McPherson did not rest on her past accomplishments. She had a burning compassion for the lost souls of the world. She must reach out further to reach more souls for Jesus. Radio broadcasting was the answer that would broaden her ministry and outreach for Christ."[70] McPherson longed to extend her ministry far beyond the walls of Angelus Temple.

69. McPherson, "The Cathedral of the Air," 2–3.
70. Duarte, "History of Radio Station KFSG," 3.

Radio, with its potential to reach vast audiences, was the ideal communication medium for McPherson and the primary way she was able to influence American religion.

McPherson's radio station was the first station in America dedicated to all Christian programming. Although radio preaching was not a novelty at this time, "McPherson was the first to bombard the airwaves around the clock."[71] This afforded McPherson an influence on American religion greater than most other radio preachers of her day. The "Cathedral of the Air" first went on the air on February 6, 1924. The first words ever spoken on radio station KFSG were those of John 3:16: "For God so loved the world, that He gave His only begotten Son, that whosoever believeth in Him should not perish, but have everlasting life."[72] "The call letters, KFSG, were chosen to convey the invitation, 'Kall Four Square Gospel.' The two towers for the station were mounted atop Angelus Temple and the studios were located within Angelus Temple on the second foyer. Thus, Radio Station KFSG became the nations' first 'Cathedral of the Air,' the first missionary station, licensed to and maintained by a church for a dedicated Christian ministry."[73]

McPherson's first experience with radio preaching came nearly two years earlier in 1922. In one of her autobiographies, McPherson described the scene that took place during a revival tour in northern California and undoubtedly influenced her later decision to pursue a regular broadcast ministry:

> A unique and interesting diversion came one Sunday morning, when, by special invitation of the Rockridge Radio Station of Oakland, the writer was accorded the gracious honor of being the first woman in the world to preach a sermon over the wireless telephone. Tens of thousands on the Pacific Coast are talking radio just now, and thousands of receiving sets are in private homes, hospitals, hotels, clubs, halls and public buildings. But in addition to being heard for a radius of 2,000 miles across the continent and by ships at sea, this was the day of the enormous blossom festival, where some 50,000 people were assembled at Saratoga. Saturday night they had danced in the open air to radio music, but this Sunday morning they were to hear the voice of a preacher coming out of the open heavens and falling through the air—the voice I mean, not the preacher.

---

71. Witham, *City upon a Hill*, 236. Witham also notes that McPherson "often gave twenty sermons a week to fill the hours."

72. Duarte, "History of Radio Station KFSG," 7.

73. Duarte, "History of Radio Station KFSG," 7. Duarte further notes that KFSG "operated on a non-commercial basis supported by its listeners."

> All the way across the ferry, our hearts beat nervously as mother and I talked of the great possibilities and prayed for the words to speak. When facing the machinery and electrical apparatus of the sending station, our nervousness was increased, especially when we found a newspaper camera man there for a picture and story, also neighbors assembled to hear the sermon. But, after putting them all out except the operator, I felt more at ease—that is, as much as it is possible for one to feel facing that great horn and having only its dark, mysterious looking depths for a visible audience.
>
> But closing my eyes, I looked to the Lord for help and began to speak—taking my text from Luke 4:18, "The Spirit of the Lord is upon me, for He hath anointed me to preach the gospel to the poor; He hath sent me to heal the broken-hearted; to preach deliverance to the captives, and the recovering of sight to the blind; to set at liberty them that are bound and to preach the acceptable year of the Lord."
>
> In a moment I found myself talking into that great receiver—talking somehow as I had seldom talked before. The room with its electrical apparatus was forgotten, and all I could think of was the thousands at the Blossom Festival, the sailor boys, mothers' boys on the ships at sea, the sick in the homes where receivers had been installed, and I prayed and preached and prayed again and did most everything but take up the collection.
>
> When the doxology was pronounced and the beaming operator turned some little adjustment, shutting off the apparatus and we dared speak again, the room filled with those who had been listening through receivers in the other room and the long-distance phone began to ring as people, one after the other, enthusiastically declared that they had heard every word and had been thrilled and blessed by a message from the Lord coming through the air that Sunday morning.[74]

McPherson's first encounter with radio broadcasting gave her a taste of the fame and notoriety she craved. McPherson wrote of the opportunity to be "the first woman in the world to preach a sermon" over the radio; the tens of thousands of people far and wide who would hear; the impressive equipment; the celebrity trappings, including photographers and reporters; and the instant gratification that came with the phone ringing with enthusiastic feedback from listeners. Radio gave McPherson the opportunity to broadcast not only the Foursquare Gospel, but to augment her own fame. McPherson's use of radio helped transform American religion by contributing to a

---

74. McPherson, *This Is That*, 422–24.

Christian celebrity culture that had certainly existed before McPherson, but now had radio technology giving it momentum on a vast scale.

Shortly after this experience, McPherson set in motion her plan to build radio station KFSG. Throughout 1923, as she was busy raising money for this massive undertaking, McPherson described gospel broadcasting with unbridled enthusiasm:

> What a wonderful day we are living in! What an unprecedented opportunity for the preaching of the Gospel to every creature is now afforded! Years ago a preacher whose voice could be heard for half a mile was lauded and thought to have accomplished a most remarkable feat. But think of it, seated in the radio studio, or standing in the pulpit of Angelus Temple, we will now be heard for thousands of miles without lifting the voice above that of the ordinary conversation.[75]

McPherson's ability to transform the theological landscape of American culture was greatly enhanced with a radio station where she controlled all content. In the event that some people were not moved by the wonders of radio, McPherson reminded her readers of Christ's imminent second coming: "The days, weeks, and months speed by with almost incredible rapidity. We know not how soon our Lord shall come, though we believe that He is near, even at the door."[76] McPherson believed that Christ was "at the door" and, therefore, that it was incumbent upon God's people to baptize radio for evangelistic purposes. Furthermore, if the church did not act on this opportunity, McPherson assured her readers that Satan would: "Certainly the Radio is the greatest means of spreading the Gospel the world has ever known. Satan ha[s] almost irretrievably captured the moving pictures. Do not let him get the Radio tied up so that none may use it for the Word of God."[77] For McPherson it was simple: Christians had to get involved in radio broadcasting, or the devil would use radio for his own destructive purposes. McPherson was not about to let the devil or any government official stop her from broadcasting. Sometimes the difference between the two was not obvious for McPherson:

> In the early years of radio, audiences could hear the evangelist all over the FM band rather than on her assigned frequency. Secretary of Commerce Herbert Hoover, who was cracking down on the many broadcasters engaged in this practice, decided

---

75. McPherson, *This Is That*, 594.
76. McPherson, *This Is That*, 594.
77. Duarte, "History of Radio Station KFSG," D13.

to shut down McPherson's station temporarily to compel her compliance. The devil may have captured the film industry, but McPherson intended to put up a fight before he commandeered her radio station. Hoover claimed that she had telegrammed him in response: "Please order your minions of Satan to leave my station alone. You cannot expect the Almighty to abide by your wave length nonsense." Shortly thereafter, nonetheless, she complied with his directives.[78]

McPherson's ministry over the air had garnered the attention of the Secretary of Commerce. It is likely that McPherson orchestrated her defiance to put herself and KFSG in the news. By depicting herself as a good soldier in the Lord's army opposing the evil forces of darkness, McPherson's celebrity status increased. This event helped transform American religion by embracing the forms of an entertainment industry and its promotion of meaning through identification with celebrities.

In addition to broadcasting the regular Sunday services of Angelus Temple, KFSG offered its listeners a wide variety of Christian programming throughout the week. This constant programming helped accelerate a religious shift toward McPherson's hybrid pentecostal faith. The November 1925 edition of *The Bridal Call* offered what amounted to a program guide:

> We will be on the air each Sunday from 10:30 to 12:30; 2:30 to 4:30 and in the evening from 7:00 till the end of the services with the wonderful altar call and later with the organ program, announcements, psalm and prayer.
>
> During the week we come to you with the Sunshine Hour each morning, except Monday, at 10:30. This will brighten and happify you all day.
>
> Wednesday afternoon we bring you the glorious Divine Healing service wherein thousands have learned to know the Great Physician, Jesus Christ.
>
> Thursday evening we bring you the Baptismal service and you may hear the waters of the beautiful Angelus Temple Baptistry splash as the converts are buried with their Lord in baptism.
>
> Every Friday evening you will hear our thousand Crusaders singing and their ringing testimonies and then the sermon by Aimee Semple McPherson, who has been called to gather these young people as Crusaders for Christ.
>
> Saturday evening promptly at 7:30 tune in; it will be the Divine Healing service again. You will enjoy messages, the singing,

---

78. Sutton, *Aimee Semple McPherson*, 81–82.

the organ, the silver band, the great choirs and all that goes with KFSG, the Radio With a Soul.

Then in late afternoons, we are on the air from 3:30 to 4:30 daily, except Monday. Tuesday and Wednesday you may enjoy us while you are having your dinner, if you will, from 6:30 to 7:30.

All our messages are sent out with a loving prayer that they will reach the hearts of God's children and also of those who need Him so—and then that the hearers will come along to Angelus Temple.

This is Radio KFSG signing off. God bless our Church of the Air.[79]

Radio was effective in contributing to the swelling attendance at Angelus Temple during the 1920s and 1930s. The evidence shows that many "hearers [came] along to Angelus Temple." By acting as a "net" to bring people into the fold, radio extended McPherson's influence even in her southern California locale.

The person responsible for the day-to-day operations of KFSG was Kenneth Gladstone Ormiston, a former radio operator with *Los Angeles Times* radio. Ormiston became famous for being at the center of a firestorm surrounding McPherson in 1926. The event also increased McPherson's fame. She was accused of having an affair with Ormiston and staging a kidnapping to cover it up. For months, the scandalous allegations created a hurricane of media attention. By constantly going to the airwaves to declare her innocence and shape public opinion, McPherson demonstrated the power of radio as a communications medium. Much like today, McPherson used radio "to redefine herself in the face of relentless hostility."[80] For example, the *Los Angeles Times* reported on how McPherson broadcast a plea for a forty-eight-hour period of fasting and prayer in an effort to clear her name. McPherson also solicited money during the broadcast for what she initially called a "fight-the-devil fund" but later renamed "the Aimee Semple McPherson defense fund." According to the article, McPherson announced that she would "put up in the church a big thermometer to register as contributions increased. She said it would say beside it: 'What we think of Aimee Semple McPherson.'"[81] Another example of McPherson using radio to rally support came on the eve of her preliminary hearing in the kidnapping case. Before thousands of people at Angelus Temple and all who were listening through radio, McPherson "fired a broadside at District Attorney

---

79. McPherson, *Bridal Call Foursquare*, 35.
80. Sutton, *Aimee Semple McPherson*, 111.
81. "Throngs Hear Fast Plea."

[Asa] Keyes and his office." She proceeded to talk of her innocence and the "merciless persecution" that had been brought against her. To help in the cause, McPherson brought her children into the broadcast:

> At one stage of the service, the evangelist called to her arms her daughter and son . . . who were seated to her right and left. With the two folded in her arms, she began to speak: "Do you believe the mother of two such lovely children could—" The remainder of the statement was lost in the fervent and voluminous applause of the congregation.[82]

By taking advantage of the persuasive power of radio, McPherson was able to manage her image and rally support. McPherson's use of radio helped transform American religion into a celebrity culture by making herself the central message of the broadcast.

By broadcasting McPherson's Angelus Temple sermons, radio station KFSG quickened a transformation of American religion into another form of entertainment. Radio was able to bring something of the experience of seeing McPherson in person into people's homes. Tona Hangen describes a typical Sunday night service at Angelus Temple—the entertainment-oriented services that helped make McPherson famous:

> McPherson's revival meetings were spectacles of entertainment, music, and emotion-rousing preaching. To the accompaniment of a huge organ, a fourteen-piece orchestra, brass band, and hundred-voice choir, she performed "illustrated sermons" every Sunday night for twenty years. Her illustrated sermons drew on popular culture for subject matter and were executed with elaborate costumes rented from Hollywood studios and huge sets with special effects, thanks to the help of her vaudeville-trained stage manager, Thomas Eade. She appeared in the uniform of a motorcycle traffic cop to proclaim that her audience was speeding to hell, or dressed up like a navy ensign to sail the "Good Ship Bounty." Sermons re-created the eruption of Vesuvius, the destruction of Sodom and Gomorrah, Humpty Dumpty's fall, and Revolutionary troops at Valley Forge with snow drifting down to the stage. One 1925 sermon featured an "Eye of the Needle" through which she tried to lead a camel rented from the Barnes Zoo; another, a Garden of Eden complete with live macaw.[83]

---

82. "McPherson Assails Keyes."
83. Hangen, *Redeeming the Dial*, 63–64.

McPherson was a celebrity, and radio brought her into people's living rooms. Radio gave listeners the opportunity to imagine what it must have looked like at the temple as they heard McPherson describe the events associated with each sermon and the audience's rapturous response. Religion at the temple was being cast as entertainment. Radio helped spread this entertainment-oriented religion to the masses.

By packaging Christianity in simple revivalist themes, McPherson's ministry moved American religion toward a theological minimalism that was ill-equipped to resist certain aspects of secularization. With the exception of occasional sermons to warn listeners of modernism's encroachment and to persuade people of America's Christian roots, McPherson stuck close to her Foursquare Gospel themes on the airwaves.[84] She regularly proclaimed the simple message of Jesus as savior, baptizer, healer, and coming king. This nonsectarian, charismatic message was well received by many people. Although McPherson's message helped preserve religion in American culture, the cost was a shift toward theological minimalism among the populace. The hundreds of thousands of KFSG listeners had to imagine McPherson's dramatics, but they could hear her renditions of classic revivalist themes, which were in essence what McPherson's Foursquare Gospel embodied. For example, in a sermon broadcast in 1939 entitled "Life Begins at Foursquare," McPherson described Jesus as Savior, while exhorting her listeners to be born again:

> The sinner from head to foot is rags . . . it doesn't matter what we've done. We may have given into the church offering and we may have given to the poor and we may have done wonderful things at hospitals—wonderful things in themselves. But unless we've been born again—no matter how many lodges we belong to or how many unions or how many churches we've joined—unless we've been born again through the precious blood of Jesus, all our righteousness is but filthy rags.[85]

On the thirty-third anniversary of the Azusa Street revival, McPherson, with constant "Amens" and "Hallelujahs" in the background, explained how Jesus is the Baptizer with the Holy Spirit. "Being filled is not enough,"

---

84. Sutton, *Aimee Semple McPherson*. Unlike Sutton, the perspective of this study is that McPherson's ministry career was more concerned with the advance of her pentecostal faith than with the restoration of "Christian America." They were not one and the same.

85. Aimee Semple McPherson, "Life Begins at Foursquare," sermon broadcast, February 10, 1939.

McPherson declared, "you must be filled to overflowing."[86] She continued, striking an evangelistic note,

> Whenever anyone is saved and filled with the Spirit . . . it is like a fire in a dry field—everything catches fire around it. Everyone who is really saved and has the Holy Ghost is like a honeybee—they're busy for the Lord, they're piling up something else. And friends, I'll tell you, if you really are saved and filled with the Spirit, you'll never be content to live by yourself alone, you'll want to win others to Jesus.[87]

McPherson concluded the sermon by drawing out what she perceived as the ecumenical implications of the great revival on Azusa Street:

> The fire is still falling. Thirty-three years have come and thirty-three years have gone. Today I believe there are millions of people baptized with the Holy Ghost. You'll find them in India, China, the Philippines, Africa, at home and abroad. . . . Though Pentecost has spread—here, there, yonder, across continents, seas, oceans, caught the rich, the poor, the high, the low—yet we are all baptized by one Spirit into one body. Amen?[88]

For McPherson, Jesus was not only a savior and baptizer, but also a healer. In one broadcast McPherson compared the person who refuses divine healing to a person who, perhaps out of fear, fails to swim because they are "fighting the water." McPherson's intention was to motivate people to yield to the power of God to heal them, which McPherson believed was always available to those who "give [their] life to Christ—body, soul and spirit."[89] McPherson believed that one of the reasons people became sick was Satan's work to make people less effective for God, but she also believed that joyful service to the Lord would come to those who realized the healing that comes by faith through the cross of Christ: "Beloved, I believe the moment Jesus Christ makes Himself manifest to you, you will realize that He Himself suffered; He took upon His own body every pain, every ill, who Himself has borne our infirmities. He put His shoulder under the yoke—you cannot help but love it and spread the joyful news along."[90]

---

86. Aimee Semple McPherson, "Many Members, One Body," sermon broadcast, April 16, 1939.

87. McPherson, "Many Members, One Body."

88. McPherson, "Many Members, One Body."

89. Aimee Semple McPherson, "Divine Healing," sermon broadcast, February 18, 1939.

90. McPherson, "Divine Healing."

Finally, McPherson broadcast a message of the imminent return of Christ for his church. This fourth pillar of McPherson's Foursquare Gospel gave her ministry urgency and helps explain the almost frantic pace she kept for nearly three decades of gospel work. This urgency, as well as McPherson's ecumenical hopes, is demonstrated in a sermon from 1924:

"Behold, the Lord is near—He is even at the doors. Know, Oh church, that the cup of the Gentiles is almost full—the Christ is coming back."

> Wake up—wake up—wake up! Work, for the night is coming when man's work is done! Work now. Roll up your sleeves and go at it! Stop preaching mere politics! Stop cooking up oyster suppers and fixing strawberry festivals. Stop showing moving pictures on Sunday night when you should be preaching the Gospel and getting people saved! Stop fighting other preachers and lifting up the sword to pierce the heart of other ministers! Whether we see eye to eye with them or not, the time is at hand—let us stop squabbling and fighting over doctrinal differences. Let us stop fighting each other. Let us join hands, join hearts, voices and forces, and turn to fight the enemy—modernism, higher criticism, agnosticism and worldliness.
>
> "In fundamentals—unity! In non-essentials—liberty! In all things—charity!"
>
> We are relay stations for Christ. Let us speed the message out and away till it leaps the sea and girdles the globe, and all men hear the cry—"Behold, the Christ is coming! He is even at the door!"[91]

McPherson's charismatic ecumenism helped transform American religion. It fostered a theological minimalism that promised an experience with God. McPherson's goal was to restore to the church the old-time religion and her Foursquare Gospel was her effort to do so. "Oh, I love the Old Time Religion! I love the old time power!" McPherson cried. "What we need today is a great movement back to God, back to the Bible, back to the faith of our fathers, back to the Old Time Religion."[92] This move back, according to McPherson, left no room for sectarian squabbles over religion. Controversial polemics were abandoned in favor of an experiential religion better suited to realize the potential broadcast media held out to reach the masses.

The music broadcast over KFSG contributed to the transformation of American religion by eschewing substantive theology. Not only were the radio sermons representative of McPherson's Foursquare Gospel, but the

---

91. McPherson, "Premillennial Signal Towers," 29.
92. McPherson, "Premillennial Signal Towers," 29.

music stayed close to her revivalist themes as well. In fact, McPherson wrote many of the gospel songs heard over the radio. As Charles Fuller would later do, McPherson chose simple gospel songs that minimized doctrine while incorporating repetitive phrases that made for easy singing and memorization. For example, McPherson's "Under His Wings" spoke of Christ's willingness to heal: "To those that love Him, the Lord shall rise, There's healing under His wings. Rise as the sun within the skies, There's healing under His wings." Then the chorus, "Under His wings, Under His wings, Under His healing wings. Under His wings, Under His wings, Under His healing wings, healing wings."[93] In "Empty Pitchers," McPherson exhorted worshippers to come to Christ to be filled with the Spirit: "Pitchers, Pitchers, here bring your empty pitchers; Pitchers, Pitchers, Fill them to the brim. Pitchers, Pitchers, Here bring your empty pitchers, come fill your empty pitchers and give praise to Him."[94] The point of the gospel songs was to give listeners a simple religion without complex doctrine and theology. While these songs were well-suited for radio broadcasting and its potential for reaching the masses, by eschewing substantive theological hymns these songs helped accelerate a move toward theological minimalism in America.

The listener correspondence to KFSG demonstrates that, at the popular level, McPherson was effective in preserving religion in American culture consistent with her rendition of the pentecostal faith. Through broadcast media McPherson's ministry contributed to the transformation of American religion. The correspondence to the station indicates that listeners loved the old-time religion that McPherson offered. For example, in 1925, a listener from North Dakota wrote, "I cannot tell you how pleased we were to tune in on your services last Sunday evening and how much we enjoyed them. How we would have loved to have been there and to have seen the many going to the altar, but we thank God that we have the privilege of at least hearing the services over the Radio. May you have many faithful years in His service."[95] A listener in New York wrote, "Last night I had the pleasure of hearing your radio station. . . . A woman was leading the church service and her voice was very clear. I greatly enjoyed her sermon."[96] A woman in Nebraska wrote enthusiastically, "I want to thank you for the fine spiritual service heard last Saturday night over the radio. Please tell the lady who spoke that she got me shouting at the end and I kept it up all day Sunday."[97] Many of the letters

93. McPherson, "Under His Wings," 180.
94. McPherson, "Under His Wings," 182.
95. Duarte, "History of Radio Station KFSG," D24.
96. Duarte, "History of Radio Station KFSG," D25.
97. Duarte, "History of Radio Station KFSG," D25.

to the station were general words of gratitude for the programming, but some letters specifically mentioned conversion experiences. For example, one listener wrote,

> RESCUED! While listening in over Radio to the Sunshine Hour, a dear soul trembling on the brink of eternity was reclaimed last Thursday. Though he was a great sufferer from dropsy, he sang God's praises and shouted all day. At the close of the day, as the sun was going down, the Lord took him home. His wife says, "God bless Sister, and Angelus Temple." If it had not been for the radio her husband would have passed away unsaved.[98]

The correspondence reveals listeners from every part of the United States as well as parts of Canada, New Zealand, Australia, and the Cape Verde Islands off the coast of Africa.[99] This demonstrates the wide reach of McPherson's broadcasts and the influence she had on religion in America and around the world.

McPherson's death on September 27, 1944, brought to a close a life and ministry that left an indelible mark on American religion. Newspaper reports surrounding her death wrote of McPherson's "34 years of spectacular evangelism frequently punctuated by sensational episodes in her personal life"[100] and how she became "a legend of evangelism around the world."[101] Over ten thousand people attended the three-hour public service at the temple, an event described as a "spectacular demonstration" that included over five hundred floral arrangements, seventy-five city police officers, and an impromptu eulogy by McPherson's son Rolf that left many attendees sobbing.[102] Reporting on the funeral, the *Los Angeles Times* noted McPherson's worldwide influence: "That her fame is world-wide was typified by

---

98. Duarte, "History of Radio Station KFSG," D21. While conversion experiences were reported, not all stories about McPherson's broadcast were positive. One news story reported how the radio station was at the center of a failing marriage: "Paul V. Ellis is a follower of Aimee Semple McPherson, at a distance, his wife, Mrs. Clara A. Ellis, declared yesterday in a divorce suit she filed. Instead of letting Mrs. Ellis sleep of nights, Ellis insists in tuning in Angelus Temple on the radio and running the loud speaker full blast, the complaint declares." See "Radio Disciple Angers Wife."

99. Duarte, "History of Radio Station KFSG," 10–11; D21-30. It is not clear how many listeners tuned in to KFSG on a weekly basis at the peak of McPherson's radio ministry. However, Epstein, *Sister McPherson*, notes, "Hundreds of thousands of people believed that McPherson's broadcasts represented God's entrance into their homes and hearts. Hundreds claimed to be healed when at McPherson's encouragement they placed their hands upon the radio speaker horn as it vibrated with her voice" (285).

100. "Aimee McPherson Dead at 53."

101. "Thousands at Aimee Rites."

102 "Thousands at Aimee Rites."

instructions of a London Daily Mail correspondent here to cable 1000 words on the funeral. His newspaper has only four pages during the wartime paper shortage, but Sister McPherson, in war as in peace, is news."[103] In addition to newspapers, national periodicals commemorated McPherson's death: "*Life* did a multipage, fully illustrated spread on the memorial services, *Time* and *Newsweek* each chronicled McPherson's life and death, and *Variety* recounted her efforts to mix evangelism with show business."[104] Sutton is surely right in his conclusion that "the overwhelming response to the death of the evangelist reaffirmed her status in life. By linking the old-time religion to the modern world, she had indeed ushered Pentecostalism into the mainstream of American culture."[105] Still, McPherson's Pentecostalism was a nonsectarian religion suitable for radio and mass audience appeal. Her charismatic ecumenism eschewed substantive theological content. This, ironically, left the American church more vulnerable to the secularizing trends within the modernism it sought to counter.

CONCLUSION

Aimee Semple McPherson's ministry accelerated a movement in America toward an experiential religion with an ecumenical appeal for world evangelization. As one of the most celebrated Christian figures of the early twentieth century, McPherson's ministry helped make the American church more accepting of important aspects of secularization. McPherson eschewed substantive theological discourse in favor of a doctrinal minimalism capable of crossing denominational lines. McPherson's ministry transformed religion in America. Radio played a major role in this transformation. Through her use of broadcast and print media as well as her dynamic illustrated sermons, McPherson became perhaps the most recognized public Christian of the early twentieth century. Her religious empire, headquartered in the bustling Los Angeles of the 1920s, gave McPherson the opportunities she needed to foster her fame and to recast religion in terms of entertainment. McPherson's superstar status cannot be understood simply by attributing it to a "rollicking self-promotion," as Grant Wacker has argued.[106] McPherson saw herself as God's chosen vessel to bring revival to the world. In all her ministry labors, McPherson acted in accord with this self-conscious exceptionalism. McPherson never seemed

103. "Thousands at Aimee Rites."
104. Sutton, *Aimee Semple McPherson*, 271.
105. Sutton, *Aimee Semple McPherson*, 271.
106. Wacker, *Heaven Below*, 33.

conflicted between her popularity and the preaching of the gospel because the rise of her fame meant the rise of Christ's.

The religious work that flowed out of Angelus Temple on a weekly basis served as a resistance movement against the secularizing trends of modernism. By avoiding a strict sectarianism, McPherson was able to forge relationships across denominational lines and avoid many of the doctrinal fights still raging in the 1920s and 1930s. The Foursquare Gospel, with its doctrinal minimalism and emphasis on subjective experience, was designed for mass appeal. It was a gospel ideally suited for the medium of radio. Radio offered McPherson the promise of a church with no boundary lines—the opportunity to realize her ecumenical dreams of a Foursquare Gospel revival. The following two stanzas from her "Radio Fantasy" of 1924 summarize it well:

> The Cathedral of the Air am I,
> The Church with no boundary line.
> And under my broad, canopied expanse
> I house the sons of men—
> The black, the white, the yellow;
> The brown and red man, too.
>
> Brothers all sit side by side
> In the church with no color line.
> The rich and the poor, the old and the young,
> The sad and the gay of heart, the strong and the
> weak, the sick and the well,
> All worship at my shrine.[107]

The "Cathedral of the Air" was capable of bringing all kinds of people together. This was the promise of religious radio. However, by casting religion for mass appeal, radio altered religion. This was one of the unintended consequences of McPherson's radio career.

---

107. McPherson, "Cathedral of the Air," 1.

4

Broadcasting Orthodoxy

Walter Maier and the *Lutheran Hour*

THIS CHAPTER ARGUES THAT Walter Maier's ministry accelerated a movement in America toward a simple orthodoxy. Maier was fully convinced of the confessional Lutheranism in which he was raised and trained. For Maier, Lutheranism was orthodoxy. The message he broadcast, however, eschewed Lutheran particulars for the bold proclamation of the basic convictions shared by Christian fundamentalists generally. In helping preserve the influence of Christianity in American culture, Maier's ministry helped transform American religion. This shift toward a simple orthodoxy, ironically, contributed to the secularization of the American church.

Radio played a major role in Maier's influence, and it was primarily through broadcasting that Maier contributed to the transformation of American religion. In 1931, the *Lutheran Hour* Committee of Concordia Seminary declared that "one of the greatest missionary offensives ever waged in the Christian Church was launched when the initial *Lutheran Hour*, the first of a long series of radio programs exalting the crucified and risen Savior, was broadcast over a coast-to-coast network of thirty-six stations."[1]

This declaration was no exaggeration. What began in 1930 on a network of thirty-six stations eventually blossomed into an international

---

1. Maier, *Lutheran Hour*, 309.

ministry broadcast on 1,236 stations. These stations "beamed [Maier's] sermons each week to an estimated 20,000,000 listeners in what was probably the largest 'parish' in church history."[2] The scope of the broadcast during its twenty years under Maier's leadership was breathtaking: "More people could hear it over more stations than any other non-government radio program in the world. Maier's messages were translated into 35 languages, aired from 55 countries, and heard in 120 nations and territories."[3]

During the first year of the *Lutheran Hour*, each weekly broadcast cost $4,500, with an annual cost of well over $200,000. The prospects for survival, let alone for growth, seemed daunting—but grow it did. Like other fundamentalist radio programs during the golden age of radio, the *Lutheran Hour* found an audience receptive to Maier's unwavering commitment to simple Protestant orthodoxy as an alternative to modernism. Maier was a confessional Lutheran. On the radio, however, his message avoided Lutheran distinctives in favor of basic Christianity.

This message carried far beyond Lutheran circles. Unlike the robust theology of the *Book of Concord*, Maier preached an accessible orthodoxy similar to Charles Fuller's "old-time religion" and Aimee Semple McPherson's foursquare fundamentalism. To accommodate Christianity to the new medium of radio, Maier forsook Lutheran particulars in favor of a gospel more compatible with the fundamentalism of his day. Like other radio preachers at the time, Maier wanted to reach as many people as possible with his message. And because the long-term viability of the *Lutheran Hour* depended on the donations of his faithful listeners, Maier needed a message that appealed to as many people as possible. Therefore his gospel had more in common with Paul Rader than with Philip Melanchthon.

Paul Maier states in his biography that among the several "paradoxes" that marked Walter Maier was this combination of Protestant orthodoxy and evangelical appeal:

> His theology was unqualifiedly Lutheran, but his message was welcomed by clergy and laity in every faith. Much of church life in the United States was in spiritual doldrums when he began his ministry, and he became one of the chief spokesman for a vigorous reassertion of classic Christianity as an antidote to the religious depression. That he helped occasion the contemporary 'return to religion' seems clear, for by 1950 he had preached to more people than any other person in history. Such

---

2. Maier, *Lutheran Hour*, 1.
3. Maier, *Lutheran Hour*, 1.

a grass-roots impact also helped to firm up orthodoxy at the theological level.⁴

A simple orthodoxy and a passion for its propagation marked Maier's radio ministry. Maier accommodated Christianity to the medium of radio. Maier was fully convinced of the truth of the confessional Lutheranism in which he was raised and trained. The message he broadcast, however, eschewed the particularities of Lutheran theology. His audience tuned in not for instruction in Lutheran theology, but for the bold proclamation of the basic convictions shared by fundamentalists generally.

THE MISSOURI WAY

The Lutheran Church-Missouri Synod nurtured in Walter Maier a love for doctrine and a desire to see truth spread throughout world.

German immigrants created the Missouri Synod in Chicago in 1847. Led by the strong hand of Carl F. Walther, these Lutherans were determined to safeguard orthodox doctrine from the corrosive influences of Americanization. In the nineteenth century some Lutherans challenged the insistence on strict orthodoxy and promoted closer identification with broader American Protestantism. Walther believed that such sentiments threatened not only orthodox essentials, but Lutheran particulars as well. The Missouri Synod's founders feared the loss of Lutheranism. Carl Meyer summarized their fears:

> Rationalism had crept into the Lutheran Church also to the detriment of sound, confessional Lutheranism. A readiness to join in religious worship with other churches and an indifference to doctrine were other characteristics of this period of Lutheranism in America. . . . Some of these Lutherans were ready to compromise with the prevailing American Protestantism and to give up their Lutheranism for the sake of becoming "American."⁵

The denomination grew quickly, and key leaders sensed the need for a revised constitution. The original 1847 version was ill equipped to deal with the changing realities of the young denomination. By 1854 the new

---

4. Maier, *Lutheran Hour*, 2. Also, by way of comparison, see Carter, "Walter A. Maier": "As a public exponent of Protestant orthodoxy at precisely the time in which neoorthodoxy was making inroads in America, Maier may indeed have aided in the postwar religious revival by making historic, doctrinal Protestantism an option worth considering in the American popular religious supermarket" (275).

5. Meyer, *Brief Historical Sketch of the Lutheran Church-Missouri Synod*, 4–5.

constitution was complete. This document delineated the determination on the part of the founders to maintain doctrinal purity while promoting the expansion of the "kingdom of God." For example, in chapter 1 of the constitution, six reasons were given for forming a synodical organization. Reason 3 included "the joint extension of the kingdom of God and the establishment and promotion of special church enterprises (seminary, agenda, hymnal, Book of Concord, schoolbooks, Bible distribution, missionary endeavors within and without the church, etc.)."[6] In chapter 2 they committed themselves to doctrinal orthodoxy. They would grant fellowship to other Christians on two conditions only:

> 1. Acceptance of Holy Scripture of the Old and New Testaments as the written Word of God and the only rule and norm of faith and life. 2. Acceptance of all symbolical books of the Evangelical Lutheran Church (to wit: the three Ecumenical Symbols, the Unaltered Augsburg Confession, its Apology, the Smalcald Articles, the Large and Small Catechism of Luther, and the Formula of Concord) as the pure, unadulterated statement and exposition of the divine Word.[7]

The Synod began with a clear affirmation of the Bible as the word of God. In addition, the *Book of Concord* stood as the "pure, unadulterated statement and exposition of the divine Word." This foundation remained intact throughout the intense controversy with modernism in the early 1920s. Maier embraced the vision of Missouri Synod Lutheranism.

Walter Maier was born to German immigrants in Boston on October 4, 1893. Emil William Maier was a professional organ builder. It was under the tutelage of his parents that Maier learned the great creeds of Christendom and witnessed their doctrine in action. It fact, it was largely the example of his parents that led Maier to pursue vocational ministry:

> Probably the greatest incentive to a profession in the church was the example set by his parents. Later in life, Walter said, "My earliest clear recollection is that of my father on his knees in the bedroom, praying." Even more a source of religious inspiration to the family was his mother. In church and community circles Anna Maier was now being called "the woman everyone loves." She saw to it that Christianity animated the life of her family and made no secret of her dream that at least one of her sons would

---

6. "Constitution of the German Evangelical Lutheran Synod of Missouri, Ohio and other States," 149.

7. "Constitution of the German Evangelical Lutheran Synod of Missouri, Ohio and other States," 149–50.

enter the ministry. Years later, when asked to cite the most influential factor in his life, Walter replied, "The prayers, support, and outstanding example of my parents."[8]

However, it was not merely by example that Emil and Anna fostered in their son a love for the Lutheran faith. Piety was not enough. Therefore, when as a twelve-year-old boy Maier began to sense a call to pursue training for the ministry, his parents made preparations for him to attend Concordia Collegiate Institute, a Lutheran boarding school in suburban New York. At the Concordia Institute Maier began the serious study of Latin and Greek and German. The Lutheran academy in New York promoted an intellectual hunger that led him to obtain a BA degree from Boston University, a BD from Concordia Seminary in St. Louis, and finally a PhD from Harvard University in Semitic studies.

As an adult, Maier immersed himself in denominational work. After being ordained to the ministerium of the Missouri Synod in 1917, Maier's ministry career included an assistant pastorate in his childhood church (Zion Evangelical Lutheran), a post as the first executive secretary of the Walther League, the youth auxiliary of the Missouri Synod, and finally, a professorship in Old Testament Interpretation and History at Concordia Seminary in St. Louis. In each of these positions Maier exhibited his allegiance to theological orthodoxy and passion for "Bringing Christ to the Nations—and the Nations to the Church."[9] For example, as editor of the *Messenger*, the monthly publication of the Walther League, Maier worked to "present thinking church people with the spiritual features not available in secular periodicals."[10] While some within his denomination criticized Maier for writing in a manner "too heavy" for the average reader, thousands of people disagreed. Under Maier's editorship the circulation of the *Messenger* soared from seven thousand to eighty thousand.[11]

As a young professor, Maier was asked to give an address at the Lutheran Day Festival at Ocean Grove, New Jersey. The gathering of nearly ten thousand people took place in the summer of 1925. The climax of Maier's sermon was indicative of his life's ministry. After cataloging many of the sins that beset the nation, Maier prescribed one remedy only—a return to the

---

8. "Constitution of the German Evangelical Lutheran Synod of Missouri, Ohio and other States," 10.

9. The motto, "Bringing Christ to the Nations—and the Nations to the Church" was one of several mottos coined by the Lutheran Layman's League. This ministry arm of the Missouri Synod was dear to Walter Maier and played a pivotal role in advancing his radio ministry. See Maier, *Man Spoke*, 113–14.

10. Maier, *Man Spoke*, 74.

11. Maier, *Man Spoke*, 74.

bedrock hope of the cross: "The hope of our country lies along the path that leads backward past all the failures and fancies of deluded minds, through all the tinseled attractions and tarnished temptations of the present day, backward, to the glory-crowned heights of Calvary."[12] For Maier, hope was not to be found in Protestant modernism's innovative renovations of Christianity for a modern age, but in a reaffirmation of Protestant orthodoxy.

Walter Maier's ecclesiastical heritage nurtured in him a commitment to Lutheran orthodoxy and a desire for its global propagation. The Lutheran Church-Missouri Synod formed Maier's thought, theologically and philosophically. Surprisingly, he studiously avoided Lutheran distinctives in the broadcast booth.

THE LUTHERAN HOUR

Walter Maier's theology did not fundamentally change when it was introduced to the medium of radio. In an essay on Maier, Guy Carter noted that "as a theologian, Maier never deviated a hair's breadth from the official teaching of the Missouri Synod or the Lutheran orthodoxy he had been taught at Concordia Seminary under Franz Pieper's presidency."[13] But his radio broadcasts did not promote Lutheranism. Instead, he promoted the specific concerns of fundamentalism: opposition to evolution, higher criticism, the social gospel, communism, and atheism. By focusing narrowly on fundamentalist issues, Maier was able to attract a broad conservative audience. In a newspaper article in 1939, Maier was quoted on the theme of his broadcasts:

> The broadcasts are pointed against all Scripture-ridiculing and Christ-denying forces, the infidelity of modernism, the irreligion of Communism and the immorality of atheism. They protest against the open and subtle attacks on the Christian home and the separation of Church and State. They indict the anti-Christian and anti-moral teachings frequently inculcated by anti-religious culture.[14]

Maier maintained that "a modern application of the gospel was not to compromise its authenticity."[15] Walter Maier was able to proclaim Protestant orthodoxy in language that resonated with the world at large. His gospel was simple and he offered his listeners basic fundamentalist Christianity.

12. Maier, *Man Spoke*, 80.
13. Carter, "Walter A. Maier," 275.
14. *St. Louis Star-Times*, November 2, 1933.
15. Maier, *Man Spoke*, 212.

Although the first broadcast of the *Lutheran Hour* did not air until 1930, Maier's formal "campaign" for a Lutheran broadcasting station began as early as 1923. Maier used an editorial in the *Walther League Messenger* to make his case. The editorial is instructive, among other reasons, for its demonstration of Maier's identification with the fundamentalism of his day. Maier began the editorial by describing a radio program that was an "insult" to biblical Christianity:

> The other night we adjusted the head-piece of our radio set, found the sensitive spot on the crystal and broke into a lecture on the subject: "How Old is Man?" that made our ears tingle because of its open and unveiled contradiction to the Bible. When the lecture was over the question suggested itself: "How many of our people and other sincere Christians have just heard this insult to Biblical Christianity?[16]

Maier surmised that many others had "heard similar slurs . . . repeated almost every week."[17] He feared the thought of many people each Sunday hearing "wishy-washy moral talks" and "misnamed sermons" on the radio.[18] For this reason, Maier believed, "the hope presented itself that at some point in the not distant future our Lutheran church might establish a broadcasting station that would send a one hundred percent Gospel message from coast to coast, yes, even to the ships that ply the oceans, and, with the continued improvement of radio, even to Europe."[19]

Maier was certainly right when he predicted that "the radio sermon is destined to play a somewhat important part in American life."[20] His campaign for radio included recognition of some of the objections to the church embracing this new technology. For example, to the objection that broadcasting sermons would keep people away from church, Maier argued that the simple solution was to not broadcast during the time of church services. He even suggested that there was evidence that broadcasting sermons actually helped increase church attendance because some "people hear the message at home and often become interested enough to make the personal acquaintance of the pastor."[21] For Maier, it seemed obvious that the potential benefits of broadcasting the faith outweighed the risks:

16. Maier, "Why Not a Lutheran Broadcasting Station?" 314.
17. Maier, "Why Not a Lutheran Broadcasting Station?" 314.
18. Maier, "Why Not a Lutheran Broadcasting Station?" 314.
19. Maier, "Why Not a Lutheran Broadcasting Station?" 314.
20. Maier, "Why Not a Lutheran Broadcasting Station?" 314.
21. Maier, "Why Not a Lutheran Broadcasting Station?" 314.

It is evident, of course, that the transmission of radio services cannot be a substitute for the regular worship in the church. Yet there are distinct services it can render and which will be of no small benefit to our church. We think first of all of our shut-ins, who have no opportunity to attend services and who would welcome the spoken word of cheer and comfort. If the radio could not accomplish anything more than assist us in reaching these unfortunate people, it would be a very profitable and desirable investment. But it can do much more. It can bring the message of pure Lutheran Christianity to uncounted thousands of people whom we could otherwise not reach. It can assist us in removing the misunderstanding which makes people view our faith as that of a foreign church. It can help to serve those of our brothers and sisters in faith who live in localities where there is no Lutheran church. It can assist preventing our people from hearing other sermons and addresses which might injure spiritual growth. It can offer a powerful and effective antidote against the many and varied forms of unbelief that are so often sent out to the listening world. It can be of frequent and valuable service to our congregation, our societies, our homes in so many and such different ways that we will do well not to underrate its importance, but to use the opportunities which it affords for spreading the Gospel.[22]

Maier's stance in this editorial is defensive (against modernism) and supportive (of orthodoxy). Furthermore, it is clear that Maier was already answering the objections to a radio broadcast, such as radio taking people away from the regular church meetings. Recognizing that "the radio sermon was destined to play a somewhat important role in American life," Maier was methodically laying the groundwork for a dream that would be realized several years later.

Early in 1930, Maier began negotiations with the National Broadcasting Company (NBC) to establish a weekly radio program. NBC executives explained to Maier that they contracted with the Federal Council of Churches to donate airtime for Protestant programming and would not give time to one denomination alone. Additionally, NBC's policy did not allow broadcast time to be sold for religious programming. Undaunted, Maier was put in contact with radio executives at the Columbia Broadcasting System (CBS), who were willing to offer religious time on a commercial basis. Given the prohibitively high network costs, Maier enlisted the help of the Lutheran Layman's League, whose motto was, "To Aid Synod with Word and Deed in Business and Financial Matters." Maier was confident that the

---

22. Maier, "Why Not a Lutheran Broadcasting Station?" 314.

League would champion the cause given their involvement in the establishment of radio station KFUO on the campus of Concordia Seminary in St. Louis in 1924. By late summer in 1930, the necessary funds were raised and a contract with CBS was established for a weekly half-hour program beginning in October. The premiere broadcast of the *Lutheran Hour* was on Thursday, October 2, 1930, at 10:00 p.m. (ET). Originating on station WHK in Cleveland, the program was carried on thirty-six stations in cities across America with short-wave outlets sending the program well beyond.[23]

Maier sought to promote a simple orthodoxy. It was a fundamental purpose of the weekly program. In the inaugural broadcast of the *Lutheran Hour*, for example, Maier positioned his program within classical Protestant orthodoxy and squarely against any compromise with modernity:

> These Thursday evening messages, sent out by the oldest Protestant Church (very appropriately in the year in which the world pauses to observe the four-hundredth anniversary of the first Protestant statement of faith, the Augsburg Confession), are not to be speculations which misguided men like to call modern, yet which, in principle and often in detail, are nothing but twentieth-century restatements of ancient, hoary fabrications of heathen minds; not a series of pessimistic lamentations on the sordid and sensual materialism of our mechanical age; not a program in which blatant bigotry and narrow sectarianism can raise a selfish voice; but a succession of uncompromising and unhesitating messages, which without fear or favor will offer an unshaken acknowledgement and glorification of a changeless Christ for a changing world.[24]

With the fundamentalist-modernist controversy at fever pitch, Maier was determined to distance himself from the vast menu of theologically liberal programs dominating radio. Nor was Maier satisfied with most of the fundamentalist radio programming at the time.

In the opening program of the third season of the *Lutheran Hour* (1935–36) Maier answered the question, "What is the message of this broadcast?":

> With many and conflicting voices on the air, some that appeal to reason and intellect, some that would inflame passions and prejudices, we promise that these weekly broadcasts have no political aims. This microphone will not be employed to fan the

---

23. Maier, *Man Spoke*, 115.

24. Maier, *Lutheran Hour*, 45–46. It is possible that Maier had in mind Harry Emerson Fosdick, featured preacher on "National Vespers," and Father Charles Coughlin when he spoke these words.

fires of class hatred, bigotry, and intolerance. The facilities of our network have not been drafted to flood the American nation and our Canadian neighbors with economic theories, financial strategies, and social speculations. Rather do we acknowledge as our own the apostle's determination "not to know anything . . . save Jesus Christ, and Him crucified" (1 Cor. 2:2).[25]

For Maier, the paramount issue of the day was the gospel of Jesus Christ. He deplored the extent to which "religious" microphones around the nation were being employed for purposes other than the proclamation of the timeless truths of Christianity.[26] Maier believed that the *Lutheran Hour* broadcasts would be "one of the most effective contributions of American Lutheranism to the restatement and reemphasis of America's supreme need: Faith in Scriptural truth as the inspired revelation of God, stalwart loyalty to Christ as the divine Savior of humanity, and a profound and practical appreciation of His Church as the pledge of Heaven for a righteous nation."[27] For Maier, America's

---

25. Maier, *Man Spoke*, 170. It is likely that Maier had Father Charles Coughlin in mind when he railed against the religious use of radio for the spread of particular "economic theories" or "financial strategies."

26. See for example, Maier's frustration over the conduct of Father Charles Coughlin in Maier, *Man Spoke*, 187-88, and Maier, *Christ for Every Crisis*, 11-12. Maier appears to have been particularly interested in the radio ministry of Coughlin, which is indicated by two files dedicated to Coughlin news stories in his archives at Concordia Historical Institute. Much of the content of these files is newspaper articles involving Coughlin's controversy with Rep. John J. O'Connor and Coughlin's silencing by the Vatican in 1937. Maier addressed Coughlin directly, "The Rev. Charles E. Coughlin, radio priest, was assailed tonight by Dr. Walter A. Maier of St. Louis, Mo., before the annual Luther day meeting as a 'clerical demagogue' who sought to have 'the canons of his church shape the political life of the nation.' . . . Dr. Maier said: 'it is the supertragedy of our age that many churches have proved unworthy of their trust, that instead of working for men's souls, churches are fighting over their bodies. Look at them as they pass in review, these highly publicized preachers, typical of widespread trends in the away-from-Christ movement. Here is a priest ripping off his Roman collar to scream out clerical endorsement of a puppet candidate. Don't tell me that this clerical demagogue of Royal Oak is repudiated by his own church. He talks personally with Rome by radiophone and his bishop is solidly behind him. Has the Vatican ever disavowed him? If ever Coughlinism should triumph, which God in his mercy may prevent, his church would capitalize the triumph and the radio priest would be the voice of his church. Don't tell me that this chameleon cleric at the Shrine of the Little Flower does not use his position and influence for the benefit of his creed and its system. We have evidence that he does and that he represents an unholy combination which admittedly would place the canons of his church above the constitution of the United States" (Associated Press, August 1, in Walter Meier Papers at Concordia Historical Institute). There is no year on the clipping, but given Maier's assertion that Coughlin had the blessing of the Vatican, it must have been before 1937, the year Coughlin was silenced by the Vatican. The year was most likely 1936, given a similar news story, "Catholics Chided on Coughlin Stand."

27. Maier, *Lutheran Hour*, vii.

supreme need lay in hearing the timeless truth of Christ crucified, or as the book of Jude said it, "the faith once delivered to the saints" (Jude 3). In addition, modernism was an enemy that needed to be defeated. "The Lutheran Church does not tinker with the Bible," asserted Walter Maier. "The Lutheran Church does not compromise with the world; it does not yield ground to modernism—and by the grace and mercy of God it never will."[28] Maier advocated a simple orthodoxy, but he also advocated Lutheranism as the true expression of simple orthodoxy. A pamphlet written by the Lutheran Hour Radio Committee positioned the *Lutheran Hour* firmly against modernism:

> Remember we have but one aim, and that is to exalt Christ, and Him crucified, as the divine Savior, in the hearts and lives of millions. It is our avowed objective to bring the Christ of the Cross to the nation and to the homes of its people. To this end we will wage an uncompromising battle against the cancer of modernist unbelief. We will fight atheistic Communism, protest against the intrusion of churchmen into the political life of the nation, and raise our voices against the loosening of the home ties and the breakdown of family life. We will cry out against any antichristian and antimoral teachings in the schools of the nation. First and last, this radio crusade for Christ will offer, not economic theories, not political programs, not legislative proposals, but the Word of God and its divine help for the solution of our personal and national perplexities.[29]

Maier's radio program was simultaneously a vigorous reaffirmation of a simple orthodoxy and a war against modernism.

Maier's commitment to a simple Protestant orthodoxy can be seen in his doctrine of Scripture. For example, Maier outlined his understanding of the uniqueness of the Bible:

> Now it is fundamentally vital that we realize that this Bible is Christ's Word, God's Word, a divine book. . . . Externally, of course, the Bible has much the same appearance as any other volume of its size and proportions. But because it is God-breathed; because, as we are expressly assured, "all Scripture is given by inspiration"; because the men who wrote the various books of the Bible "spake as they were moved by the Holy Ghost," we believe the Bible . . . presents to us the Word of God, written by men who were chosen and supernaturally endowed by God for

---

28. Letter dated July 15, 1931, Walter Maier Papers.
29. Walter Maier Papers.

that purpose and who, through the divine process of inspiration, were given the exact, literal messages they have recorded for us.[30]

On another occasion Maier asked, "Is the Bible merely human, or is it gloriously divine?" Maier answered by declaring that the Bible is "the Word of Truth and Power . . . heaven's perfect verity."[31] Like the fundamentalists, Maier asserted that the Bible was "inspired," "inerrant," "God-breathed," "infallible," and "authoritative," among other designations consistent with confessional Protestantism.[32] Over the seventeen years of the *Lutheran Hour*, Maier pressed the inspiration and inerrancy of the Bible repeatedly.

For Maier, the divine origin of the Bible was not merely an academic debate. An orthodox commitment to Scripture was imperative, for it was the very foundation of the church: "The entire Christian faith, the work of the whole Church of Christ, the eternal hope of millions for their salvation, stands or falls with the claim that the Bible is the errorless, divinely inspired 'Word of God.' Attack this basic truth, and you are undermining the foundation upon which all Christianity rests."[33] Maier saw the *Lutheran Hour* as a ministry of the word, broadcasting "the infallible truths of Scripture."[34]

Maier sought to advance traditional trinitarianism as part of his commitment to Protestant orthodoxy. For example, in the inaugural broadcast of the third season of the *Lutheran Hour*, Maier committed the program to God in traditional trinitarian fashion:

> Heavenly Father: In Thy name and for the far reaching testimony to the love of Thy Son, Jesus Christ, the only, but all-sufficient Savior from sin and sorrow, we to-day begin this third series of broadcasts. Send us Thy Spirit, so that, as the hymns, prayers, and messages wing their way over the nation and beyond its confines, men may raise believing hearts to the cross and in Christ's ever-valid redemption find the divine answer to every question of body and soul.[35]

Maier proclaimed the oneness of God while detailing several of his perfections:

---

30. Walter Maier Papers.
31. Walter Maier Papers.
32. See, for example, Maier, *Christ for the Nation!* 21–22, 132–42; Maier, *Lutheran Hour*, 10–11, 20; Maier, *Radio for Christ*, 45–60; Maier, *Jesus Christ Our Hope*, 153–66.
33. Maier, *Radio for Christ*, 47–48.
34. Maier, *Christ for Every Crisis*, 12.
35. Maier, *Christ for the Nation*, 11.

> Contrary to the crude extravagances of heathen worship with its immense pantheons of hundreds, yea, thousands and tens of thousands of gods, there is, as all Christendom confesses on the basis of plain Scripture passages, but one God, infinitely exalted and immeasurably supreme, above the strongest, the best, the purest, the greatest, and the most permanent that earth and heaven combined contain.[36]

He took particular issue with the "modern" renditions of God's doctrine so prevalent in his day:

> Contrary to the refined speculations of a skeptical age, in which God is held to be an idea, an impersonal force, a mere abstraction found in flagrant flowers and blue skies, in laughing waters and wooded groves; contrary to all the loose, hazy, doubtful, shallow thoughts of God that are so popular in our modern books and periodicals, He who to-night tells every one of us, "I am the Lord, thy God," is an absolute personality, an individual, definite, personal God; a God who wills and works; a God who plans and directs; a God who creates and sustains; a God who bears a very vital and personal relation to every human being that has ever walked the face of the globe.[37]

Maier moved from the doctrine of God's oneness to an affirmation of God as Trinity: "But when we have acknowledged God as the one personal, definite Being, this by no means exhausts the Biblical statements regarding His essence and nature. For in this personal unity there is a blessed, holy Trinity."[38]

Maier defended the deity of Christ as part of his commitment to orthodoxy. For example, to combat the prevailing tendency among liberal theologians to acknowledge only Christ's humanity, Maier made forceful pleas to regard Jesus as fully human and divine. For instance, in the middle of a sermon, Maier paused to remind his listeners that Jesus Christ was not merely human:

> Let me stop for a moment to tell you again what I have told you before and what, pray God, we shall incessantly continue to repeat as long as we use the facilities of this marvelous Gospel-messenger, and that is that you are listening to the representative of a Church which bases all its preaching on this glorious, victorious truth, so often misunderstood, so unfairly misrepresented,

---

36. Maier, *Lutheran Hour*, 56.
37. Maier, *Lutheran Hour*, 56.
38. Maier, *Lutheran Hour*, 56–57.

and so systematically denied, namely, that Jesus Christ is not a mere human being as you and I are, that He is not merely the greatest man, the most exalted hero, the most stupendous mind of which history knows, but that He is, beyond all possibility of doubt and hesitation, what St. Peter declares Him to be—"the Son of the living God."[39]

Confessing the deity of Christ was, for Maier, a matter of eternal consequence. He believed that holding to the deity of Christ was absolutely essential for the church:

> When Saint Paul deliberately calls Christ "God, blessed forever" (and I accept the interpretation of these words that the Christian Church has always adopted), he expresses the central truth of Christianity, the apex fact of all history. The one blessed conviction which distinguishes Christianity from all other creeds is its reverence for Jesus Christ as the God of glory. . . . By accepting or rejecting this foundation truth you and I are saved or lost forever.[40]

Maier believed emphatically that "the eternal value of the cross and the promise of shed blood are rooted in the deity of Jesus Christ." Furthermore, "when the enemies of the Cross take away the divine Savior and substitute the human Christ, they have torn the heart from the hope of humanity."[41]

> Maier answered what he believed was the all-important question: "Who is Jesus?"
>
> May every one of you be given the faith and the fortitude to behold the Cross and to join me in the confession of faith I repeat once in every broadcasting season—words of a man, it is true, yet to me of all human utterances closest to divine Scripture—the statement of the hero whose name is perpetuated in our broadcasts, Martin Luther's, four-century-old, but ever new, declaration of loyalty to the Lord: "I believe that Jesus Christ, true God, begotten of the Father from eternity, and also true man, born of the Virgin Mary, is my Lord, who has redeemed me, a lost and condemned creature, purchased and won me from all sins, from death, and from the power of the devil, not with gold or silver, but with His holy, precious blood and with His innocent suffering and death, that I may be His own and live under Him in His kingdom and serve Him in everlasting righteousness, innocence,

---

39. Maier, *Lutheran Hour*, 5.
40. Maier, *Cross from Coast to Coast*, 192.
41. Maier, *Cross from Coast to Coast*, 196.

and blessedness, even as He is risen from the dead, lives and reigns to all eternity. This is most certainly true."[42]

By citing Martin Luther's *Small Catechism* and his exposition of the second article of the Apostles' Creed, Maier summarized his orthodox position on Christ and redemption. In one sweeping statement he affirms the two natures of Christ, the Virgin Birth, Christ's atoning work, resurrection, rule, and reign. For Maier, Lutheranism was orthodoxy.

Maier's simple orthodoxy included homespun advice on how to live the Christian life. In this Maier did not divorce doctrine from practice. Similar to Harry Emerson Fosdick and Aimee Semple McPherson, Maier wanted to help people fare better in this life. One newspaper article described Maier's practical advice to listeners this way:

> Most of the flood of correspondence he gets is from people who have problems confronting them and they come to him for their solutions. It keeps twenty persons busy answering just the everyday garden variety of query, but he saves the tough ones for himself. Six special assistants are needed to take care of these personal replies.
>
> What do they write about? The majority want to thank him for the inspiration they receive from his messages. This out of the way, they ask advice mainly on personal problems. The answers are keyed by Dr. Maier on the following creed: "Marriage shall be held in esteem; divorce shall be checked; a decent regard for childhood shall be instilled and the ravages of race suicide checked; above all, a spiritual atmosphere shall be inculcated in the home."[43]

For Maier, orthodox Christianity addressed issues such as the breakdown of morality, especially regarding the American family. For example, Maier commended the "Christ-conscious family" as the only way of properly esteeming marriage: "The Christ-conscious family will esteem marriage as the divine institution which it is, ordained by God Himself for the bestowal of multiplied benedictions and blessings. In the Christ-exalting family there will be an intensity and continuance of pure, self-sacrificing love, which binds husband and wife together in devoted companionship as the better or worse of life's destiny predominates."[44] Maier believed a Christ-centered home was the best hope for children as well: "The Christ-centered family will thank God for the precious children that His bounty bestows upon

42. Maier, *Jesus Christ Our Hope*, 6.
43. *St. Louis Star-Times*, November 3, 1939.
44. Maier, *Christ for Every Crisis*, 49–50.

them, and these children, brought up 'in the nurture and admonition of the Lord,' will love, honor, and obey their parents in unbroken devotion."[45] For Maier, orthodox Christianity had everything to do with properly esteeming marriage and rightly raising children. It also had everything to do with the health of a nation. For example, in a sermon broadcast on 1 Timothy 5:4, in which the Apostle Paul teaches about the priority of showing godliness in the home, Maier tied the prosperity of the nation to the spiritual health of American homes: "What America needs is repentance, a deep, personal, unreserved sorrow over sin and a clear knowledge of what unforgiven sin means in its misery here on earth and its endless suffering hereafter. And when the text reminds us to show godliness in the home, we realize that our repentance can well begin with the sins violating our family happiness."[46]

"If American families are to help form the blessed foundation we need for individual and national happiness," Maier declared over the air on another occasion, "they must stand before the Lord in banishing the strife and quarrel that mars many a household."[47] Maier believed that national happiness depended on the family.

Maier's simple orthodoxy, consistent with the fundamentalism of his day, included warnings about things such as communism, atheism, and Hollywood morality. For example, in a sermon entitled "America, Return to God!" Maier lamented the fact that "millions in the United States have left God. Atheism, the absolute denial that there is an almighty Father above, has reached new and shocking heights."[48] In another sermon Maier warned of a "poet, reputedly an atheist and a self-acknowledged Communist" whose "poems are not only blasphemous but ultra-Red" who was invited to speak at the University of Minnesota. In that same sermon, Maier warned his listeners of a similar spread of communism at Columbia University in New York.[49] Not only were communism and atheism a deep concern for Maier, but also what he perceived as the corrupting values of a burgeoning Hollywood culture. If these values went unchecked by Christians, Maier believed, the future of America was in grave danger:

> If, then, we continue to build homes with loose family morality and nonchalant ideas concerning marriage ties, as this unruffled

---

45. Maier, *Christ for Every Crisis*, 50.
46. Maier, *Peace through Christ*, 69.
47. Maier, *Rebuilding with Christ*, 268.
48. Maier, *America, Turn to Christ!* 137–38.
49. Maier, *Radio for Christ*, 184. Maier's anti-Communism and warnings against atheism caught the attention of the *New York Times*. See, for example, "Professor Maier Sees War on Faith."

disregard of God's holy will is featured in many of our motion-pictures (and 77,000,000 Americans pay to see these every week); if free love and a host of unspeakable perversions are championed in gangrenous fiction (and your children can often secure this printed virus now for a cent a day—the cheapest means of moral suicide ever known); if myriads of American youth continue to see the standards of the jungle paraded with the lust and liquor of night clubs and road-houses (and these breeding-places of vice are springing up almost overnight as quickly as poisonous toadstools), just so long we must look to the future with unsuppressed concern.[50]

For all of this, Maier blamed, in large part, modern education philosophy and its rejection of the Bible in any orthodox sense:

> The modern philosophy of education from beginning to end is often based on a code which flatly contradicts the Bible. . . . They tell us that the Bible is just another book, which may be viewed in part as good literature but which must be denied all authority, since it is saturated with superstition and error, leaving only those parts to be retained which can be endorsed by modern science . . . we see that many schools are deliberately engaged in destroying the Christian hope of our boys and girls.[51]

Maier warned against what he saw as the evils of modernism—evils that lead to an "anti-Biblical" and, ultimately, "Christless culture."[52] For Maier, the answer was a return to simple Protestant orthodoxy.

One of the distinguishing features of the *Lutheran Hour* was its commitment to a simple Protestant orthodoxy. Maier was determined to reach as many people as possible with his rendition of the old-time gospel. To this end, the particulars of a robust Lutheran theology and practice were not emphasized on the *Lutheran Hour* broadcasts.

Maier believed that "while the technique, illustrations, idiom, style, application, and communication of [the gospel's] preaching must be modernized, the essential truths remain constant."[53] What the world needed most was to beat back modernism and reaffirm the timeless truths of the Bible, such as the sufficiency of Holy Scripture, God as Trinity, and Jesus Christ

---

50. Maier, *Christ for the Nation!* 48.

51. Maier, *Radio for Christ*, 182–83. Maier's condemnation of modern educational philosophy was documented in the *New York Times*. See, for example, "Dr. W.A. Maier Assails 'Subversive' Trends."

52. Maier, *Radio For Christ*, 183.

53. Maier, *Man Spoke*, 96.

as the Son of God and man. As he applied his message to the particular circumstances of his day, Maier sought to bring the ancient faith to a modern people.

TRANSCENDING LUTHERANISM

Walter Maier's commitment to proclaim simple Protestant orthodoxy gained him an audience that transcended Lutheranism. His gospel struck a nerve with countless people who were hungry for the "good old religion" that came from the pages of sacred Scripture and had been taught by the church for centuries. For Maier, confessional Lutheranism in its most basic expression consisted in the great truths of the Bible that humanity desperately needed.

Maier's reach beyond Lutheranism was not accidental, but intentional. When asked by a friend if Maier's dream for a radio program was for a distinctly "Lutheran" message, he answered, "Exactly, a 'Lutheran Radio Hour,' preaching an authentic Christianity sometimes missing in a few of the 'modernized' versions I've heard, although it should have a very broad appeal—not sectarian—appeal."[54] For Maier, the best expression of Protestant orthodoxy was Lutheranism. In other words, Lutheranism was "authentic Christianity." Still, Maier conceded that radio would not support Lutheran particulars beyond what fundamentalist Christians could embrace generally. Years later, Maier described the range of subjects he covered on the *Lutheran Hour* broadcasts during World War II, demonstrating that his radio program maintained the "very broad appeal" he originally envisioned:

> I have emphasized the disastrous consequences following widespread warfare. I have denounced the tyranny and despotism of Nazism, Fascism, and Communism; but I have tried not to blind myself to the serious dangers confronting our own national life: the breakdown of the home, godless education, rampant crime, corruption of justice, class struggle, radical, anti-Scriptural theories of government and administration, the disloyalty to Christ in modernist circles, and particularly the religious indifference that keeps more than half our population away from the Church.[55]

Maier's intentional efforts to transcend Lutheranism were evidenced in his *Lutheran Hour* prayers. For example, before a sermon on Jesus Christ as the world's only hope, Maier offered a prayer that any fundamentalist of his day could embrace:

---

54. Maier, *Man Spoke*, 111.
55. Maier, *Courage in Christ*, iii.

> Great and Glorious God: In the name of Jesus Christ, our Savior, through the power of Thy Holy Spirit, our Comforter, and with the promise of Thy grace, our Lord of love, we begin this new season of our radio ministry. We have but one purpose: to proclaim the Gospel of full, free and final forgiveness through faith in the cleansing blood and the life-giving death of our merciful Redeemer. Without Thee, Triune God of mercy, might and majesty, we can do nothing; but with Thee we can maintain and spread this mission of the air throughout the world, even though the legions of our enemies are multiplied a thousand-fold. Therefore, we entreat Thee, bless our broadcast! Use this message of word and song in warning the wicked, calling sinners to repentance, comforting the afflicted, recalling the unfaithful, sustaining the bereaved, and, above all, in bringing souls to Thee in Christ, our only hope and our sure Salvation.[56]

In this prayer listeners heard classic orthodox themes such as God as Trinity, forgiveness in Christ, the Holy Spirit as comforter, and the love of God. Listeners also heard Maier's plea for souls to come to Christ. There was nothing distinctly Lutheran about this simple orthodox prayer.

In another prayer, Maier demonstrated his primary concern that people come not necessarily to Lutheranism, but to Christ:

> O' Christ, Though Lamb of God, that takest away the sin of the world: Have mercy upon us for our many sins of uncleanness, selfishness, greed, hatred! Have mercy upon us, we pray again, as we realize the eternal penalty of our unforgiven transgressions, but turn for pardon to Thee, who in Thine own holy body on the cross of Calvary, the altar of Thine atoning love, didst offer Thyself to ransom us from ruin and restore us to our heavenly Father! Show us that we can come to Thee in every need of soul or body and find peace for our restless hearts, comfort for our sorrows, healing for all agonies. O Jesus, precious Savior, through this broadcast earnestly warn those who are destroying themselves through unbelief! Send Thy Spirit to call them, if necessary through hardship and reverse. To repentance and faith! Let many who are children of wrath be born again as children of grace![57]

Maier's primary concern was for the masses to learn of the forgiveness found in Jesus Christ, not the particulars of Lutheranism.

---

56. Maier, *Jesus Christ Our Hope*, 1.
57. Maier, *Jesus Christ Our Hope*, 17.

During the seventeen seasons of the *Lutheran Hour*, fan mail was the only available means to estimate audience size. By this measurement, Maier's growth was explosive:

> After the first few broadcasts, well over 15,000 communications had been received, not including thousands sent directly to local stations or CBS in New York. Radio officials were surprised at the immediacy of the response, which they thought would build up only through months of broadcasting. Soon the listening audience was estimated at five million hearers, and after just two months on the air, network newcomer Maier was receiving more mail than such top secular shows as *Amos 'n' Andy*, or any other religious program in America.[58]

By the eleventh season of the *Lutheran Hour*, the audience was estimated at twelve million people. This number climbed to fifteen million by the twelfth season and to twenty million by the fifteenth season.[59] Table 1 illustrates the growth of the *Lutheran Hour* during the seventeen seasons under Maier's leadership.

Much of the listeners' correspondence that flooded the *Lutheran Hour* contained testimonials of how helpful the "thoroughly orthodox and evangelical" messages had been to them. For example, a listener from Portland, Oregon, wrote,

> As a superintendent of the American Sunday-school Union permit me to tell you of the help and pleasure I get out of your splendid Thursday night religious programs. Not myself a Lutheran, I find that no finer, clearer, and more helpful and more thoroughly orthodox and evangelical message is being more splendidly received by the Lord's people in this section.[60]

A woman from Montreal, Quebec, dismayed at her church's drift toward modernism, wrote, "We belong to the United Church of Canada, but our Church is governed by a Modernist of the States, and we cannot enjoy his sermons. He knocks out every prop of our good old religion, and we have stopped listening to him. It is a great joy to hear a real Gospel sermon coming in over the radio once a week, especially when the blessed blood of Jesus is mentioned."[61] A Presbyterian pastor in Richmond, Virginia, summarized the uniqueness of Walter Maier among the radio personalities in his day:

---

58. Maier, *Jesus Christ Our Hope*, 119.
59. Hangen, "Man of the Hour," 120.
60. Maier, *Lutheran Hour*, 317.
61. Maier, *Lutheran Hour*, 318.

I desire to express the delight and appreciation with which I greet your sermons. They are the only religious discourses of their kind, and you can console yourself by reflecting that you are unique on the radio and that there is no competition as far as I have been able to learn. I, of course, hear the pompous vapidities and glittering generalities of others, and it is refreshing to hear the apostolic Gospel of the crucified and risen Son of God coming with a note of authority and yet at the same time with pleading evangelistic note beseeching men to look to the Lord Jesus and be reconciled to God. That is the Gospel that created the Church and has kept it alive.... I hear some sermons that are orthodox, but those of the Lutheran Hour are not only orthodox, but spiritual and dynamic, with the cross at the center.[62]

Table 1. Growth of the *Lutheran Hour*, 1930–50[63]

Season	Year	Total stations	Mail received
1	1930–31	36	57,000
2	1935	11	16,000
3	1935–36	10	70,000
4	1936–37	31	90,000
5	1937–38	62	125,000
6	1938–39	66	140,000
7	1939–40	171	176,508
8	1940–41	374	200,000
9	1941–42	346	260,000
10	1942–43	450	330,000
11	1943–44	540	335,000
12	1944–45	609	340,000
13	1945–46	809	403,367
14	1946–47	905	400,000
15	1947–48	1,022	410,000
16	1948–49	1,100	450,000
17	1949–50	1,236	over 500,000

62. Maier, *Lutheran Hour*, 317–18.

63. From Hangen, "Man of the Hour," 120. Due to financial difficulties the *Lutheran Hour* was off the air for three years (1932–34) before resuming in 1935.

This Presbyterian pastor cherished the "apostolic Gospel" he heard proclaimed on the *Lutheran Hour*. In addition, he commended Maier for not only being orthodox in his doctrine, but for giving sermons that were "spiritual and dynamic, with the cross at the center." According to this listener, Maier's messages were "the only religious discourses of their kind" on the radio.[64]

Not all of Maier's listeners responded with praise. In fact, some took issue with his simple Christianity, considering Maier a simpleton who was in need of some new material. One listener, for example, implored Maier to be more like Harry Emerson Fosdick:

> Dear Dr. Maier:
> For a long time I have been wanting to ask you a question. Do you use the same sermon on the air every Sunday afternoon? Always, the blood, the blood, and a tirade against those who would interpret the Gospel according to practical needs. Although you use a high sounding vocabulary, your message, if analyzed, is nothing but a childish faith and a hopeless superstition. Really what you say is nothing more than a constipation of real thought and a diarrhea of words, and it seems to appear in the same style and form every Sunday. And the way that you tell it (with your bombastic talent and irritating voice)—you would have your hearers believe that you and only you have probed into the secrets of the Bible. I can hardly think that you believe some of the drivel that you preach, for you speak as do most arrogant bluffers. Not one word do I say against the Source of your message, it is the way that you interpret that Source that puzzles me, and causes me to turn the dial to a musical Sunday afternoon. You have a great opportunity to bring an intelligent message to a public sorely in need of true enlightenment, but instead you keep on with this idea—scare a person to death, and then he will believe. What is the I.Q. of your hearers? Why don't you write another sermon? Why not forget the bloody Christ and tell more of the Christ who lives in men? Why not admit that *there is* some truth outside of the Bible? Why not listen to Fosdick? Is Christ a "boogey man," as you would have us believe? Finally, to repeat, please write a new sermon, and tone down on your voice. A soft voice will turn away wrath. And probably keep your writer from turning the dial—probably.[65]

---

64. Correspondence commending Maier's orthodoxy abounds in the primary sources. For further examples see Maier, *Christ for Every Crisis*, 154–55; *Christ, Set the World Aright*, xiv; *America, Turn to Christ*, xvii–xviii.

65. Letter with no date, no place, from "One of Many," Walter Maier Papers,

A critic listening in Los Angeles bemoaned Maier's fundamentalism with its "ranting" and "fault-finding":

> Responding to your invitation for comments on the program broadcast by your organization over the Columbia network last evening, February 26, permit me to suggest that your speaker would have been more impressive had he been less declamatory, less ranting, and less fault-finding. If you Fundamentalists have a message for the people, why can you not present it in a cheerful, genial manner? Why this constant looking on the dark side of life, seeing only evil and recalcitrance, and devoting your time to scolding and expressions of bitterness? I know you have a worthy exemplar in Jeremiah, but what did his wailings accomplish?[66]

Walter Maier's radio ministry was not lost on the popular media of his day. For example, Maier notes in his biography that "more than eight hundred newspapers carried the story of the *Lutheran Hour* in its inaugural weeks. Both the *New York Herald Tribune* and the *New York Post* regularly selected it as a recommended program for Thursdays, and editorials acclaiming its high quality appeared in various periodicals."[67] In addition, *Time* magazine described Maier as the "Chrysostom of American Lutheranism," and upon his death the *New York Times* declared that he was "one of the world's best known Lutheran preachers."[68]

The *Time* magazine article is important for the way it shows the *Lutheran Hour*'s emphasis on Protestant orthodoxy and antimodernism. The occasion for the story was Maier's recent filling of the Chicago Stadium (twenty-five thousand people) for the opening of the eleventh season of the *Lutheran Hour* in 1943:

> They heard sacred music on the stadium organ, listened to scripture reading, recited the Apostolic Creed, pledged allegiance to the flag, roared Luther's battle hymn, *A Mighty Fortress is Our God*, put $15,260 into the collection, heard Indiana's Lutheran Governor Henry F. Schricker talk about the church in the postwar world, and, best of all, saw and heard Dr. Maier's initial

---

emphasis original. In the early 1930s, given the enormous amount of written correspondence coming into the program, Maier began to reply to his critics with a simple acknowledgement of their opinion and regret for the disagreement. "Dear Sir, I hereby wish to acknowledge receipt of your letter. I am sorry you do not agree with me. Yours very truly, Walter A. Maier."

66. Clifford Howard, February 27, 1931, Los Angeles, Walter Maier Papers.
67. Maier, *Man Spoke*, 120.
68. Maier, *Man Spoke*, 1–2.

> broadcast of the current Lutheran Hour. . . . To Boston-born Dr. Maier, who was 50 last week, the way to Christ is through the Bible. He is a Fundamentalist and glories in the name: "I don't quote Scripture with my fingers crossed." He has no use for "sawdust" sermons, bases his own on "the Word of God, the divinely and literally inspired record of our Heavenly Father for the guidance, instruction, and salvation of His children." Vast numbers of Bible-loving people, both Protestant and Catholic, write to thank him for stressing his Bible message. . . . Except when he is on tour, Maier broadcasts from a St. Louis studio. He perspires so profusely that he takes off his shirt. When he has to wear shirt and coat before an audience his collar is wilted and his clothes sopping. Even so, he stays to shake hands with his listeners, often standing three hours to do it. He says he likes it, that his hand never gets sore. . . . Maier talks for 19 ½ minutes. He literally shouts into the microphone at a machine-gun pace. Radio engineers have tried all sorts of tricks to modulate the tone. Once or twice they persuaded him to slow down, but it took the punch out of what he said, people wrote in to ask if he was sick and fan mail dropped off 1,000 letters a day. Now Dr. Maier just shouts and lets the engineers worry about it.[69]

Another significant profile of Walter Maier and the *Lutheran Hour* came from the *Saturday Evening Post* in June of 1948. This article positioned Maier squarely in the company of the fundamentalists of his day and described him as a radio preacher determined to proclaim classic Protestant orthodoxy to the masses. The author of the story, Hartzell Spence, began by noting the irony of Walter Maier's radio career given his academic training:

> In the early days of radio a professor of ancient languages at Concordia Lutheran Theological Seminary in St. Louis, Missouri, presented to his colleagues a startling idea. "The radio," he said, "is a great gift from God. We should use it to preach the gospel."
>
> The proposal was far removed from the special field of its proponent, the Rev. Dr. Walter Arthur Maier. He was a student of the antiquities, a man who could recite in Hebrew long sections of the Book of Genesis. He had won his doctor-of-philosophy degree at Harvard University, in semantics, which is the science that deals with the meanings of words in the various evolutions of languages. He had taught Arabic at Harvard, and he spoke the complex Semitic tongues which are difficult for the

---

69. *Time*, October 18, 1943, vol. XLII, no. 16: 46, 48–49, Walter Maier Papers.

Western mind to grasp. He had translated the New Testament into Chinese. He wrote weighty tomes on ancient subjects.

Now he had emerged from the cocoon of the religious campus with a proposal so alien to his natural bent that his fellow professors were a little shocked. But he pleaded his case so eloquently that in 1927 the seminary established a radio station in the attic of an old building, and Doctor Maier went on the air fifteen times a week with sermons, book reviews and discussions of family problems. People began to write him letters, and he to answer them. Before long he was inundated by his correspondence. It was plain to everyone at Concordia that the erudite professor had hold of something that might well be bigger than himself.[70]

Spence accurately labeled Maier a fundamentalist and recognized how he "hewed to a line that his colleagues prophesied would fail":

> They told him his viewpoint was too narrow, that the constant repetition of a single theme would not attract listeners in a modern world, even when that theme was the mighty Biblical concept of the power of faith to redeem sinners. But Maier holds doggedly to a stern, unyielding, absolutely fundamentalist doctrine. Divorce, birth control, intoxicating liquors, luxurious living and easy morals are particular targets of his invective. With biting scorn he dismisses all modern religious notions which cannot be sustained by chapter and verse from the Testaments. The Devil is his personal enemy. And sin is SIN, not just a difference of opinion over right and wrong.[71]

Spence was right to highlight not only Maier's fundamentalist doctrine, but also his crusade against what he perceived as the crumbling moral standards of his time. Maier spent considerable airtime decrying, for example, the weakened family values of the modern age. For example, in a radio broadcast shortly after the close of World War II, Maier sounded the alarm over the state of the American family. He asked his listeners this searching question: "Above all, what does the Almighty, who perceives even the unspoken thought, hear within the walls of your house?"[72] Maier suggested that what God heard was not good. Maier singled out children:

---

70. Hartzell Spence, "The Man of the Hour," *Saturday Evening Post*, June 19, 1948, Walter Maier Papers.
71. Spence, "The Man of the Hour."
72. Maier, *Rebuilding with Christ*, 268.

> Today is Mother's Day. How many American mothers will receive no flowers, no gifts, no cards, not even a loving thought, from their children, because their sons and daughters—proud, self-sufficient, sometimes too successful—have forsaken their mother, deserted their father?[73]

But children were not the only ones to blame. Parents were at fault as well:

> Many of our homes do not stand before the Lord because parents neglect their little ones. Not only have more parents than ever before cruelly deserted their offspring, but masses of our boys and girls, their fathers absent, their mothers preoccupied or unconcerned, live on without discipline, counsel, and especially spiritual guidance.[74]

For Maier, the sins that beset the home and left the nation morally impoverished stemmed from neglect of God: "All these sins that weaken the home, provoke divine wrath, and undermine the nation, stem from the first and most fatal domestic weakness—rejection of God."[75]

Like his fundamentalist colleagues on the air, such as Aimee Semple McPherson, Paul Rader, Charles Fuller, and others, Maier believed in absolute right and wrong. Spence noted this emphasis by highlighting the centrality of the Bible to Maier's understanding of truth and falsehood: "To the doctor there is only one Truth. All else is false. In his sermons he sets up all the philosophies that are not founded on the Bible, bowls them over like so many tenpins, and leaves standing one kingpin, Holy Writ."[76] Spence explained that Maier's purpose was not always apparent to the listener. He explained it with reference to his "flamboyant oratory," which sounded much like other fundamentalists of Maier's day:

> This concise professorial logic is not apparent to the listener, because of his flamboyant oratory. An executive of the Mutual Broadcasting System, which airs The Lutheran Hour, describes Dr. Maier's speaking technique as "the soapbox delivery of a Harvard script." The radio preacher bangs away at the microphone like a Fourth of July orator of the old school. With the machine-gun delivery of a Billy Sunday he shouts at the top of

---

73. Maier, *Rebuilding with Christ*, 267.
74. Maier, *Rebuilding with Christ*, 267.
75. Maier, *Rebuilding with Christ*, 270.
76. Spence, "The Man of the Hour."

his lungs such warnings as, "If you are headed for hell, may the Almighty throw you in the dust to save your soul."[77]

Spence described Maier accurately as a vigorous fundamentalist who declared orthodoxy over the radio as if heaven and hell were in the balance:

> He drives home these words with extravagant gestures, even in the sanctuary of a radio studio in which he permits no audience. To command complete freedom of physical action, he strips down for his broadcast as though he were entering the prize ring—removes his coat, vest, shirt, and tie, and even his belt, and appears at the microphone in an undershirt. Just before he goes on the air, he loosens up his arm and shoulder muscles by calisthenics in the manner of a shadow boxer. Then he cuts loose in a voice that is the terror of radio sound engineers—stentorian, impelling. The microphone becomes his audience, and to it he delivers his discourse, pointing his finger at it in stern warning, raising clenched fists toward it as he calls for penitence and spiritual rebirth, shaking his head at it intensely, as though it were the most miserable of sinners.[78]

Maier's popularity, like other fundamentalist radio preachers of the day, was not due to his "oratorical acrobatics . . . but to the direct hold he gains on his audience":

> There is no doubt that he means you, not some other fellow. He may lead off, as he did recently, by quoting a telegram he has received from a listener who needs help. This very personal plea then becomes the springboard for a heart-to-heart talk with each one of his listeners. "Christ can change your life!" he thunders. "You are going to hell. You can save yourself!"[79]

Demonstrating the mass appeal of Maier's radio ministry, Spence described the non-Lutheran emphasis of the *Lutheran Hour*: "The wide range of his audience causes Doctor Maier to shun any denominational flavor in his discourses. Pastors of many faiths write him letters of encouragement, often saying they wished they dared speak as forthrightly from their own pulpits."[80] Spence's analysis advances the argument that Maier used radio broadcasting to advance simple Protestant orthodoxy devoid of Lutheran particulars.

77. Spence, "The Man of the Hour."
78. Spence, "The Man of the Hour."
79. Spence, "The Man of the Hour."
80. Spence, "The Man of the Hour."

From the beginning of his radio ministry, Walter Maier was intentional about transcending Lutheranism. In an effort to reach as many people as possible, Maier did not preach a sectarian theology, but a simple orthodoxy compatible with the fundamentalism of his day.

CONCLUSION

In this chapter I argued that Maier, to accommodate Christianity to the new medium of radio, forsook Lutheran particulars in favor of a gospel more compatible with the fundamentalism of his day. Maier's vigorous reaffirmation of simple Christianity struck a nerve with millions of people in the tumultuous decades of the 1930s and 1940s. The Lutheran Church, Missouri Synod, was Maier's ecclesiastical home. This ecclesiastical affiliation nurtured in Maier a love for doctrinal truth and a passion to see that truth spread throughout the world. Armed with biblical truth and motivated by a zeal for its propagation, Maier proclaimed a simple Protestant orthodoxy over the airwaves for seventeen seasons of the *Lutheran Hour*. In the dedicatory address of the Walter A. Maier Study at the Concordia Historical Institute in 1981, William Kramer summarized the essence of Maier's message: "Dr. Maier preached the Law in all its severity to prepare the hard ground; he preached the Gospel in all its beauty to heal the wounds in the lives of people."[81] The flood of mail that came pouring into the *Lutheran Hour* each year testified to the tremendous success of the program. People heard the words of "the old Gospel" and responded by the thousands.

What happened to Maier's Lutheranism when it moved to the medium of radio? Although much of it stayed intact, other particulars were left behind.[82] The medium of radio did not lend itself to strong polemics or intricate details of one's theological system. In addition, Maier needed to appeal to as many people possible to keep the *Lutheran Hour* financially viable. At its peak, the *Lutheran Hour* commanded a $25,000 per week budget. Although the show was supported in part by Maier's speaking engagements and the Lutheran Laymen's League (an organization of forty-five thousand men that helped support the program financially), the majority of the *Lutheran Hour* budget was sustained by the donations of millions of loyal listeners around the world. Maier simply could not afford

---

81. Kramer, "Walter A. Maier Dedicatory Address," 100.

82. Radio broadcasts, as far as I can tell, never took up distinctly Lutheran positions on issues of polity, liturgy, sanctification, the Lord's Supper, or baptism to name several things that were "left behind" in the move to radio.

to cut off listeners by being too robustly Lutheran in his message. It appears that Maier's longing to reach the world with the message of a simple Christianity merged well with the constraints of broadcast media, constraints that made the *Lutheran Hour* an agency for broad evangelical religion more than an agency for Lutheranism.

5

"All We Do Is Toward Evangelism"

Charles E. Fuller and the *Old Fashioned Revival Hour*

THIS CHAPTER ARGUES THAT Charles Fuller's ministry contributed to the transformation of American religion by defining it primarily in terms of evangelism. Fuller's success uncovered a particular mood in America: one tired of the militant fundamentalism of the early decades of the century but not ready to abandon the fundamentals of the faith for theological liberalism. Fuller epitomized a new evangelicalism that would eventually dominate the airwaves. By defining evangelical Protestantism in terms of evangelism, Fuller's radio program became a unifying force within the broader evangelical movement. Although Fuller's ministry helped preserve the influence of religion in the culture, it altered the religion it aimed to preserve.

In the twilight of his career as the world-renowned host of radio's *Old Fashioned Revival Hour*, Charles Fuller addressed a classroom of students at Fuller Theological Seminary. His aim was to impress upon his listeners the importance of evangelism by describing what marked his broadcast for over thirty years:

> Paul said, "Woe to me if I preach not the Gospel." Not everyone has the specific gift of evangelism, but whatever your particular spiritual gift, you should be evangelistic. All we do is toward

evangelism. There should be a definite purpose in preaching, and that is to realize that the people you are talking to are those that are alienated from Christ, dead in trespasses and sins, and walking according to the course of this age, energized by the prince of the power of the air, the spirit that now works in the children of disobedience. And people need to know that they are bound for everlasting separation unless they repent and believe the Gospel. So, that's been the heart of the "Old Fashioned Revival Hour" all these years.[1]

Although evangelism was not the only concern of Fuller's ministry labors, it was preeminent.[2]

Radio was the means that Fuller employed to preach the "good old Gospel" and the "simple truths" of the Bible. He did this in the hope that countless thousands would turn from their sin and embrace Jesus Christ as their personal Savior. Before there was Billy Graham, there was Charles Fuller. The microphone was his pulpit, and at the peak of his popularity he broadcast the faith on over six hundred stations to an estimated weekly audience of twenty million people around the world. Some weeks, thousands of letters from listeners would flood the office. Long-time friend of the Fullers and editor of the *Sunday School Times* Charles Trumbull believed that natural explanations for Fuller's success would not suffice: "The story of the Old Fashioned Revival Hour is one of the most amazing miracles of God's grace and power in the field of Christian evangelism during our lifetime."[3]

Charles Fuller and the *Old Fashioned Revival Hour* stand out among the many personalities and events of the 1940s and 1950s that make up what Garth Rosell calls "the surprising work of God"—a religious awakening in America that saw fundamentalists emerge from the shadows of mainstream culture while transforming the religious landscape in America and around

1. Fuller, *Give the Winds*, 48.

2. Fuller, *Give the Winds*. Fuller gives two reasons for his father's importance: "I believe his life is important because, more than anyone else, he used radio to get the Gospel out to the world in that era before television became the primary mass communication medium. His life is also significant because in his zeal to get the Gospel out, he never forgot how necessary is the time-consuming, expensive, and difficult task of training young people to be preachers of the Gospel themselves" (9). Although it is certainly true that Charles Fuller believed that training the next generation of preachers was important (e.g., he was on the board of Biola, taught at Los Angeles Baptist Seminary, and helped found Fuller Theological Seminary), his unwavering commitment for over thirty years to radio evangelism demonstrates the priority of evangelism in his life.

3. Wright, *Old Fashioned Revival Hour and the Broadcasters*, 13. Trumbull might not have been the most objective admirer of Fuller and the *Old Fashioned Revival Hour* given that Fuller's Gospel Broadcasting Association advertised the program regularly in the *Sunday School Times*.

the world. Evangelicalism was reborn.[4] Evangelicalism's rebirth was needed after decades of battling what James DeForest Murch calls the "Great Apostasy." Liberalism, Murch notes, had been on the march since the dawn of the twentieth century and was threatening to undermine biblical Christianity: "A new interpretation of Christianity commonly known as 'liberalism' challenged the 'faith once for all delivered to the saints.' It refused to accept the authority of the Holy Scriptures and the historic creeds of Christendom, and began to project its heresies into every root and branch of the Christian Church."[5] A new band of Christian soldiers was needed to contend for orthodox belief. Charles Fuller was part of that band.

Fuller prided himself on not being innovative or novel in his interpretation of Christianity. His goal was to give his millions of listeners "old-time religion."[6] With liberalism encroaching upon American Christianity, Charles Fuller pressed an effective counteroffensive over the airwaves. By adapting religion to radio, Charles Fuller was able to resist some of the secularizing trends of the mid-twentieth century. The *Old Fashioned Revival Hour* helped maintain religion as a vital force in American culture. However, by creating a program that catered to a particular niche, namely revivalist Christianity with its emphasis on evangelism, the *Old Fashioned Revival Hour* may have made American Christianity more vulnerable to particular aspects of secularization.

THE MAKING OF AN EVANGELIST

Fuller's childhood nurtured in him a love for the simple truths of Protestant Christianity and a longing to see the simple gospel spread around the world.

Charles Fuller was born in 1887 in Los Angeles. He was the last of four children to Henry and Helen Day Fuller. Henry Fuller owned and managed a furniture store. In 1889, Henry, to give his wife some relief from her constant asthma attacks, purchased seventy acres in the drier Redlands area to enter the orange industry. Fuller's Fancy Oranges proved to be a lucrative business. Charles Fuller grew up in a Methodist home with parents who were "dedicated Christians." Daniel Fuller gave a window into his father's childhood and commented on the mark his parents' religious practice made on Charles:

---

4. Rosell, *Surprising Work of God*.

5. Murch, *Cooperation without Compromise*, 19.

6. That Fuller's rendition of "old time religion" was associated with dispensationalism, a theological system founded in the late 1800s, is just one of the ironies of Fuller's ministry.

Family devotions were held each morning. His father would read a portion of Scripture and then the family would gather around his mother and sing hymns as she accompanied them on the pump organ. But though he sat through these daily devotions at home as well as two church services each Sunday, Charles Fuller had no great interest in spiritual things in these days. Nevertheless his parents' faithfulness in exposing him to the Christian faith did leave an indelible impression upon him. In later years he would mention in his broadcasts, often with tears in his voice, those times when family would gather around the organ to sing hymns.[7]

These early religious experiences shaped Fuller's adult ministry. His religious nurture helps explain Fuller's emphasis on the simple doctrines of Protestant Christianity as well as the religious sentimentalism, reminiscent of his childhood family gatherings around the organ, that he brought to the radio.

Perhaps the greatest influence on Charles Fuller's future zeal for evangelism was watching his father participate in global missions. When Charles was a teenager, his father's orange business was prospering. With his earnings Henry Fuller began an aggressive campaign to support world evangelism. To educate himself on the state of various missionary fields around the globe, Henry took two "world tours"—one in 1902 and another in 1905. On the first tour Henry wrote a letter from India scolding English and American Christians for their lack of missionary support:

> The real cause and want of greater success in missions is in so-called Christian lands. The man or woman in England or America that gives a few dimes to missions and one hundred dollars to build and adorn some costly home church that never prays for a foreign mission, that breathes a sigh of relief when the missionary collection is raised, knows of and cares but little for missionary work. With the scanty funds with which missionaries are provided, I think they are accomplishing real miracles.[8]

Toward the end of his life, through the Immanuel Missionary Fund he created, Henry Fuller "was supporting, in full or in part, fifty-five missionaries and Christian workers around the world."[9]

---

7. Fuller, *Give the Winds*, 15. Philip Goff notes the influence of Charles Fuller's parents on his religious development: "Charles Fuller came by his missionary interests honestly. Both his parents were dedicated Methodists in an era when the Holiness movement attracted many to the 'deeper life' and a concern for world evangelism." In, "We Have Heard the Joyful Sound," 68.

8. Quoted in Fuller, *Give the Winds*, 16.

9. Fuller, *Give the Winds*, 16. In recognition of Charles's commitment to missions,

In 1910 Charles Fuller graduated cum laude with a degree in chemistry from Pomona College. He was a standout football player and was elected class president his senior year. Charles was also a member of his college debate team. Meanwhile, Grace Payton, Charles's future wife and partner on the *Old Fashioned Revival Hour*, was studying at the Cumnock School of Expression in Los Angeles. Daniel Fuller notes the significance of Charles studying debate and Grace training at the Cumnock School: "It would seem that God was training both Charles and Grace to improve their ability at public speaking, since He would use them as a team to spread the Gospel by radio."[10]

FULLER'S CONVERSION TO FUNDAMENTALIST CHRISTIANITY

In 1916, Charles Fuller was recently graduated, newly married, and managing an orange-packing company in Placentia, California. Grace Fuller suffered from tuberculosis for nearly three years following a stillbirth. In an effort to get some relief, Grace, with her mother accompanying her, sought refuge in the San Bernardino Mountains. With his wife gone and having read in the newspaper that the former wrestler and boxer Paul Rader would be preaching at the Church of the Open Door in Los Angeles, Charles made plans to go. Charles was deeply moved by the sermon. Indeed, the revival service sparked in Fuller had what can only be described as a radical spiritual change[11] that set him on a trajectory away from a successful career in the orange business and into a life of vocational ministry. Once back in Placentia, Charles wrote Grace to tell of this powerful encounter and the change in him it had wrought:

> There has come a complete change into my life. Sunday I went up to Los Angeles and heard Paul Rader preach. I never heard such a sermon in all my life. Ephesians 1:18. Now my whole life aims and ambitions are changed. I feel now that I want to serve God if He can use me instead of making the goal of my life the making of money. I may have a call to go to the mission field in Africa.[12]

Henry Fuller in 1922 chose him to administer the Immanuel Missionary Fund.

10. Fuller, *Give the Winds*, 20. Fuller continues, "As Grace Fuller read the letters over the radio in later years, many were impressed with her unaffected yet beautiful, flowing diction" (21–22).

11. Fuller, *Give the Winds*, 33–35.

12. Fuller, *Give the Winds*, 34–35.

Fuller immediately began to study the Bible and theology vigorously. When Grace returned from her time of convalescence, she noticed how "instead of spending his spare time poring over the Saturday Evening Post he now read his Bible for long periods."[13] It was also during this time that Charles became interested in studying the theological system of dispensationalism with its emphasis on the second coming of Christ. Books such as William E. Blackstone's *Jesus Is Coming* and Arno C. Gaebelein's works on Daniel and Revelation helped establish a theological foundation in Fuller that would remain throughout his ministry career.

THE BIBLE INSTITUTE OF LOS ANGELES

Charles Fuller's passion for revivalism, evangelism, and the central doctrines of dispensationalism was further formed while a student at the Bible Institute of Los Angeles (Biola). Enrolling in 1919 and leaving in 1921, Fuller was confirmed in "fundamental Christianity" as a student at Biola. The Bible institutes in the early twentieth century became havens for theological students wanting to reject modernism and the theological liberalism that accompanied it.[14] Fuller saw in Biola the opportunity to become further grounded in the fundamentals of the faith with an emphasis on revivalism and evangelism. Biola was just one of several Bible institutes that served as the training ground for fundamentalists such as Charles Fuller. Joel Carpenter observes,

> The largest and most important of the fundamentalist Bible institutes by the early 1930s were the Bible Institute of Los Angeles (known as BIOLA), Gordon College of Theology and Missions in Boston, Moody Bible Institute in Chicago, National Bible Institute in New York City, Northwestern Bible and Missionary Training School in Minneapolis, Nyack Missionary Training Institute (in Nyack-on-the-Hudson, New York), the Philadelphia School of the Bible, and the Bible Institute of Pennsylvania (also in Philadelphia). Two other schools that were founded in the 1920s but were developing rapidly were Columbia Bible College in South Carolina and the Prairie Bible Institute in Three Hills, Alberta.[15]

---

13. Fuller, *Give the Winds*, 35.

14. Carpenter, *Revive Us Again*, 16. Carpenter observes, "Without a doubt, the most important terminals in the fundamentalist network were its Bible institutes."

15. Carpenter, *Revive Us Again*, 17.

Carpenter explains why these Bible institutes had become so popular within the ranks of fundamentalism:

> For fundamentalist pastors and parishioners who were weary of the theological tensions they felt with their denominational neighbors and wary of the perspectives emanating from their denominational agencies, Bible schools often became denominational surrogates. These agencies provided educational and other religious services, a support structure for fellowship and inspiration, and opportunities to participate in such "Christian work" as evangelism and foreign missions.[16]

One of the professors at Biola who influenced Fuller the most was Reuben Torrey.

> Reuben Torrey was a dispensationalist. The text that he wrote for his classes in Bible doctrine, entitled *What the Bible Teaches*, sounds the dispensational note when it declares that the Church will be raptured out of the earth before the Great Tribulation. The large auditorium that he wanted was completed in 1913, and at its dedication a *Scofield Reference Bible* was placed in its cornerstone.[17]

Fuller had already been studying dispensationlism, but sitting under Torrey's teaching grounded him in the system. Biola also laid "a heavy emphasis on evangelism, soul winning, foreign missions, and all forms of Christian service."[18] It was during his time at Biola that Fuller became deeply committed to evangelism. Charles practiced it with an urgency consistent with the dispensational premillenialism he was taught.[19]

While at Biola, Charles and Grace were active members of Placentia Presbyterian Church. Fuller's commitment to fundamentalist Christianity provoked a clash with the Placentia Presbyterian Church.[20] The clash came

---

16. Carpenter, *Revive Us Again*, 17.
17. Fuller, *Give the Winds*, 42.
18. Fuller, *Give the Winds*, 44.
19. Fuller cites evidence of his father's growing zeal for evangelism during his Biola years in *Give the Winds*, 43–48. Charles distributed gospel tracts and kept records of whom he talked with about the gospel. Also, on camping trips he and Grace would seek out the people who lived in the "out-of-the-way places—for the miners, the lumberjacks, and the sheepherders—who did not have much chance to hear the Gospel."
20. Fuller, *Give the Winds*, 53. Fuller observed that "tensions within the church were bound to emerge when this young elder, so deeply involved in the main industry of the area, became himself an avid and highly capable representative of the chief characteristics of the Fundamentalist movement. Although quite orthodox, the Placentia Presbyterian Church did not completely fit the Fundamentalist profile, and therefore a

when Charles and the students of the Sunday school class he was teaching began to act independently of the church. For example, in 1922, Charles and his students began financially supporting an independent missionary and advertising the Placentia Bible Class without mentioning the church.[21] Daniel Fuller speculated that his father had imbibed a fundamentalist mood at odds with the church's:

> My conclusion from the evidence is that Charles Fuller had come to feel that this class was now doing some things that the church itself should have been doing all along. From his exposure to men like Paul Rader, Reuben Torrey, Thomas Horton, and the many capable leaders of what is known as the Fundamentalist movement, he had been imbued with a spirit characterized by such things as aggressive evangelism, enthusiastic Bible teaching, and the hearty singing of the Gospel songs made popular by Daniel B. Towner, Charles Alexander (Reuben Torrey's song leader during his evangelistic campaigns), and Robert Harkness (his campaign pianist). Charles Fuller's mood was also characterized by an interest in biblical prophecy and in the Zionist movement, which seemed to be the beginnings of a remarkable fulfillment of biblical prophecy. Then, too, he was influenced by the Victorious Life movement (stemming from the Keswick Conferences of England), which he had learned about from Charles Trumbull, the editor of the widely read *Sunday School Times* who had held several Victorious Life Conferences in Southern California.[22]

The Bible class became Calvary Church in 1925, with Charles Fuller as its pastor. For eight years Fuller led Calvary Church with sermons that "sounded the evangelistic note" and taught the dispensational system he had embraced.[23] But the pastorate was not to be his primary ministry. The walls of the local church could not contain this evangelist to the world.

THE OLD FASHIONED REVIVAL HOUR AND THEOLOGY IN AMERICA

Charles Fuller's radio career contributed to the transformation of American religion by broadcasting religion primarily in terms of evangelism. For

---

clash between Charles Fuller and this church was inevitable."

21. Fuller, *Give the Winds*, 52–53.
22. Fuller, *Give the Winds*, 53.
23. Fuller, *Give the Winds*, 63–64.

Fuller, evangelism was paramount. Fuller used the *Old Fashioned Revival Hour* to advance the old-time gospel as well as religious sentimentalism—the longing for a time when Protestant Christianity was united around the simple proclamation of the gospel. Fuller was determined to make religion accessible to the masses, and he knew sectarianism or controversial polemics were ill-suited to building audiences of sufficient size to answer radio's potential. Fuller succeeded in preserving the influence of religion in American culture; however, by eschewing substantive theological content, Fuller's ministry contributed to the secularization of the American church.

Fuller showed a childhood interest in electric technology, and this interest surely influenced his migration to radio ministry as an adult. In hindsight, it seems natural that Fuller dedicated his life to broadcast ministry. Daniel Fuller recounts the childhood signs pointing to an adult career in radio:

> Through the dimes earned by gopher tails he ordered a telegraph set from a mail-order catalog. When it arrived, he busied himself in learning Morse code and in stringing wire through the ranch house so that he could transmit messages between several points. Then, too, on his way home from high school he would sometimes stop at the Southern Pacific railway station nearby and persuade the old station manager, Jim Rimpaw, to let him practice sending and receiving real messages on the railroad circuits. He became so good at it that before long Mr. Rimpaw was even allowing him to send instructions to the main dispatcher in Los Angeles.
>
> Charles Fuller also installed a buzzer down at the ranch gate so the postman cold signal the family that he had left mail in the box. In addition he set up a telephone connection between his house and the neighbors' who lived a few hundred yards away. Later as a senior in high school, Charles also had the first amateur wireless telegraph receiver in the Redlands area. One hot July day he bounded down the stairs from his room waving a slip of paper. "Listen to this," he cried excitedly. "I just took a message from the wireless station on Catalina Island. Some congressman has just hooked a tremendous bass weighing three-hundred pounds!"
>
> "Oh, pshaw!" his father muttered. "You're just joking." He went back to his paper. But the next day in the Los Angeles Times the same story appeared which Charles had reported the day before. "Look here, Dad—just as I told you!" he exclaimed. His father's only words were, "Well, I'll be jiggered."[24]

24. Fuller, *Give the Winds*, 16–17.

Adding to Fuller's childhood intrigue with broadcast technology was the euphoric mood of the age, when radio was beginning to show its promise for religious broadcasting.[25] As an adult Fuller became engulfed in the national excitement over radio technology and the general consensus among Protestants that broadcasting the faith was good for the church. In 1922, the year after Fuller graduated from Biola, the number of licensed radio stations in America exploded: "In 1920 just one station, KDKA, Pittsburgh, was licensed to render a regular broadcasting service. In 1921 it was joined by a few others. Then, in 1922, more than five hundred broadcasting stations went on the air."[26] Demand for licenses was so great that during the spring of 1922 "the Department of Commerce ran out of three-letter combinations and began assigning four-letter combinations."[27] Fuller's growing burden for evangelism, nurtured by the rigors of personal Bible study and formal training at Biola, came of age at a time when radio was beginning to permeate the culture.

Fuller began broadcasting his messages in 1924: "Charles Fuller had preached the Gospel from time to time on radio ever since 1924 when he gave Bible lessons two mornings a week over Biola's 750-watt radio station, whose call letters then were KJS."[28] The event that Fuller used to count the number of years he had been in radio ministry was a Sunday evening in 1925 when he took musicians from Calvary Church in Placentia to Los Angeles to broadcast a program over Biola's station.[29] In February 1929, Charles Fuller gave a radio broadcast that left an indelible mark on him and set the trajectory of his public ministry. The broadcast took place in Indianapolis, Indiana, at the Defenders of the Christian Faith Conference.[30]

25. Barnouw, *Tower of Babel*, 1:96; Hangen, *Redeeming the Dial*. Barnouw's point was about radio broadcasting in general, but the American church and its rush to use radio technology was certainly part of the overall radio euphoria. Earlier in this same volume, Barnouw compares the desire for radio technology in the United States with the "Oklahoma land rush or California gold rush" (4). In *Redeeming the Dial*, Hangen addresses the religious use of radio in the 1920s: "Individuals and denominations scrambled to get in on the new market as the public appetite for radio broadcasting grew. By 1924, a church or religious organization held one out of every fourteen licenses, and the number of stations operated by religious groups climbed from twenty-nine in 1924 to seventy-one in 1925. In 1924, churches or other religious organizations controlled 10 percent of the more than six hundred radio stations in the United States" (22).

26. Barnouw, *Tower of Babel*, 4.

27. Barnouw, *Tower of Babel*, 100. Barnouw continues, "Perhaps the most arresting testimony to the impact of the radio boom was the simper message put up by a minister in front of his church in Louisville, KY: 'God is always broadcasting'" (104).

28. Barnouw, *Tower of Babel*, 75.

29. Barnouw, *Tower of Babel*, 75.

30. Wright, *Old Fashioned Revival*; Smith, *Voice for God*; Fuller, *Give the Winds*, 74–75.

On short notice Fuller was asked to fill in for the regular speaker of a local gospel radio program. Maier gave a four-point exposition of Mark 4:35–41, where Jesus calmed the storm on the Sea of Galilee. His points were titled, "a Great Peril; a Great Plea; a Great Peace; and a Great Personage."[31] Both Fuller and the regular speaker for the radio program were surprised by the "many letters and phone calls that came in telling of the blessing people had received from this straightforward Gospel message."[32] During the long train ride back to Los Angeles, Fuller awoke in his Pullman berth with an overwhelming burden to pursue a regular radio ministry:

> A sense of the great opportunity that radio afforded for getting out the Gospel overwhelmed him. He was weary from the heavy speaking schedule that he had just completed and wanted to go back to sleep, but it seemed God kept impressing upon his heart that he should take the first opportunity that presented itself to begin preaching regularly on the radio. He was awed by the problems that would have to be overcome in order to fulfill such a task. How could he have a program with sufficient appeal to sustain a regular listening audience? How would he pay for a regular broadcast? Would people continue to respond enthusiastically to his preaching, or was his recent experience in Indianapolis just a fluke? After tossing in his berth for some time, Charles Fuller finally told the Lord that he would go on the radio regularly if God would open the door. Having said yes to God, he slept soundly the rest of the night.[33]

As the pastor of Calvary Church, Charles Fuller showed an unflagging commitment to broadcasting the gospel. It was this commitment that eventually resulted in his resignation from the church to pursue radio ministry full-time. Late in 1929, Fuller was presented with the opportunity to broadcast the evening service of Calvary Church on a new station with the call letters KREG. The cost was supposed to be minimal because the station was supported by a number of wealthy men who wanted to emphasize cultural, educational, and religious programming. However, technical problems arose with the building of the station and financial provisions were less than expected, so KREG determined that it would have to receive support from commercial advertisers as other stations were doing. By the end of January 1930, Fuller was confronted with the reality of having to pay his own way if he wanted a regular radio program. Fuller was undaunted. He sent a letter to

---

31. Fuller, *Give the Winds*, 74.
32. Fuller, *Give the Winds*, 74.
33. Fuller, *Give the Winds*, 75.

his congregation enlisting their support and announcing the establishment of a radio fund. This marked the beginning of an exercise in raising support that would occupy him for over thirty years.[34]

Having tasted success on a regular broadcast through the spring of 1930,[35] Fuller longed for more exposure through the airwaves. To increase his coverage, Fuller canceled the contract with KREG and negotiated a new contract with the 1000-watt KGER in Long Beach, thirty miles away. Fuller explained why in a letter to his congregation:

> Radio KGER is considered by many as one of the best 1000-watt stations west of Chicago. This station covers an area populated by more than four million people. What an opportunity, therefore, to preach the Gospel, which is the power of God unto salvation![36]

Not only was Fuller working to get better coverage for Calvary's Sunday services, but he was also exploring other program formats to get the gospel out over the airwaves and extend his personal ministry. For example, in 1931, when Biola officials decided to sell their radio station because the institution could no longer justify the expense, Fuller, as chairman of the Biola board, contracted with the Columbia Broadcasting System (CBS) to air a Sunday afternoon program on seven stations from San Diego to Seattle. The half-hour program, "The Pilgrim's Hour," was dedicated to Gospel music and expository preaching. It was an effort to "place the Bible Institute before its friends" and relied solely on the contributions of listeners.[37] The effort helped Biola. It also helped extend the reach of Fuller's ministry.

---

34. Fuller, *Give the Winds*, 79.

35. Fuller, *Give the Winds*, notes that after two months of broadcasting on KREG, "Charles Fuller contracted for an additional hour of broadcasting time each Sunday evening. Following the hour-long broadcast of the regular church service, he would broadcast a program called the 'Happy Hour,' a time of special music put on by the young people of the church. By now he was anxious to get some idea of how many were listening so he announced that a telephone would be installed at the pulpit and that in between the musical numbers of the 'Happy Hour' he would attempt to answer any questions about the Bible that people would phone in. Charles Fuller recalled in later years that it was with bated breath that he waited to see if there would be any calls. But no sooner had he told people they could call than more calls than he could handle began pouring in" (81). Undoubtedly, this instant gratification from the listening audience would contribute to Fuller's decision in later years to do the *Old Fashioned Revival Hour* in front of a live audience of thousands at the Long Beach Municipal Auditorium.

36. Fuller, *Give the Winds*, 82.

37. Fuller, *Give the Winds*, 84. "The Pilgrim Hour" was canceled at the end of spring of 1931 due to a lack of contributions. In September of that year, Fuller, "suffering great financial losses himself," resigned from the Biola board.

This helps explain another program that Fuller commenced in the fall of 1931 while at Calvary Church, the "Calvary Church Radio Bible Class." The one-hour, Thursday-evening show originated from the KGER studios in Long Beach. Daniel Fuller argues that "this new broadcast was significant because it was an extension of Charles Fuller's radio ministry that was somewhat independent of Calvary Church."[38] With Fuller's longing for a larger radio ministry, independence from Calvary Church was inevitable. Daniel Fuller explained:

> Churches need a leader who is basically a pastor. Charles Fuller, however, was never content to simply be a pastor. His heart was in heading up a mission to spread the Gospel by radio. But Don Milligan, the youth director, loved to visit people, and gradually the church shifted their allegiance to him. . . . Charles Fuller's constant urge to extend his ministry had finally made it impossible for him to work from a church as his base of operations.[39]

Resolved to pursue an independent radio ministry, Charles Fuller officially resigned from the pastorate at Calvary Church in March 1933.

With his personal finances becoming desperate amid the Great Depression, conventional wisdom would not have deemed this an opportune time to pursue a listener-funded radio ministry.[40] Daniel Fuller recounted some of what was going on nationally and locally when his father's first independent broadcasts began in Long Beach:

> March, 1933, was not a very auspicious time to launch out alone on a radio ministry. The morning after his last sermon at Calvary Church, Franklin Roosevelt closed all the banks. Only those banks could open thereafter whose financial condition was sound, and there was a period of several weeks when people were very short of cash. Five days later, Long Beach suffered a severe earthquake which killed 115 people and inflicted $40,000,000 damage. United States Marines were guarding the city against looters, and only after arguing with a sergeant could Charles Fuller proceed to the KGER studio for his first Sunday morning broadcast from Long Beach.[41]

38. Fuller, *Give the Winds*, 85. Charles Fuller would eventually drop the words "Calvary Church" from the name of the program, calling it simply "The Radio Bible Class." Daniel P. Fuller, *Give the Winds*, finds the name change significant in the development of his father's radio career: "This indicates more of that trend in which Charles Fuller's ministry was shifting away from Calvary Church" (85).

39. Fuller, *Give the Winds*, 85–86.

40. Fuller, *Give the Winds*, 87–96.

41. Fuller, *Give the Winds*, 96.

Having left Calvary Church determined to continue his three weekly broadcasts (Sunday morning, Sunday evening, and Thursday evening), Fuller created the Gospel Broadcasting Association as the governing organization of his radio ministry. This nonprofit corporation was officially recognized by the state of California on August 15, 1933. Fuller would direct the association until his death in 1968.[42]

In August 1934 Charles Fuller began referring to his Sunday evening broadcast as "The Radio Revival Hour." In October 1934, the evening broadcast expanded from a half hour to an hour on the air, and the "hour-long old-fashioned revival service" would be aired each Sunday for the next twenty-three years.[43] Through trial and error, Fuller found a format for the program that he would use throughout the peak years of the *Old Fashioned Revival Hour* broadcasts. Before the program moved from Hollywood's KNX (a local CBS station) to the Mutual Broadcasting System in 1937 to begin coast-to-coast coverage, Fuller explained some changes in the program to his listeners:

> After the change, we are making plans for a better Sunday night program—more varied, interesting, and more spiritual—but continuing our policy of singing the *old songs* and giving only the *old Gospel*. We are not called to discuss politics or plans for fixing up the world, much as it needs fixing. We are called to preach *Christ* and men and women are hungering to hear. We are praying—God is working. You have assured me you are going to continue to stand by financially and with prayer, so I am eagerly looking forward to increased opportunities for reaching the lost before it is too late.[44]

Fuller employed a combination of entertainment and Bible teaching in an effort to win people to Christianity. In an announcement on the air in 1937, Fuller explained why the name of the program was officially changed to the *Old Fashioned Revival Hour*:

> Each Sunday by God's grace we have an hour to broadcast the old songs and the old Gospel which is the power of God unto salvation. Our one message is Christ and Him crucified, and we endeavor by God's grace to beseech men and women to be reconciled to God in Christ Jesus, never closing a broadcast but

---

42. Fuller, *Give the Winds*, 97.
43. Fuller, *Give the Winds*, 108.
44. Fuller, *Give the Winds*, 115, emphasis original.

that we give every one an opportunity to accept Christ as their personal Savior—this is truly an *old-fashioned revival hour*.[45]

The formula proved immensely successful. Philip Goff outlines the staggering statistics of the program during its peak years:

> 256 stations in 1940, a gain of 100 stations in just one year; 341 stations by 1941, with twenty-three full-time secretaries to handle the bags of mail that arrived daily; 456 stations in 1942, by far the most widely heard program in the nation. In fact, the show had outgrown the network that had pushed it to such heights: Mutual Broadcasting accounted for only half the stations on which Fuller's broadcast ran. Fuller's Gospel Broadcasting Association, meanwhile, generated one-eighth of Mutual's income. By 1944, the show ran on 575 stations and short-wave bands around the world, boasted twenty million listeners, and required an annual budget of more than 1.7 million dollars.[46]

Other radio programs had large audiences as well. Even some religious broadcasts, such as Walter Maier's *Lutheran Hour*, could boast a similar global reach. For example, Dennis Voskuil notes that with its move from CBS to the Mutual Broadcasting System in 1934, Maier's program quickly became

> one of the most popular religious broadcasts of all time. . . . In 1945 "The Lutheran Hour" was being broadcast over 224 mutual stations and was being transcribed to another 450 stations in twenty-six countries. *Time* estimated that twelve million people listened regularly to Maier's program, which received approximately three hundred thousand letters per year.[47]

However, no radio broadcast was able to unite Protestant conservatives like the *Old Fashioned Revival Hour*. By focusing almost exclusively on evangelism, Fuller gave his constituency a doctrinal minimalism that exceeded Maier's, one that nearly every group could support. Goff explains,

> Without a doubt, the program's purpose was to bring lost souls to a saving knowledge of Jesus Christ. It was, plainly, *the* common denominator for Protestant fundamentalists, a group that had divided over doctrinal differences and had been ostracized by cultural losses in the 1920's. Charles Fuller purposefully stayed away from the debates that were already

---

45. Quoted in Fuller, *Give the Winds*, 122.
46. Goff, "We Have Heard the Joyful Sound," 71.
47. Voskuil, "Power of the Air," 80.

beginning between separatist and constructive fundamentalists during the war. The show reflected his interest to provide over the air what Charles Trumbull had furnished with the Sunday School Times: a popular medium whereby evangelicals could put aside differences and concentrate on the important matters at hand, namely, domestic revivalism and foreign evangelism.[48]

By uniting evangelicals around evangelism, Fuller was able to build an audience of sufficient size that took advantage of radio's potential, something that sectarianism or controversial polemics could never do. This accommodation to radio was driven by pragmatism—a distinguishing mark of the *Old Fashioned Revival Hour*:

> Pragmatism drove the "Old Fashioned Revival Hour" in both tone and appeal. The program's noncontroversial manner united disparate fundamentalists and various conservative Protestants throughout the nation. "We are allied with no denomination," Fuller wrote his listeners in 1937. "We are fundamental, premillennial and our desire is to bring up no controversial questions, but only to preach and teach the Word of God." It proved a familiar and powerful format. By ignoring doctrinal differences that split denominations, he emphasized a revivalist style that united an otherwise factious movement.[49]

This approach also helps explain Fuller's involvement in the founding of the National Association of Evangelicals (1942) and the National Religious Broadcasters (1944), two groups founded upon a doctrinal minimalism that allowed for maximum participation. Fuller's pragmatism enabled him to unify "disparate fundamentalists and various conservative Protestants throughout the nation." In doing so, American religion was being homogenized into sentimental evangelicalism.

The format for the *Old Fashioned Revival Hour* was a model of consistency. The show opened with H. Leland Green leading the choir in the theme song, "Jesus Saves," with Rudy Atwood at piano. Charles Fuller came on the air with announcements and words of encouragement before more gospel songs were played. At the appointed time Charles welcomed his wife, Grace (who he addressed endearingly as *honey*), so that she could read the customary sample letters of the thousands that had come into the offices the week of the broadcast. After another song it was time for Charles to give the sermon for the evening. This format was undoubtedly something that millions of listeners came to depend on in the uncertain times of economic

---

48. Goff, "We Have Heard the Joyful Sound," 84, emphasis original.
49. Goff, "We Have Heard the Joyful Sound," 70.

depression and war. The *Old Fashioned Revival Hour* was simple, entertaining, and easily accessible due to a basic Bible message that called people to come to Christ for salvation.

SINGING THE OLD-TIME RELIGION

The music played on the *Old Fashioned Revival Hour* was tailored to the new medium of radio. It too fostered theological minimalism. The music was designed to evoke feelings of nostalgia in the audience—a longing for a simpler time when Protestant Christianity was largely united around its confident proclamation of the simple message of the gospel. The gospel songs were not theologically sophisticated, but were easily accessible with catchy melodies and lyrics. What Joel Carpenter observes about Paul Rader's Chicago Tabernacle music in the 1920s and early 1930s was true for Fuller's music as well:

> Tabernacle music became radio-tailored as well. Gospel songs had to have a message that was simple and patently obvious, a lively tempo, or a stirring melody, and they had to do their work within one or two verses. . . . Like radio jingles, the gospel choruses being composed by the Tabernacle musicians had to be easy to memorize, with catchy melodies and rhythms that almost sang themselves, so that people would find themselves humming and singing them again and again.[50]

For example, the *Old Fashioned Revival Hour* opened with the simple and rousing "Jesus Saves," a song that fit Carpenter's criteria perfectly:

> We have heard the joyful sound, Jesus saves, Jesus saves;
> Spread the tidings all around, Jesus saves, Jesus saves;
> Bear the news to every land, Climb the steeps and cross the waves,
> Onward!—'tis our Lord's command, Jesus saves, Jesus saves.
> Give the winds a mighty voice, Jesus saves, Jesus saves;
> Let the nations now rejoice, Jesus saves, Jesus saves;
> Shout salvation full and free, Highest hills and deepest caves,
> This our song of victory, Jesus saves, Jesus saves.[51]

Another simple gospel song that became closely identified with the *Old Fashioned Revival Hour* was "Heavenly Sunshine."[52]

---

50. Carpenter, *Revive Us Again*, 128.

51. Fuller et al., *Old Fashioned Revival Hour Songs*, song 1. The numbers in all references to songs denote song number, not necessarily page number.

52. Daniel Fuller tells the story of how this song came to be a part of the program in *Give the Winds*, 147–48.

> Heavenly sunshine, heavenly sunshine,
> Flooding my soul with glory divine;
> Heavenly sunshine, heavenly sunshine,
> Hallelujah! Jesus is mine![53]

These songs eschewed substantive theological content and provided a least-common-denominator evangelicalism that served as a unifying factor among conservative Protestants.

The *Old Fashioned Revival Hour* songs fall into several distinct categories. Each category contributed to the transformation of American religion by depicting religion in simple terms. One of those categories includes songs that portray Jesus as immanent and salvation as a simple act of "letting Jesus come into your heart."[54] He is described as a dear friend who ensures that "all things are possible" to those who "only believe."[55] These songs fit Fuller's evangelistic goals in that they made coming to Jesus for salvation sound easy. One song, "Come Just As You Are" provides an example:

> Ye who are troubled and burdened by sin, Come just as you are;
> Come to the Saviour, a new life begin, Oh, come just as you are;
> Come just as you are, Oh, come just as you are;
> Turn from your sin, let the Saviour come in,
> And come just as you are.[56]

Another song, "There's An Open Heaven Tonight" had a similar message:

> There's a sacred and blessed retreat that is known,
> To the Saviour and sinner who meet alone,
> And this spot is available all of the time.
> To the soul that is seeking His will,
> There's an open heaven tonight,
> There's an open heaven tonight.
> With Jesus up there and the Comforter here,
> There's an open heaven tonight.[57]

In these songs scant attention was given to the doctrinal formations of repentance and faith, nor did they include any clear Christology. The audience was encouraged to come to "Jesus," who was a "Saviour" and a "sacred and blessed retreat," but those terms were not clearly defined in a doctrinal sense. Such topics as hell and suffering received scant attention, lest they

---

53. Fuller, Green, and MacDougall, *Old Fashioned Revival Hour Songs*, 2.
54. Fuller, Green, and MacDougall, *Old Fashioned Revival Hour Songs*, 8.
55. Fuller, Green, and MacDougall, *Old Fashioned Revival Hour Songs*, 3.
56. Fuller, Green, and MacDougall, *Old Fashioned Revival Hour Songs*, 15.
57. Fuller, Green, and MacDougall, *Old Fashioned Revival Hour Songs*, 7.

disrupt the program's sentimentalist appeal. Doctrinal substance could evoke antagonism and drive listeners away. Pragmatic concern for attracting the largest possible audience required avoiding troubling themes.

Another category of songs that simplified religion reminded Fuller's listeners of their "pilgrim" status in this world while they awaited arrival in their heavenly home. These notes were struck in songs such as "Lord, I'm Coming Home," "My Home, Sweet Home," "Sweet By and By," "The Eastern Gate," and "Look Away to Heaven."[58] These themes came together perfectly for Fuller in "I'm a Pilgrim":

> I'm a pilgrim, and I'm a stranger;
> I can tarry, I can tarry but a night!
> Do not detain me, for I am going
> To where the fountains are ever flowing.
> I'm a pilgrim, and I'm a stranger,
> I can tarry, I can tarry, but a night![59]

These simple songs did little to advance any substantive doctrinal understanding of the Christian life. This aversion to theological substance ironically promoted the secularization of the American church. This transformed religion was ill-equipped to answer the questions of modernity.

As a "fundamental Christian," Fuller wanted to arm his listeners for the battle against modernism and theological liberalism in the culture. Not only this, he was convinced that the devil was real and that the Christian was engaged in spiritual warfare. Therefore, the *Old Fashioned Revival Hour* employed many "battlefield" songs. These songs did not advance a robust theology, but simply called Christians to the battle against modernism and the devil. For example, Fuller wanted his listeners to be able to say, "I am on the battlefield for my Lord":

> I was alone and idle. I was a sinner too;
> I heard a voice from heaven say there is work to do.
> I took the Master's hand, and I joined the Christian band,
> I'm on the battlefield for my Lord.[60]

Capturing the mood of the day was the appropriately titled "The Fight Is On":

> The fight is on, the trumpet sound is ringing out,
> The cry "To arms!" is heard afar and near,
> The Lord of hosts is marching on to leads, and victory will assure;

---

58. Fuller, Green, and MacDougall, *Old Fashioned Revival Hour Songs*, 29, 29, 33, 72; Fuller and Green, *Old Fashioned Revival Hour Songs*, songs 2 and 93.

59. Fuller and Green, *Old Fashioned Revival Hour Songs*, songs 2 and 46.

60. Fuller, Leland, and MacDougall, *Old Fashioned Revival Hour Songs*, 24.

> Go buckle on the armor God has given you,
> And in His strength unto the end endure.
>
> The fight is on, O Christian soldier,
> And face to face in stern array,
> With armor gleaming and colors streaming,
> The right and wrong engage today!

With the nation at war in the 1940s and the theological and cultural battles between fundamentalists and modernists still raging, the battlefield songs resonated with Fuller's audience. These songs, however, did not do much more for Christians than energize them emotionally.

Fuller's radio ministry accelerated a movement away from theological substance in the American church and toward a religious sentimentalism. The songs that perhaps connected the most with his audience were those that harkened back to a simple religion of former times when the nation was not at war and modernism was not infiltrating the American church. Fuller tapped into a longing for a nostalgic Christianity on the part of millions of Americans. Songs such as "The Old-Fashioned Meeting" captured this sentiment well:

> Oh, how well I remember in the old fashioned days,
> When some old fashioned people had some old fashioned ways;
> In the old fashioned meetings, as they tarried there,
> In the old fashioned manner, how God answered their pray'r.
> 'Twas an old fashioned meeting, in an old fashioned place,
> Where some old fashioned people, had some old fashioned grace:
> As an old fashioned sinner I began to pray,
> And God heard me, and saved me in the old fashioned way.[61]

A similar theme was found in "Old-Time Religion":

> It was good for our mothers,
> It was good for our mothers,
> It was good for our mothers,
> And it's good enough for me.
>
> 'Tis the old-time religion,
> 'Tis the old-time religion,
> 'Tis the old-time religion,
> And it's good enough for me.[62]

---

61. Fuller, Leland, and MacDougall, *Old Fashioned Revival Hour Songs*, 12.
62. Fuller, Leland, and MacDougall, *Old Fashioned Revival Hour Songs*, 82.

The song added six more verses to the chorus: "makes me love everybody"; "it has served our fathers"; "it was good for Daniel"; "it was good for Paul and Silas"; "it will do when I am dying"; and "it will take us all to heaven." In other words, if the "old-time" religion does all of this, why would Americans want anything else?

Every week, millions of listeners tuned in to the *Old Fashioned Revival Hour* to imagine a religion of old—one that was simple, uncomplicated, and devoid of knotty theological questions. Under the direction of Charles Fuller, H. Leland Green, and Rudy Atwood, the *Old Fashioned Revival Hour* songs helped deliver this experience, but in doing so theology in America may have been weakened by stripping the gospel of important layers of doctrine. The songs sung on the *Old Fashioned Revival Hour* broadcasts served to foster a theological minimalism in an effort to reach as many people as possible. Deeply theological hymns were not appropriate for radio. The lyrics had to be simple and easy to memorize, and the melodies catchy. More than teach, the simple gospel songs worked to create a feeling about religion largely lost in modern America. The fundamentalist-modernist controversy, with its intense doctrinal battles, helped create a longing in conservative religious circles for a simpler time when Protestant Christianity was largely united around the proclamation of the simple gospel message. Fuller's *Old Fashioned Revival Hour* tapped into this mood with its simple gospel songs. In doing so, religion in America was changed. This religious transformation left the American church vulnerable to certain aspects of modernity and, therefore, contributed to the secularization of the American church.

PREACHING THE OLD-TIME RELIGION

By depicting Christianity primarily in terms of evangelism, Charles Fuller's *Old Fashioned Revival Hour* homogenized conservative Protestantism around the activist concern for conversion. Although this emphasis on evangelism was ideally suited for radio with its potential to reach the masses, Fuller's theological minimalism promoted the secularization of the American church.

Fuller's emphasis on evangelism was heard in the sermons that he preached each week on the *Old Fashioned Revival Hour*. For example, Fuller reminded his audience about the purpose of the program: "I especially ask you to pray today that many who have tuned in to the broadcast now in darkness may find the faith, the dynamic living faith that Job had, and be converted. We're not putting on the broadcast for any entertainment, but for the salvation of souls, the preaching of the Word."[63]

Regardless of the Scripture that Fuller chose to preach, he always pled with the listener to come to Christ for salvation. The following example is representative: "Will you come in childlike faith today, in the simplicity of childlike faith and take God at His word and receive Christ as your Savior and become a son of God through faith in Him?"[64] In one edition of the monthly newsletter *Heart to Heart Talk*, which Charles Fuller sent to the thousands of people on the *Old Fashioned Revival Hour* mailing list, he took the opportunity to rehearse his goal in preaching over the radio:

> I am not gifted as many men are for preaching—but I love God and His Word, and I have a burning desire to see men brought to Christ while there is yet time. I'd rather preach the Word than anything in this world, and my constant prayer is that I may be able to make it so simple and plain that everyone can understand, and as I pray, or as I preach, that the Holy Spirit may open the eyes of sinful men and women to behold the beauty of Christ—and that is what He has been doing.[65]

Fuller made a commitment to his listeners: as they prayed for and financially supported the program, he would tell people about the saving gospel of Jesus Christ. Evangelism was paramount.

Fuller's emphasis on evangelism was consistent with his training at Biola, where he had been taught to always, in every sermon, preach Christ: "It was Reuben Torrey who taught Charles Fuller never to preach a sermon on any subject without bringing in the cross of Christ and also to repeat often what the Bible says about heaven."[66] The evidence indicates that Fuller stayed true to his professor's admonition. Sermons broadcast on the *Old Fashioned Revival Hour* always emphasized the urgency of the evangelistic task. For Fuller, evangelism was the essence of Christianity.

One way in which Fuller made sure to mention the cross of Christ during each broadcast was an interpretation method called *typology*.[67] This

---

63. The *Old Fashioned Revival Hour* broadcast, April 11, 1954.
64. The *Old Fashioned Revival Hour* broadcast, April 11, 1954.
65. Charles Fuller, *Heart to Heart Talk*, May 16, 1936, Charles E. Fuller and Grace Payton Fuller Papers,
66. Fuller, *Give the Winds*, 44.
67. Charles Fuller learned this method of interpretation at Biola as well. Fuller, *Give the Winds*, explains, "Mrs. Anna Dennis showed him how to give concrete illustrations of the truths of God's Word from the Bible itself. She taught him to understand how the incidents in the history of Israel and details regarding the construction of the Tabernacle in the wilderness were types of Christ and His work of redemption" (44).

method of biblical interpretation portrays an element in the Old Testament as prefiguring or foreshadowing something in the New Testament. Fuller spent many broadcasts unpacking what he saw as "types" of Christ in the Old Testament. In fact, based on listener response, one of his most popular sermons was his series on "The Tabernacle in the Wilderness."[68] In this series Fuller made elaborate use of typology for evangelistic purposes. For example, in the introductory sermon of the series, Fuller explained,

> The Tabernacle shows forth in types (illustrations) the glorious Gospel of Christ which is "the power of God for salvation for everyone who believes." The furnishings of the Tabernacle which we shall study in detail are used to show us God's way of approach to Himself. Jesus is the Brazen Altar, Jesus is the Laver, Jesus is the Showbread, Jesus is the Light of the World, Jesus is the Altar of Incense. He is the blood-sprinkled Mercy Seat in the Holy of Holies. Let me repeat: *No one comes to the Father except through Jesus Christ!*[69]

Fuller, likewise, utilized typology for evangelism when he preached from the sixth chapter of Genesis:

> Noah's ark is one of the clearest, most comprehensive types of the believer's salvation in Christ to be found in all the scripture. Last Sunday remember we told you that the O.T. contains pictures—God's art gallery—foreshadowing N.T. truths. For in the O.T. are the *shadows* of things to come—in the N.T. the *substance*. These O.T. types point toward the work of the Lord Jesus Christ in His threefold office of Prophet, Priest and Coming King.
>
> We will close for tonite with this 7th point—leaving the remaining five for our next broadcast—the ark had only *one door* to it. Likewise the tabernacle—brazen altar. Just one door—no other name—no other foundation—no other way. So beloved friends there is only one way of escape from eternal death—through Christ.[70]

Biblical interpretation methods were used by Fuller to serve his evangelism goals. This practice contributed to the transformation of American religion by defining Christianity primarily in terms of evangelism.

---

68. Not only was this series published in pamphlet form, but also a brochure was made and mailed to listeners that sketched in detail the tabernacle and how it prefigured the person and work of Christ.

69. Fuller, *Tabernacle in the Wilderness*, 2–3.

70. Charles Fuller, "The Ark," sermon manuscript, June 6, 1940, Charles E. Fuller and Grace Payton Fuller Papers, emphasis original.

Another distinguishing mark of Fuller's radio sermons that also helped advance his evangelistic purposes and transform American religion was the theological system of dispensational premillennialism.[71] Religious historian George Marsden explains that "in his radio ministry, Fuller sometimes sent out dispensational charts detailing God's plan for each of the biblically revealed dispensations and pointing out prophecies that showed that our own era was in the last days. Jesus might return at any moment."[72] Not only was the imminent return of Jesus a hallmark of the dispensational system, it also had within it "a bracing jolt of pessimism."[73] Unlike

> the prevailing postmillennialism which taught that Christ's kingdom would grow out of the spiritual and moral progress of this age, dispensational premillennialists said that the churches and the culture were declining and that Christians would see Christ's kingdom only after he personally returned to rule Jerusalem. They thus offered a plausible explanation of the difficulties the church was facing.[74]

The imminent return of Christ and the moral decline of the churches and culture were dominant themes in Fuller's radio preaching, and he utilized both to persuade his listeners to come to Christ for salvation. The following excerpt from Charles Fuller's *Heart to Heart Talk* is an example of what millions of listeners heard each week over the airwaves:

> No one who knows his Bible and its prophecy concerning world conditions in the last days, leading up to Christ's return, can doubt for one moment that we are living in those days. This means that time is short—we must work almost feverishly. It also means that Satan, who hates God with a venomous hatred from the pit, is working as he has never worked before, with all his helpers, to thwart God's plans. Satan is seeking in this pleasure-mad age to debauch men and women, even our boys and girls, for drinking is increasing tremendously, liquor being sold even from the corner grocery store. We know how liquor

---

71. Not only is a commitment to dispensational premillennialism seen in Fuller's radio broadcasts, but also in the founding of Fuller Seminary in the 1940s. George Marsden notes the letter Fuller sent in March 1946 to renowned dispensationalist and president of Dallas Theological Seminary Lewis Sperry Chafer asking him to recommend men who might help lead the new school. The letter also expresses hope that Daniel Fuller might be attending Dallas Seminary the following autumn. See Marsden, *Reforming Fundamentalism*, 20–21.

72. Marsden, *Reforming Fundamentalism*, 20.

73. Hart, *That Old-Time Religion in Modern America*, 38.

74. Marsden, *Understanding Fundamentalism and Evangelicalism*, 39.

> weakens the will power, and people will do things when drinking, which they would never think of doing when sober—so sin of every type is rampant, and increasing because of drink. Then there is a horrifying moral looseness which has increased amazingly even in the last year. There is a breaking down of honor and honesty in public office, which is appalling. All of this is the result of Satan's work, through his legions of helpers, and truly, the days are growing darker. But on the other hand, "God is still on the throne," and is permitting the Gospel to be preached with power in such an unusual way (even unthought of a few years ago) being carried through the air, the very realm of Satan who is "the prince of the power of the air"—so that every one may hear, often without choosing to do so, in the homes, in the shops, on the highways—even hundreds of miles from church.[75]

For Fuller, as bad as things were, there was always hope because "God is still on the throne." Christ would return soon and make all things right, but in the meantime, people had to hear the good news so that they could believe and be saved. This simple message of salvation was the heart of Fuller's old-time religion. As complicated as some of the dispensational schemes could be, Fuller's message was consistently simple with its emphasis on coming to Jesus for salvation.[76]

Dispensationalism contributed to the transformation of American religion by making evangelism paramount. With the moral decline of the nation inevitable and Christ's imminent return certain, it is easy to see how conservative Christianity became primarily defined by the evangelistic task. Fuller fitted this emphasis to radio and discovered that radio was well-suited for the job. For example, the urgency to believe and evangelize in the light of the imminent return of Christ was Fuller's closing words in the October 1946 broadcast:

> Over the past weeks, [our] hearts have been greatly encouraged. Reports of revival fires are burning brightly in various sections of the land. Keep on praying for revival—keep on reading the Word of God daily, especially the book of Romans. We are admonished to let the Word of God dwell in us richly—and

---

75. Fuller, *Heart to Heart Talk*, May 16.

76. Hart, *That Old-Time Religion in Modern America*, 35. Hart notes the irony of dispensationalism's appeal among fundamentalists: "Dispensationalism's appeal was ironic since some of its teachings were no less complex than those propounded in the halls of university divinity schools and seminaries." In Fuller's broadcasts, however, the intricacies of the system were minimized in favor of a simple salvation call. This further demonstrates Fuller's movement away from the fundamentalism of his day.

when this takes place and we walk in the light of God—walking obedient to God's Word—revival fires will increase. We are very close—I firmly and honestly believe, to the closing hours of the Times of the Gentiles. May we be awake—watching for the Bright and Morning Star—for Christ to come and take His own—home to be with Him forever. In the meantime, may we work and pray for the salvation of souls—a great deal of work to be done.[77]

What Fuller meant when he said, "We are very close . . . to the closing hours of the Times of the Gentiles," is that Jesus is set to return any moment; therefore, be ready. The most important task in the meantime is evangelism.

Evangelism was central in Fuller's ministry due to a deeply pessimistic outlook about any moral progress in the culture. As an antimodernist dispensationalist, Fuller did not subscribe to liberal notions of progress:

And hence you have coming to the front in these closing days a manifestation of the sins of the flesh. It's thrown at you from all sides. And Satan, the old serpent of Genesis 3—the devil, the father of lies—is the god of this present evil world system. . . . And when you pick up your daily newspaper and read of the drunken brawls and murders and rapings and robberies and shootings and suicides and graft and corruption and cheating on income taxes and evasions and fraud in high places, bear in mind you're reading about the natural man who walks according to the course of the age, an evil age, an age ruled over by none other than Satan the prince of the power of the air, the ruler over the powers of darkness. I'm giving it to you straight; I'm not mincing words.[78]

Fuller was merely describing what was obvious to millions of people who had lived through two world wars and a national economic depression. Moral decline was the norm until the second coming of Christ. Dispensationalism helped make sense of what Fuller's audience had experienced and impressed upon them the urgency of evangelism. Darryl Hart observes,

In fact, one of the many ways Christians could know that the end of history and Christ's return was near was by the degree to which society deteriorated. In the last days, as dispensationalist teachers like Chafer reminded audiences, wars, famines, pestilence, immorality, and tyranny would be obvious and

---

77. Charles Fuller, untitled sermon manuscript, October 17, 1948, from Charles E. Fuller and Grace Payton Fuller Papers.

78. Charles Fuller, "Conditions of This World," sermon broadcast, December 9, 1951.

widespread. These dire circumstances would emphasize the wickedness of human endeavor and the need for God's activity to make things right. This was a forceful rationale for evangelism and revivals. Because the times were so unsettling, evangelicals could point to contemporary crises as part of the reason for nonbelievers to convert and for evangelicals themselves to be more vigilant in spreading the message of Christianity.[79]

As bad as conditions were in the world, millions of people each week knew they could tune in to the *Old Fashioned Revival Hour* and hear Fuller declare the simple gospel—the old-time religion in a new and often painful world. Furthermore, because this world was steadily marching toward a cataclysmic end with the imminent return of Christ, what mattered above all else was evangelism. Fuller's emphasis on evangelism contributed to the transformation of American religion.

What listeners of the *Old Fashioned Revival Hour* heard each week was a thinner gospel than the one that earlier Protestants preached. Fuller's preaching, with its emphasis on moral decline, the second coming of Christ, and the need to believe, effectively diluted the gospel by taking away its theological depth. This theological minimalism may have actually had the perverse effect of leaving Christians more vulnerable to the very worldliness and spiritual warfare Fuller sought to combat. Although Fuller's *Old Fashioned Revival Hour* set itself to oppose secularization, its aversion to theological substance ironically promoted the secularization of the American church.

RESPONDING TO THE OLD-TIME RELIGION

The correspondence sent to the *Old Fashioned Revival Hour* demonstrates the profound influence that the program had on American religion. During the *Old Fashioned Revival Hour*'s peak years in the 1940s thousands of listener letters arrived weekly at the Gospel Broadcasting Association offices. The letters offered overwhelming support for the program while relaying stories of how the show was a blessing in the writers' lives. Two distinct themes emerge from the correspondence. First, many of the letters tell a conversion story—how a listener had begun to trust in Christ because of the broadcast.[80] Second, many of the letters include words of appreciation for

---

79. Hart, *That Old-Time Religion in Modern America*, 38.

80. Fuller, *Give the Winds*, 171. Specifically, "Miss Rose Baessler, Charles Fuller's secretary from 1940 to 1963, estimated that during the 1950s, an average of four hundred conversions a week were reported by letter. And of course many other converts never

Fuller's "old-time religion." By their own testimony, the listeners loved the simple Christianity Fuller offered.

Stories of conversion and comfort dominate the letters to the *Old Fashioned Revival Hour*. For example, a letter from Tennessee told of how one person "accepted the Lord Jesus Christ" through Charles Fuller "preaching the Gospel plain."[81] A letter from Alaska thanked Fuller for teaching "the plain truth and the way of salvation" while noting the comfort received in hearing Fuller "speak often of our Lord's return."[82] A woman from Minnesota wrote,

> I first heard your broadcast in Oakland, California and the Lord began dealing with me then, through your preaching. After moving to a town in Wisconsin, I listened to you there; then two years ago we moved to Minneapolis. It seemed to me as if you were following me everywhere I went and speaking directly to me. Finally, one Sunday afternoon, I just asked God to take over and surrendered my life to Him. About one month later my husband was converted. Truly we have a wonderful Saviour and I know the meaning of forgiveness now.[83]

The radio became the altar for countless people who listened to the *Old Fashioned Revival Hour* and decided to follow Jesus: "Right by my radio, at long last, I have accepted the Lord as my Saviour. I have listened to you for a long time and you have convinced me that I am a sinner in need of a Saviour."[84]

The letters demonstrate that many Christians listened to the program because they appreciated the simplicity of Fuller's old-time religion. A listener from Iowa exclaimed, "Oh how I love your 'Old Fashioned Revival Hour!' Tis a great comfort in this bewildered, sinful, confused world."[85] A listener from the Los Angeles area wrote, "We are still enjoying the Sunday evening broadcasts from KNX and sincerely hope they may continue, for so many are listening and receiving real help from them. We feel there is such a

---

bothered to write." From this, Goff, "We Have Heard the Joyful Sound," concludes, "If one estimates that the same number holds true during the show's more popular years, then more than five hundred thousand people reported conversions" (95).

81. Charles Fuller, Script, November 22, 1942, Charles E. Fuller and Grace Payton Fuller Papers.

82. Grace Fuller, *Heavenly Sunshine*, 18.

83. Fuller, *Heavenly Sunshine*, 22–23.

84. Fuller, *Heavenly Sunshine*, 23.

85. Vernon C. Losee to Charles Fuller, January 24, 1950, Charles E. Fuller and Grace Payton Fuller Papers.

need for the old fashioned kind of gospel preaching, and you seem to be the only one of that type that we have succeeded in getting over the air."[86] The *Old Fashioned Revival Hour* also brought comfort in the 1940s to soldiers far away from home:

> Your broadcast comes on just after lights out at 10:00 p.m. As the boys are still laying awake in the darkened barracks, the chorus choir starts singing "Jesus Saves" & then the quarte[t] with their wonderful numbers. Truly one can feel a holy rush come over this barracks, & it makes such a deep thrill to go through my being. You'll never know how much your broadcast has meant to me, & I know the boys who bunk with me, in these trying and difficult times. It seems I look forward to it so much during the day, that I can hardly wait. God bless you brother, & keep you on the air till Jesus comes to take His own from this sin-cursed blood-soaked earth.[87]

The letters also reveal the sacrificial giving from the audience, which helped sustain the broadcast for so many years. Indeed, without a sponsor or any major donor underwriting the program, Charles Fuller knew that the *Old Fashioned Revival Hour* depended on the prayers and financial contributions of its listeners to meet the weekly budget.[88] Fuller boasted about this fact in the May 1937 issue of *Heart to Heart Talk*:

> Recently the Pacific coast manager of the [Mutual] network said to me, "Mr. Fuller, each week when the large check for station time comes in from the Gospel Broadcasting Association, I am amazed that a religious program could make it." Well—millions of people do like to hear jazz orchestras and how to apply makeup—how to train the pup and how to make Hungarian goulash—millions of us do enjoy the symphonies, but millions also love to hear the Gospel and sweet spiritual songs over the air, and though there aren't many mighty or wealthy among that number, still there are enough who are rich in faith though poor in this world's goods and can each give a little help to keep the Gospel on the air.[89]

---

86. Script, October 18, 1936, Charles E. Fuller and Grace Payton Fuller Papers.

87. Quoted in Goff, "We Have Heard the Joyful Sound," 75.

88. Goff, "We Have Heard the Joyful Sound," 69–70. Goff explains Fuller's dependence on his listening audience during the program's rise on the Mutual Broadcasting System: "Mutual's growth accelerated more than anyone anticipated, but the Fullers miraculously kept apace. In early November 1937, the show ran on eighty-six stations with a weekly budget that had tripled in only six weeks from $1,500 to $4,500, all of which came from listeners, mostly in one-or-two-dollar donations."

89. Charles Fuller, *Heart to Heart Talk*, May 15, 1936, Charles E. Fuller and Grace

Additionally, an Alabama woman's testimony is representative of the many listeners who "gave from their poverty" in support of the *Old Fashioned Revival Hour*:

> I accepted Christ as my personal Savior 37 years ago, 25th of last July. And oh how sweet it is to be saved and have no fear. I have been a tither ever since I was saved. I don't have much earthly possessions. But what a joy it is to have even a little to give. I am enclosing a little gift. It's not much. But what a joy it is even to have that much. I have often wanted to send a little offering to help keep your gospel ministry on the air. But it was such little I could give I couldn't sum up the courage to do so. But tonight I thought of the poor widow's mite and said just a little in the precious name of Jesus would be better than much for show.[90]

Fuller undoubtedly had these sacrificial givers in mind when he wrote his audience informing them of the new—and costly—transcription venture he embarked upon in 1936: "This new outlet is going to cost a good deal more. It might be nice if we had some sponsors, or a rich friend who could send in a check for $1,000 to start this new work—but we know no such person. Anyway, I like better the way God seems to have planned for our work to be carried on—letting hundreds of persons of small means do it, which fits as love offerings to Himself."[91]

Not all responses to the *Old Fashioned Revival Hour* were positive. The press was not always friendly to radio evangelists (Henry L. Mencken's rants come to mind),[92] and the mainline denominations disdained the sectarianism of fundamentalist radio preachers. Sometimes, listeners would take the time to write with their own critique. The following listener lumped Fuller in with the controversial Gerald Winrod, who had been a guest speaker at McPherson's Angelus Temple:

> Being considerably more humble and lacking the smug self satisfaction of you two "reverends" I will say merely that I believe in the Christian faith."

Payton Fuller Papers.

90. Mrs. J. R. Meadows to Charles Fuller, January 15, 1950, Charles E. Fuller and Grace Payton Fuller Papers. Fuller, *Give the Winds*, notes the primary lesson his father learned in the funding of the *Old Fashioned Revival Hour*: "Even during the days when he was on some one thousand stations and the broadcast was costing about thirty-five thousand dollars a week, he depended only on the small offerings which came in from a multitude of God's people. Thus he was conscious of being cast only upon God and His guidance in carrying on the radio work" (83).

91. Fuller, *Heart to Heart Talk*, May 16, 1936.

92. See, for example, Joshi, *Henry L. Mencken on Religion*.

Dr. Winrod's pulpit style consists of an angry roar which gives an auditor the impression that he is liable at any moment to burst forth with a string of oaths. Your's is little better. Is there any reason why your remarks cannot be delivered in more than one tone? Neither of you could pass an audition at any radio station.

But both of you are guilty of bringing to the great work you supposedly serve infantile minds and amateurish expression. You may both be sincere but your "ham actor" delivery removes even the suggestion of sincerity to an intelligent listener.

There are many excellent schools of public speaking in Los Angeles. Why not avail yourself of their advantages? You could gain greatly from a real study of your Bible and from the great divines and students who have written works inspired by it.

The time has passed when people are satisfied with platitudes shouted from the pulpit.[93]

Another letter began, "I have had the misfortune of tuning in on your Sunday sermon for some time now, and at each conclusion I am left with a cold feeling of depression." The woman then proceeded to lament Fuller's emphasis on sin ("Why emphasize sin—sin—sin, when your real desire is to make people good?") and pled with him to "try preaching about good for a change." Still, even his critics seemed to have trouble changing the dial; for instance, one letter confessed, "Hope overcomes experience—I will listen again next Sunday."[94] Although this listener did not agree with Fuller's old-time religion and its emphasis on sin, there was something attractive about the program. Fuller's religion was simple, inviting, and entertaining. By avoiding sectarianism and controversial polemics, Fuller was able to take advantage of radio's potential and reach the masses.

Through tireless promotion over the airwaves of old-time religion, Fuller became a radio celebrity. Like Aimee Semple McPherson before him, Fuller seemed to revel in the spotlight. For example, although Fuller did not build anything like the Angelus Temple, he did broadcast the *Old Fashioned Revival Hour* live each week in front of three to six thousand people at the Long Beach Municipal Auditorium.[95] Moreover, just as McPherson went on a national "tour" to fund her shrine in Echo Park, Fuller oftentimes took to

---

93. Mrs. Edward L. Cox (Jean), West Hollywood, CA, to Charles Fuller, November 14, 1938, Charles E. Fuller and Grace Payton Fuller Papers.

94. Mrs. R. E. Mattice, Los Angeles, CA, to Charles Fuller, Charles E. Fuller and Grace Payton Fuller Papers.

95. Fuller began broadcasting from the Long Beach Auditorium in 1943 and did so for the next thirteen years—the program's "golden years." See Fuller, *Give the Winds*, 176.

the road to conduct "radio rallies" to raise the profile of the *Old Fashioned Revival Hour* and win new donors.

Fuller knew that the press was a powerful tool in getting the word out about his radio show. He welcomed the many instances of friendly press coverage of his revival meetings across the country as well as the positive descriptions of the *Old Fashioned Revival Hour*. Headlines across the nation told of the conquests of the "Famous Radio Preacher." For example, a newspaper in Dallas announced, "Near-Traffic Tie-Up Results As Crowd Storms Fair Park For Radio Evangelist's Talk."[96] The *Boston Daily Globe* reported on Fuller's gathering at the Boston Garden in 1941 with no apparent cynicism in the headline: "30,000 at Revivals Here by Rev. Charles E. Fuller."[97] Also, Bruce Adams of the "Behind Your Dial" column wrote warmly of Fuller:

> Imagine a pastor who numbers his congregation in the millions ... who preaches to an audience far larger than the total population of New York City ... an audience that never misses his sermons even though they have never seen him ... and you have a thumbnail portrait of the Reverend Charles Fuller, friendly voice of radio's Old Fashioned Revival Hour.[98]

CONCLUSION

In this chapter I argued that Charles Fuller's ministry contributed to the transformation of American religion by defining it primarily in terms of evangelism. Fuller's success uncovered a particular mood in America: one tired of the militant fundamentalism of the century's early decades not yet ready to abandon the fundamentals of the faith for theological liberalism. Fuller epitomized the "new" evangelicalism that would eventually dominate the airwaves. By defining evangelical Protestantism in terms of evangelism, Fuller's radio program became a unifying force within the broader evangelical movement. However, although Fuller's ministry helped maintain the influence of religion in the culture, it altered the religion it aimed to preserve.

Fuller was recognized as "an evangelist to the world." Given the peak years of the *Old Fashioned Revival Hour*, with an estimated twenty million listeners each week, the title seems fitting. Above all else, it was evangelism

---

96. Scrapbook, 2.38, no title for newspaper, September 1940, Charles E. Fuller and Grace Payton Fuller Papers.

97. Scrapbook, *Boston Daily Globe*, October 13, 1941, Charles E. Fuller and Grace Payton Fuller Papers.

98. Quoted in Goff, "We Have Heard the Joyful Sound," 72.

that moved Fuller. He wanted to broadcast his rendition of evangelical faith as far as possible, and with the advent of radio technology geographical boundaries vanished. However, in the process of trying to reach as many people as possible and thereby optimize broadcast technology, Fuller transformed the gospel into simple evangelism. There was no need for a robust theology for the church when what really mattered was that people "get saved" and avoid the judgment to come.

Fuller's ministry also catapulted American religion toward celebrity, accelerating a movement identified with Aimee Semple McPherson's ministry. The *Old Fashioned Revival Hour* made Fuller famous. As evidenced by the thousands of people who packed the Long Beach Municipal Auditorium each week to watch the show's live broadcast and the thousands more who attended his radio rallies around the country, Fuller himself became an attraction. In the end Fuller's emphasis on evangelism, although countering some of the secularizing trends of the twentieth century, unintentionally left the church more vulnerable to certain aspects of modernism.

6

The Church in a Digital Age

BROADCASTING THE FAITH HAS argued that religious radio in America sought to counter the secularization of American culture, but did so in a way that contributed to the dilution of theology in American religion. In seeking to sustain the influence of religion in American culture, radio preachers unwittingly altered the very religion they aimed to preserve.

The prominent radio preachers proclaimed rather diverse interpretations of the Christian message, yet each one found millions of people receptive to their message. Radio religion was consistent with the privatization of religion, but radio helped ensure that the voice of religion continued to shape the culture during some of the most tumultuous decades in our nation's history. Radio acted as what Peter Berger calls a "resistance movement," a movement that served to counter secularization in American culture.[1]

Broadcasting the faith, however, changed it. To make religion accessible to the masses, radio preachers accommodated the faith in ways suited to the medium of radio. Sectarianism and controversial polemics seemed ill-suited to building audiences of significant size to answer radio's promise. All of the prominent radio preachers felt the constraints of broadcast media. Most radio preachers embraced this nonsectarian approach. Those

---

1. Berger, "From the Crisis," 16.

who did not had to be satisfied with reaching small audiences. Still, the medium seemed better suited to reaching the masses, a goal inconsistent with sectarian preaching.

Charles Fuller distanced himself from militant fundamentalism and emphasized the need for evangelism. By defining evangelical Protestantism in terms of evangelism, Fuller's radio program became a unifying force within the broader evangelical movement. Although Fuller's ministry helped preserve the influence of religion in the culture, it simplified the Christian message to the people. Walter Maier forsook Lutheran particulars to bring "Christ to the nations." His work to advance simple Protestant orthodoxy allowed Maier to reach across denominational lines and gather a worldwide following. Aimee Semple McPherson promoted a charismatic ecumenism. McPherson used radio to promote an experience with the divine that required little theological reflection. Harry Emerson Fosdick preached simple virtues. Fosdick did this while embracing a theological liberalism at odds with the fundamentalism of his day. Fosdick's assault on the classic Protestantism of his youth found a powerful outlet in religious radio. These preachers were four of the most influential voices of religious radio from 1920 to 1950, and they all eschewed substantive theological discourse. Although religious-radio preachers set forth to oppose secularization, the lack of theological substance in their programs ironically promoted the secularization of the American church.

Successful radio also required charisma. The fact that these radio preachers attracted an adoring public helped shift religion's focus from one on God to one on man. Radio became a platform less for robust theology than for fame and notoriety. Not all radio preachers set out to be famous. However, the most dynamic personalities tended to be the preachers that gained audience share—regardless of what they preached. Content often took second place to popularity. This helps explain why the radio preachers in this study, although in some ways very different in their teaching, could be equally popular in America. Their personalities were larger than life, and by the sheer force of their persona they were able to amass audiences in the millions.

As the "Golden Age" of radio came to a close in the late 1940s, television began to supplant radio as the dominant communications medium in America. Some preachers who had done very well via radio tried to make the transition to television, but did so with little success.[2] Most radio preach-

---

2. Witham, *City upon a Hill*, 236. Witham notes that the year McPherson died she had been licensed to construct a television station. Of the individuals profiled in the present study, Harry Emerson Fosdick and Walter Maier stand out as examples. Had she lived longer, McPherson may have found television success.

ers at this time were already struggling to keep their programs on the air and could not absorb the higher costs of television.

In the early twenty-first century the internet has become nearly ubiquitous in American culture, and preachers of all kinds are scrambling to get their content online. Religious Americans are again being presented with a communication medium fraught with challenges and opportunities for the propagation of the faith. The internet, with its relatively low cost for entry compared to radio and television broadcasting, is an opportunity for American evangelicals to promote their perspectives into new avenues of influence quickly and efficiently. However, with the abundance of voices on the internet, it is difficult to gather the audience sizes observed, for example, during the golden age of radio, and the drive to set oneself apart from the masses has intensified. Additionally, unlike radio, where sectarianism and polemics were left behind in favor of a theological minimalism that could reach the masses, the internet appears to reward the more innovative and shocking content with increased online traffic. Finally, the allure of popularity, for American evangelicals in particular, has only intensified with the advent of the internet. Social networking channels such as Facebook, Twitter, and Instagram, as well as video sharing services such as YouTube and Vimeo, tempt preachers like never before to excel at self-promotion for the sake of bigger platforms of influence.

We live in a technological society. Neil Postman suggested that the great argument of the twenty-first century "is not between humanists and scientists but between technology and everybody else."[3] Postman was concerned about the uncritical acceptance of technology in American culture. For Postman, this uncritical stance toward technology is explained in two ways. First, technology is embraced uncritically because the benefits of technology to society are undeniable. Second, technology is embraced uncritically "because of its lengthy, intimate, and inevitable relationship with culture,"[4] and given this relationship with culture "technology does not invite a close examination of its consequences."[5] However, technology, Postman argued, is both a friend and an enemy. Postman even went so far as to say that "the uncontrolled growth of technology destroys the vital sources of our humanity. It creates a culture without a moral foundation."[6] Evangelical scholarship on the relationship between technology and

---

3. Postman, *Technopoly*, xii. Postman argued that in our time technology had become "a particularly dangerous enemy." For a more thorough treatment of this thesis see Ellul, *Technological Society*.

4. Postman, *Technopoly*, xii.

5. Postman, *Technopoly*, xii.

6. Postman, *Technopoly*, xii.

religion has received scant attention.[7] The church in America appears to be embracing technology uncritically. The implications of this reality for theology in America will be seen and felt in the years to come.[8] If the church follows the pattern established by the radio preachers, theology will be one of the first casualties.

---

7. An exception to this is the work of Quentin J. Schultze. See, especially, his *Christianity and the Mass Media in America*; *Communicating for Life*; *Habits of the High-Tech Heart*.

8. Murray, *Madness of Crowds*, warns of the long-term impact of technology on our societies: "There is a phrase variously attributed to the Danish computer scientist Morten Kyng or the American futurist Roy Amara, that the one thing we can say with certainty about the advent of new technologies is that people overestimate their impact in the short term and underestimate their impact over the long term. There is little doubt now, after the initial excitement, that we all massively underestimated what the internet and social media would do to our societies" (108). There can be little doubt that the church has underestimated the impact of the internet and social media for theology in America.

Bibliography

PRIMARY SOURCES

Books

Coughlin, Charles. *"By the Sweat of Thy Brow."* Royal Oak, MI: Radio League of the Little Flower, 1931.
———. *Eight Lectures on Labor, Capital and Justice.* Royal Oak, MI: Radio League of the Little Flower, 1934.
———. *Father Coughlin's Radio Discourses: 1931–1932.* Royal Oak, MI: Radio League of the Little Flower, 1932.
———. *Father Coughlin's Radio Sermons Complete: 1930–1931.* Baltimore: Knox and O'Leary, 1931.
———. *A Great Time to Be Alive: Sermons on Christianity in Wartime.* New York: Harper, 1944.
Fosdick, Harry Emerson. *Adventurous Living and Other Essays.* New York: Harper, 1926.
———. *A Series of Lectures on Social Justice.* Royal Oak, MI: Radio League of the Little Flower, 1935.
———. *As I See Religion.* New York: Grosset & Dunlap, 1932.
———. *The Hope of the World.* New York: Harper, 1933.
———. *The Living of These Days: The Autobiography of Harry Emerson Fosdick.* London: SCM, 1957.
———. *Living under Tension: Sermons on Christianity Today.* New York: Harper, 1941.
———. *The Power to See It Through.* New York: Harper, 1935.
———. *The Secret of Victorious Living: Twenty-Five Sermons on Christianity Today.* London: SCM, 1934.
———. *Successful Christian Living.* New York: Harper, 1937.
Fuller, Charles. *The Tabernacle in the Wilderness.* Grand Rapids: Revell, 1955.
Fuller, Charles E., et al., eds. *Old Fashioned Revival Hour Songs.* Winona Lake, IN: Rodeheaver, Hall-Mack, 1950.

Fuller, Mrs. Charles E. [Grace], comp. *Heavenly Sunshine: Letters to the "Old-Fashioned Revival Hour."* Westwood, NJ: Revell, 1956.
Maier, Walter A. *America, Turn to Christ! Radio Messages of the Lutheran Hour from Easter through Christmastide, 1943.* St. Louis: Concordia, 1944.
———. *Christ for Every Crisis! The Radio Messages Broadcast in the Second Lutheran Hour.* St. Louis: Concordia, 1935.
———. *Christ for the Nation! The Radio Messages Broadcast in the Third Lutheran Hour.* St. Louis: Concordia, 1936.
———. *Christ, Set the World Aright! Radio Messages of the Eleventh Lutheran Hour from New Year to the Pentecost Season.* St. Louis: Concordia, 1945.
———. *Courage in Christ: Radio Messages Broadcast in the Eighth Lutheran Hour.* St. Louis: Concordia, 1941.
———. *The Cross from Coast to Coast: Radio Messages Broadcast in the Fifth Lutheran Hour.* St Louis: Concordia, 1938.
———. *Fourth Lutheran Hour: Winged Words for Christ.* St. Louis: Concordia, 1937.
———. *Jesus Christ Our Hope: Radio Messages of the First Part of the Twelfth Lutheran Hour.* St. Louis: Concordia, 1946.
———. *The Lutheran Hour: Winged Words to Modern America, Broadcast in the Coast-to-Coast Radio Crusade for Christ.* St. Louis: Concordia, 1931.
———. *Peace through Christ: Radio Messages Broadcast in the Seventh Lutheran Hour.* St. Louis: Concordia, 1940.
———. *The Radio for Christ: Radio Messages Broadcast in the Sixth Lutheran Hour.* St. Louis: Concordia, 1939.
———. *Rebuilding with Christ: Radio Messages of the Second Part of the Twelfth Lutheran Hour.* St. Louis: Concordia, 1946.
McPherson, Aimee Semple. *The Foursquare Gospel.* Los Angeles: Echo Park Evangelistic Association, 1946.
———. *Lost and Restored: Sermons and Personal Testimony of Aimee Semple McPherson.* Los Angeles: Foursquare, 1990.
———. *The Story of My Life.* Waco, TX: Word, 1973.
———. *This Is That: Personal Experiences, Sermons, and Writings.* Los Angeles: Echo Park Evangelistic Association, 1923.

SECONDARY SOURCES

Books

Abrams, Douglas C. *Selling the Old-Time Religion: American Fundamentalists and Mass Culture, 1920–1940.* Athens: University of Georgia Press, 2001.
Adair, James R. *M. R. DeHaan: The Man and His Ministry.* Grand Rapids: Zondervan, 1969.
Ammerman, Nancy. *Bible Believers: Fundamentalists in a Modern World.* New Brunswick, NJ: Rutgers University Press, 1987.
Anderson, Robert M. *Vision of the Disinherited: The Making of American Pentecostalism.* New York: Oxford University Press, 1979.
Apostolidis, Paul. *Stations of the Cross: Adorno and Christian Right Radio.* Durham, NC: Duke University Press, 2000.

Armstrong, Ben. *The Electric Church*. Nashville: Thomas Nelson, 1979.
Arnheim, Rudolph. *Radio*. London: Faber and Faber, 1936.
Badaracco, Claire H., ed. *Quoting God: How Media Shape Ideas about Religion and Culture*. Waco, TX: Baylor University Press, 2005.
Balk, Alfred. *The Rise of Radio: From Marconi through the Golden Age*. Jefferson, NC: McFarland, 2006.
Barnouw, Erik. *A History of Broadcasting in the United States*. 3 vols. New York: Oxford University Press, 1966–70.
———. *A Tower of Babel: A History of Broadcasting in the United States to 1933*. New York: Oxford University Press, 1966.
Berger, Peter. *A Far Glory: The Quest for Faith in an Age of Credulity*. New York: Free Press, 1992.
———. *The Sacred Canopy: Elements of a Sociological Theory of Religion*. New York: Doubleday, 1969.
Berman, Marshall. *All That Is Solid Melts into Air: The Experience of Modernity*. New York: Simon and Schuster, 1982.
Blumhofer, Edith. *Aimee Semple McPherson: Everybody's Sister*. Grand Rapids: Eerdmans, 1993.
Boone, Kathleen. *The Bible Tells Them So: The Discourse of Protestant Fundamentalism*. Albany: State University of New York Press, 1989.
Bounds, Elizabeth M. *Coming Together/Coming Apart: Religion, Community, and Modernity*. New York: Routledge, 1997.
Boyer, Paul. *When Time Shall Be No More: Prophecy Belief in Modern American Culture*. Cambridge, MA: Harvard University Press, 1992.
Brinkley, Alan. *Voices of Protest: Huey Long, Father Coughlin, and the Great Depression*. New York: Vintage, 1982.
Bruce, Steve. *God is Dead: Secularization in the West*. Oxford: Blackwell, 2002.
Burg, David F. *The Great Depression*. New York: Facts on File, 2005.
Butler, Jon. *God in Gotham: The Miracle of Religion in Modern Manhattan*. Cambridge, MA: Harvard University Press, 2020.
Buxton, Frank, and Bill Owen. *The Big Broadcast, 1920–1950: A New Revised and Greatly Expanded Edition of Radio's Golden Age*. New York: Avon, 1973.
Cantril, Hadley, and Gordon Allport. *The Psychology of Radio*. New York: Harper, 1935.
Carpenter, Joel A. *Revive Us Again: The Reawakening of American Fundamentalism*. New York: Oxford University Press, 1997.
Carson, Donald A. *Christ & Culture Revisited*. Grand Rapids: Eerdmans, 2008.
Carter, Paul A. *The Decline and Revival of the Social Gospel: Social and Political Liberalism in American Protestant Churches, 1920–1940*. Ithaca, NY: Cornell University Press, 1954.
Cary, James W. *Communication as Culture: Essays on Media and Society*. Rev. ed. New York: Routledge, 2008.
Casanova, José. *Public Religions in the Modern World*. Chicago: University of Chicago Press, 1994.
Covert, Catherine L., and John D. Stevens, eds. *Mass Media between the Wars: Perceptions of Cultural Tensions, 1918–1941*. Syracuse, NY: Syracuse University Press, 1984.
Cruz, Jon, and Justin Lewis, eds. *Viewing, Reading, Listening: Audiences and Cultural Reception*. Boulder, CO: Westview, 1994.

Czitrom, Daniel. *Media and the American Mind: From Morse to McLuhan.* Chapel Hill: University of North Carolina Press, 1982.

Danbom, David B. *Born in the Country: A History of Rural America.* Baltimore: Johns Hopkins University Press, 1995.

Dillon, Michelle, ed. *Handbook of the Sociology of Religion.* Cambridge: Cambridge University Press, 2003.

Dorgan, Howard. *The Airwaves of Zion: Radio and Religion in Appalachia.* Knoxville: University of Tennessee Press, 1993.

Douglas, Mary, and Steven M. Tipton, eds. *Religion in America: Spirituality in a Secular Age.* Boston: Beacon, 1983.

Douglas, Susan. *Inventing American Broadcasting, 1899–1922.* Baltimore: Johns Hopkins University Press, 1987.

———. *Listening In: Radio and the American Imagination from Amos 'n' Andy to Edward R. Murrow and Wolfman Jack to Howard Stern.* New York: Times, 1999.

Duarte, Charles. "History of Radio Station KFSG." Unpublished manuscript. Heritage Center, International Church of the Foursquare Gospel.

Edelman, Murray. *The Licensing of Radio Services in the United States, 1927 to 1947: A Study in Administrative Formulation of Policy.* Illinois Studies in the Social Sciences 31, no. 4. Urbana: University of Illinois Press, 1950.

Ellens, Harold J. *Models of Religious Broadcasting.* Grand Rapids: Eerdmans, 1974.

Ellul, Jacques. *The Technological Society.* New York: Vintage, 1964.

Ellwood, Robert S. *The Fifties Spiritual Marketplace: American Religion in a Decade of Conflict.* New Brunswick, NJ: Rutgers University Press, 1997.

Epstein, Daniel Mark. *Sister McPherson: The Life of Aimee Semple McPherson.* San Diego: Harcourt, 1993.

Erickson, Hal. *Religious Radio and Television in the United States, 1921–1991: Programs and Personalities.* Jefferson, NC: McFarland, 1992.

Eskridge, Larry K., and Mark Noll. *More Money, More Ministry: Money and Evangelicals in Recent North American History.* Grand Rapids: Eerdmans, 2000.

Ewen, Stuart, and Elizabeth Ewen. *Channels of Desire: Mass Images and the Shaping of American Consciousness.* Minneapolis: University of Minnesota Press, 1992.

Feuerherd, Peter. *Holyland USA: A Catholic Ride through America's Evangelical Landscape.* New York: Crossroad, 2006.

Finke, Roger, and Rodney Stark. *The Churching of America, 1776–1990: Winners and Losers in Our Religious Economy.* New Brunswick, NJ: Rutgers University Press, 1992.

Fishwick, Marshall W. *Great Awakenings: Popular Religion and Popular Culture.* New York: Haworth, 1995.

Forbes, Bruce D., and Jeffrey H. Mahan, eds. *Religion and Popular Culture in America.* Berkeley: University of California Press, 2000.

Fore, William F. *Television and Religion: The Shaping of Faith, Values, and Culture.* Minneapolis: Augsburg, 1987.

Fox, Richard W., and T. J. Jackson Lears. *The Culture of Consumption: Critical Essays in American History, 1880–1980.* New York: Pantheon, 1983.

Fuller, Daniel P. *Give the Winds A Mighty Voice: The Story of Charles E. Fuller.* Waco, TX: Word, 1972.

Gasper, Louis. *The Fundamentalist Movement, 1930–1956.* 1963. Reprint, Grand Rapids: Baker, 1981.

Getz, Gene A. *MBI: The Story of Moody Bible Institute*. Chicago: Moody, 1986.
Gilbert, James. *Redeeming Culture: American Religion in an Age of Science*. Chicago: University of Chicago Press, 1997.
Goethals, Gregor. *The Electronic Golden Calf: Images, Marketing and the Making of Meaning*. Cambridge, MA: Cowley, 1990.
Graebner, Alan. *Uncertain Saints: The Laity in the Lutheran Church—Missouri Synod, 1900–1970*. Westport, CT: Greenwood, 1975.
Graham, Billy. *Just As I Am: The Autobiography of Billy Graham*. San Francisco: Zondervan/Harper, 1997.
Gritsch, Eric W. *A History of Lutheranism*. Minneapolis: Fortress, 2002.
Hadden, Jeffrey, and Anson Shupe. *Televangelism: Power and Politics on God's Frontier*. New York: Holt, 1988.
Hadden, Jeffrey K., and Charles E. Swann. *Prime Time Preachers: The Rising Power of Televangelism*. Reading, MA: Addison-Wesley, 1981.
Handy, Robert T. *A History of Union Theological Seminary in New York*. New York: Columbia University Press, 1987.
Hangen, Tona. *Redeeming the Dial: Radio, Religion, & Popular Culture in America*. Chapel Hill: University of North Carolina Press, 2002.
Harding, Susan. *The Book of Jerry Falwell: Fundamentalist Language and Politics*. Princeton, NJ: Princeton University Press, 2001.
Harmon, Jim. *The Great Radio Heroes*. Garden City, NY: Doubleday, 1967.
Harrell, David Edwin, Jr. *All Things Are Possible: The Healing and Charismatic Revivals in Modern America*. Bloomington: Indiana University Press, 1975.
Hart, Darryl G. *Defending the Faith: J. Gresham Machen and the Crisis of Conservative Protestantism in Modern America*. Phillipsburg, NJ: P&R, 1994.
———. *The Lost Soul of American Protestantism*. New York: Rowman & Littlefield, 2002.
———. *A Secular Faith: Why Christianity Favors the Separation of Church and State*. Chicago: Ivan R. Dee, 2006.
———. *That Old-Time Religion in Modern America: Evangelical Protestantism in the Twentieth Century*. Chicago: Ivan R. Dee, 2002.
Hatch, Nathan O. *The Democratization of American Christianity*. New Haven: Yale University Press, 1989.
Hill, George H. *Airwaves to the Soul: The Influence and Growth of Religious Broadcasting in America*. Saratoga, CA: R&E, 1983.
Hilmes, Michelle. *Hollywood and Broadcasting: From Radio to Cable*. Urbana: University of Illinois Press, 1990.
———. *Radio Voices: American Broadcasting, 1922–1952*. Minneapolis: University of Minnesota Press, 1997.
Holifield, E. Brooks. *God's Ambassadors: A History of Christian Clergy in America*. Grand Rapids: Eerdmans, 2007.
Holub, Robert. *Reception Theory: A Critical Introduction*. London: Methuen, 1984.
Hoover, Stewart M. *Mass Media Religion: The Social Sources of the Electronic Church*. Newbury Park, CA: Sage, 1988.
Hoover, Stewart M., and Lynn Schofield Clark, eds. *Practicing Religion in the Age of Media: Explorations in Media, Religion and Culture*. New York: Columbia University Press, 2002.

Horsfield, Peter G. *Religious Television: The American Experience*. New York: Longman, 1984.
Hudson, Winthrop S. *American Protestantism*. Chicago: University of Chicago Press, 1961.
Hunter, James Davison. *American Evangelicalism: Conservative Religion and the Quandary of Modernity*. Piscataway, NJ: Rutgers University Press, 1983.
Hutchinson, William R., ed. *Between the Times: The Travail of the Protestant Establishment, 1900–1960*. Cambridge: Cambridge University Press, 1989.
———. *The Modernist Impulse in American Protestantism*. Cambridge, MA: Harvard University Press, 1989.
Huyssen, Andreas. *After the Great Divide: Modernism, Mass Culture, Postmodernism*. Bloomington: Indiana University Press, 1986.
Innis, Harold. *The Bias of Communication*. Toronto: University of Toronto Press, 2008.
Jacobsen, Douglas, and William Vance Trollinger Jr. *Reforming the Center: American Protestantism, 1900 to the Present*. Grand Rapids: Eerdmans, 1998.
Jones, Clarence W. *Radio: The New Missionary*. Chicago: Moody, 1946.
Jones, Jacqueline. *The Dispossessed: America's Underclasses from the Civil War to the Present*. New York: Basic, 1992.
Joshi, Sunand T., ed. *Henry L. Mencken on Religion*. Amherst, NY: Prometheus, 2002.
Kamensky, Jane. *Governing the Tongue: The Politics of Speech in Early New England*. New York: Oxford University Press, 1997.
Kazin, Michael. *The Populist Persuasion: An American History*. Ithaca, NY: Cornell University Press, 1995.
Kennedy, David M. *Freedom from Fear: The American People in Depression and War, 1929–1945*. New York: Oxford University Press, 1999.
Kintz, Linda, and Julia Lesage, eds. *Media, Culture, and the Religious Right*. Minneapolis: University of Minnesota Press, 1998.
Kirby, Jack T. *Rural Worlds Lost: The American South, 1920–1960*. Baton Rouge: Louisiana State University Press, 1987.
Kolb, Robert, and Timothy J. Wengert, eds. *The Book of Concord: The Confessions of the Evangelical Lutheran Church*. Translated by Charles Arand et al. Minneapolis: Fortess, 2000.
Kyvig, David E. *Daily Life in the United States, 1920—1940: How Americans Lived through the 'Roaring Twenties' and the Great Depression*. Chicago: Ivan R. Dee, 2004.
Lambert, Farnk. *The Founding Fathers and the Place of Religion in America*. Princeton: Princeton University Press, 2003.
Larson, Edward J. *Summer of the Gods: The Scopes Trial and America's Continuing Debate over Science and Religion*. New York: Basic, 1997.
Lawrence, Bruce B. *Defenders of God: The Fundamentalist Revolt against the Modern Age*. San Francisco: Harper & Row, 1989.
Lazere, Donald, ed. *American Media and Mass Culture: Left Perspectives*. Berkeley: University of California Press, 1987.
Leach, William. *Land of Desire: Merchants, Power, and the Rise of a New American Culture*. New York: Pantheon, 1993.
Lears, T. J. Jackson. *Fables of Abundance: A Cultural History of Advertising in America*. New York: Basic, 1994.

Leibman, Nina C. *Living Room Lectures: The Fifties Family in Film and Television*. Austin: University of Texas Press, 1995.

Lichty, Lawrence W., and Malachi C. Topping, eds. *American Broadcasting: A Source Book on the History of Radio and Television*. New York: Hastings, 1975.

Longfield, Bradley J. *The Presbyterian Controversy: Fundamentalists, Modernists, and Moderates*. New York: Oxford University Press, 1991.

Loveless, W. P. *Manual of Gospel Broadcasting*. Chicago: Moody, 1946.

Lynd, Robert S., and Helen Merrell Lynd. *Middletown: A Study in Modern American Culture*. New York: Harcourt, 1929.

Lyon, Arabella. *Intentions: Negotiated, Contested, Ignored*. University Park: Pennsylvania State University Press, 1998.

MacDonald, J. Fred. *Don't Touch That Dial! Radio Programming in American Life, 1920–1960*. Chicago: Nelson-Hall, 1979.

MacLatchy, Josephine H., ed. *Education on the Air: Tenth Yearbook of the Institute for Education by Radio*. Columbus: Ohio State University, 1939.

Maier, Paul L., ed. *The Best of Walter A. Maier*. St. Louis: Concordia, 1980.

———. *A Man Spoke, a World Listened: The Story of Walter A. Maier and the Lutheran Hour*. New York: McGraw-Hill, 1963.

Marchand, Philip. *Marshall McLuhan: The Medium and the Messenger*. New York: Ticknor and Fields, 1989.

Marcus, Sheldon. *Father Coughlin: The Tumultuous Life of the Priest of the Little Flower*. New York: Little, Brown and Company, 1973.

Marsden, George M. *Fundamentalism and American Culture: The Shaping of Twentieth-Century Evangelicalism, 1870–1925*. New York: Oxford University Press, 1980.

———. *Reforming Fundamentalism: Fuller Seminary and the New Evangelicalism*. Grand Rapids: Eerdmans, 1987.

———. *Understanding Fundamentalism and Evangelicalism*. Grand Rapids: Eerdmans, 1991.

Martin, David. *On Secularization: Towards a Revised General Theory*. Aldershot, UK: Ashgate, 2005.

Martin, Lerone A. *Preaching on Wax: The Phonograph and the Shaping of Modern African American Religion*. New York, NY: New York University Press, 2014.

Martin, William. *With God on Our Side: The Rise of the Religious Right*. New York: Broadway, 1996.

Mayo, Morrow. *Los Angeles*. New York: Knopf, 1933.

McChesney, R. W. *Telecommunications, Mass Media, and Democracy: The Battle for Control of U.S. Broadcasting, 1928–1935*. New York: Oxford University Press, 1993.

McElvaine, Robert S., ed. *Down and Out in the Great Depression: Letters from the Forgotten Man*. Chapel Hill: University of North Carolina Press, 1983.

McGirr, Lisa. *Suburban Warriors: The Origins of the New American Right*. Princeton, NJ: Princeton University Press, 2001.

McIntire, Carl. *Twentieth Century Reformation*. Fundamentalism in American Religion, 1880–1950. 1944. New York: Garland, 1988.

McLoughlin, William G. *Revivals, Awakenings, and Reform: An Essay on Religion and Social Change in America, 1607–1977*. Chicago History of American Religion Series. Edited by Martin Marty. Chicago: University of Chicago Press, 1978.

McLuhan, Marshall. *Understanding Media: The Extensions of Man*. Cambridge, MA: MIT Press, 1994.

McWilliams, Carey. *Southern California Country: An Island on the Land*. New York: Duell, Sloan and Pearce, 1946.
Meyer, Carl S. *A Brief Historical Sketch of the Lutheran Church-Missouri Synod*. St. Louis: Concordia, 1963.
———. *Log Cabin to Luther Tower: Concordia Seminary During One Hundred and Twenty-five Years toward a More Excellent Ministry, 1839-1964*. St. Louis: Concordia, 1965.
———, ed. *Moving Frontiers: Reading in the History of the Lutheran Church—Missouri Synod*. St. Louis: Concordia, 1964.
Meyrowitz, Joshua. *No Sense of Place: The Impact of Electronic Media on Social Behavior*. New York: Oxford University Press, 1985.
Miller, Robert Moats. *Harry Emerson Fosdick: Preacher, Pastor, Prophet*. New York: Oxford University Press, 1985.
Moore, R. Laurence. *Religious Outsiders and the Making of Americans*. New York: Oxford University Press, 1986.
———. *Selling God: American Religion in the Marketplace of Culture*. New York: Oxford University Press, 1994.
Moser, J. G., and Richard A. Lavine. *Radio and the Law*. Los Angeles: Parker, 1947.
Muggeridge, Malcolm. *Christ and the Media*. Grand Rapids: Eerdmans, 1977.
Mugglebee, Ruth. *Father Coughlin of the Shrine of the Little Flower*. Boston: L. C. Page, 1933.
Murch, James D. *Adventuring for Christ in Changing Times: An Autobiography*. Louisville: Restoration, 1973.
———. *Cooperation without Compromise: A History of the National Association of Evangelicals*. Grand Rapids: Eerdmans, 1956.
Murray, Douglas. *The Madness of Crowds: Gender, Race, and Identity*. London: Bloomsbury, 2019.
Nadeau, Remi. *Los Angeles: From Mission to Modern City*. New York: Longmans, Green, 1960.
Neely, Lois. *Come Up to This Mountain: The Miracle of Clarence W. Jones and HCJB*. Wheaton, IL: Tyndale, 1980.
Neth, Mary. *Preserving the Family Farm: Women, Community, and the Foundation of Agribusiness in the Midwest, 1900-1940*. Baltimore: Johns Hopkins University Press, 1995.
Niebuhr, H. Richard. *Christ and Culture*. New York: Harper & Row, 1951.
Nichols, Stephen J. *Jesus Made in America: A Cultural History from the Puritans to the Passion of the Christ*. Downers Grove, IL: InterVarsity, 2008.
Noll, Mark A. *Between Faith and Criticism: Evangelicals, Scholarship, and the Bible in America*. Vancouver, BC: Regent College, 2004.
———. *The Scandal of the Evangelical Mind*. Grand Rapids: Eerdmans, 1994.
Noll, Mark, and Luke E. Harlow. *Religion and American Politics from the Colonial Period to the Present*. 2nd ed. New York: Oxford University Press, 2007.
Norris, Pippa, and Ronald Inglehart. *Sacred and Secular: Religion and Politics Worldwide*. Cambridge: Cambridge University Press, 2004.
Nye, David E. *Electrifying America: Social Meanings of a New Technology, 1880-1940*. Cambridge, MA: MIT Press, 1990.
Ong, Walter J. *The Presence of the Word: Some Prolegomena for Cultural and Religious History*. Minneapolis: University of Minnesota Press, 1981.

Parker, Everett C., et al. *The Television-Radio Audience and Religion*. New York: Harper, 1955.
Pells, Richard H. *Radical Visions and American Dreams: Culture and Social Thought in the Depression Years*. New York: Harper, 1973.
Postman, Neil. *Amusing Ourselves to Death: Public Discourse in the Age of Show Business*. New York: Penguin, 1985.
———. *Technopoly: The Surrender of Culture to Technology*. New York: Vintage, 1992.
Pratt, Henry J. *The Liberalization of American Protestantism: A Case Study in Complex Organizations*. Detroit: Wayne State University Press, 1972.
Prothero, Stephen. *American Jesus: How the Son of God became a National Icon*. New York: Farrar, Staus, and Giroux, 2003.
Pultz, David, ed. *A Preaching Ministry: Twenty-One Sermons Preached by Harry Emerson Fosdick at the First Presbyterian Church in the City of New York, 1918–1925*. New York: First Presbyterian Church, 2000.
Rader, Paul. *Life's Greatest Adventure*. London: Victory, 1938.
———. *Paul Rader's Stories of His Early Life: Interspersed by Spiritual Messages of Priceless Value*. Chicago: Chicago Gospel Tabernacle, 1928.
———. *Radio Messages by Paul Rader*. Chicago: Chicago Gospel Tabernacle, 1928.
Reeves, Thomas C. *The Empty Church: The Suicide of Liberal Christianity*. New York: Free, 1996.
Rice, John R. *Bobbed Hair, Bossy Wives, and Women Preachers: Significant Questions for Honest Christian Women Settled by the Word of God*. Wheaton, IL: Sword of the Lord, 1941.
Rose, C. B., Jr. *National Policy for Radio Broadcasting: Report of a Committee of the National Economic and Social Planning Association*. New York: Harper, 1940.
Rosell, Garth M. *The Surprising Work of God: Harold John Ockenga, Billy Graham, and the Rebirth of Evangelicalism*. Grand Rapids: Baker Academic, 2008.
Rosen, Philip T. *The Modern Stentors: Radio Broadcasters and the Federal Government, 1920–1934*. Westport, CT: Greenwood, 1980.
Rudnick, Milton L. *Fundamentalism & the Missouri Synod: A Historical Study of Their Interaction and Mutual Influence*. St. Louis: Concordia, 1966.
Sandeen, Ernest R. *The Roots of Fundamentalism: British and American Millenarianism, 1800–1930*. Chicago: University of Chicago Press, 1970.
Savage, Barbara D. *Broadcasting Freedom: Radio, War, and the Politics of Race, 1938–1948*. Chapel Hill: University of North Carolina Press, 1999.
Schlesinger, Arthur M., Jr. *The Age of Roosevelt: The Politics of Upheaval*. Boston: Houghton Mifflin, 1960.
Schultze, Quentin J., ed. *American Evangelicals and the Mass Media: Perspectives on the Relationship between American Evangelicals and the Mass Media*. Grand Rapids: Zondervan, 1990.
———. *Christianity and the Mass Media in America: Toward a Democratic Accomodation*. East Lansing: Michigan State University Press, 2003.
———. *Communicating for Life: Christian Stewardship in Community and Media*. Grand Rapids: Baker Academic, 2000.
———. *Habits of the High-Tech Heart: Living Virtuously in the Information Age*. Grand Rapids: Baker Academic, 2002.
Siedell, Barry. *Gospel Radio*. Lincoln, NE: Back to the Bible Broadcast, 1971.

Singal, Daniel Joseph. *The War Within: From Victorian to Modernist Thought in the South, 1919–1945*. Chapel Hill: University of North Carolina Press, 1982.

Singleton, Gregory H. *Religion in the City of Angels: American Protestant Culture and Urbanization, Los Angeles, 1850–1930*. Ann Arbor: UMI Research, 1979.

Sittser, Gerald. *A Cautious Patriotism: The American Churches and the Second World War*. Chapel Hill: University of North Carolina Press, 1997.

Smith, Christian. *American Evangelicalism: Embattled and Thriving*. Chicago: University of Chicago Press, 1998.

Smith, Christian, ed. *The Secular Revolution: Power, Interests, and Conflict in the Secularization of American Public Life*. Berkeley: University of California Press, 2003.

Smith, Wilbur M. *A Voice for God: The Life of Charles E. Fuller, Originator of the Old Fashioned Revival Hour*. Boston: Wilde, 1949.

Smulyan, Susan. *Selling Radio: The Commercialization of American Broadcasting, 1922–1934*. Washington, DC: Smithsonian, 1994.

Snow, Robert P. *Creating Media Culture*. Beverly Hills: Sage, 1983.

Sobel, Robert. *The Manipulators: American in the Media Age*. Garden City, NY: Anchor, 1976.

Stanley, Susie Cunningham. *Feminist Pillar of Fire: The Life of Alma White*. Cleveland, Ohio: Pilgrim, 1993.

Stark, Rodney, and Roger Finke. *Acts of Faith: Explaining the Human Side of Religion*. Berkeley: University of California Press, 2000.

Steel, Ronald. *Walter Lippmann and the American Century*. New Brunswick, NJ: Transaction, 2005.

Sterling, Christopher H., and John M. Kitross. *Stay Tuned: A Concise History of American Broadcasting*. Belmont, CA: Wadsworth, 1978.

Stone, Jon R. *A Guide to the End of the World: Popular Eschatology in America*. New York: Garland, 1993.

———. *On the Boundaries of American Evangelicalism: The Postwar Evangelical Coalition*. New York: St. Martin's, 1997.

Stout, Harry S. *The Divine Dramatist: George Whitefield and the Rise of Modern Evangelicalism*. Grand Rapids: Eerdmans, 1991.

———. *The New England Soul: Preaching and Religious Culture in Colonial New England*. New York: Oxford University Press, 1986.

Strasser, Susan. *Satisfaction Guaranteed: The Making of the American Mass Market*. Washington, DC: Smithsonian, 1995.

Summers, Harrison B., ed. *A Thirty-Year History of Programs Carried on National Radio Networks in the United States, 1926–1956*. New York: Arno, 1971.

Sumner, Robert L. *A Man Sent from God: A Biography of Dr. John R. Rice*. Grand Rapids: Eerdmans, 1959.

Susman, Warren. *Culture as History: The Transformation of American Society in the Twentieth Century*. New York: Pantheon, 1984.

Sutton, Matthew Avery. *Aimee Semple McPherson and the Resurrection of Christian America*. Cambridge, MA: Harvard University Press, 2007.

Swatos, William H., Jr., and Daniel V. A. Olson, eds. *The Secularization Debate*. Lanham, MD: Rowman and Littlefield, 2000.

Sweeney, Douglas A. *The American Evangelical Story: A History of the Movement*. Grand Rapids: Baker Academic, 2005.

Sweet, Leonard, ed. *The Evangelical Tradition in America*. Macon, GA: Mercer, 1984.
Synan, Vinson. *The Holiness-Pentecostal Tradition: Charismatic Movements in the Twentieth Century*. Grand Rapids: Eerdmans, 1997.
Taylor, Charles. *A Secular Age*. Boston: Harvard University Press, 2007.
Taylor, Ella. *Prime-Time Families: Television Culture in Postwar America*. Berkeley: University of California Press, 1989.
Teachout, Terry. *The Skeptic: A Life of H.L. Mencken*. New York: HarperCollins, 2002.
Terrace, Vincent. *Radio's Golden Years: The Encyclopedia of Radio Programs, 1930–1960*. New York: Barnes, 1981.
Todd, Mary. *Authority Vested: A Story of Identity and Change in the Lutheran Church—Missouri Synod*. Grand Rapids: Eerdmans, 2000.
Tull, Charles. *Father Coughlin and the New Deal*. Syracuse: Syracuse University Press, 1965.
Turner, James. *Without God, without Creed: The Origins of Unbelief in America*. Baltimore: Johns Hopkins University Press, 1985.
Vaca, Daniel. *Evangelicals Incorporated: Books and the Business of Religion in America*. Cambridge, MA: Harvard University Press, 2019.
Viguerie, Richard, and David Franke. *America's Right Turn: How Conservatives Used New and Alternative Media to Take Power*. Chicago: Bonus, 2004.
Wacker, Grant. *Heaven Below: Early Pentecostals and American Culture*. Cambridge, MA: Harvard University Press, 2001.
Ward, Mark, Sr. *Air of Salvation: The Story of Christian Broadcasting*. Grand Rapids: Baker, 1994.
Warner, R. Stephen. *New Wine in Old Wineskins: Evangelicals and Liberals in a Small-Town Church*. Berkeley: University of California Press, 1988.
Warren, Donald. *Radio Priest: Charles Coughlin the Father of Hate Radio*. New York: Free Press, 1996.
Watt, David Harrington. *A Transforming Faith: Explorations of Twentieth-Century American Evangelicalism*. New Brunswick, NJ: Rutgers University Press, 1991.
Weber, Timothy. *Living in the Shadow of the Second Coming: American Premillennialism, 1875–1925*. Chicago: University of Chicago Press, 1987.
Wells, David F. *God in the Wasteland: The Reality of Truth in a World of Fading Dreams*. Grand Rapids: Eerdmans, 1994.
———. *No Place for Truth: Whatever Happened to Evangelical Theology?* Grand Rapids: Eerdmans, 1993.
Wilson, John F. *Public Religion in American Culture*. Philadelphia: Temple University Press, 1979.
Winrod, Gerald B. *Persecuted Preachers*. Wichita, KS: Defender, 1946.
Witham, Larry. *A City upon a Hill: How Sermons Changed the Course of American History*. New York: HarperOne, 2007.
Worster, Donald. *Dust Bowl: The Southern Plains in the 1930s*. New York: Oxford University Press, 2004.
Wright, J. Elwin. *Death in the Pot: An Appraisal of the Federal Council of the Churches of Christ in America*. Boston: Fellowship, 1944.
———. *The Old Fashioned Revival Hour and the Broadcasters*. Boston: Fellowship, 1940.
Wuthnow, Robert. *Rediscovering the Sacred: Perspectives on Religion in Contemporary Society*. Grand Rapids: Eerdmans, 1992.

———. *The Restructuring of American Religion: Society and Faith since World War II.* Princeton, NJ: Princeton University Press, 1988.

———. *The Struggle for America's Soul: Evangelicals, Liberals, and Secularism.* Grand Rapids: Eerdmans, 1989.

Articles and Chapters

"Aimee McPherson Dead at 53 after Taking Sleeping Tablets." *Washington Post,* September 28, 1944.

"Aimee Semple McPherson: Thousands Mourn at Famed Evangelist's Funeral." *Life,* October 30, 1944.

"Air Time for Atheism." *Newsweek,* December 2, 1946.

"Air for Atheists." *Time,* August 5, 1946.

"American Council to Broadcast on American Broadcasting Network January, February, March." *Christian Beacon,* December 6, 1945.

"Atheists to Sue for Radio Time?" *United Evangelical Action,* April 1, 1947.

Ayer, William W. "Will Americans Be Allowed to Broadcast the Gospel?" *Calvary Pulpit and Monthly Messenger* 6, no. 2 (January 1944) 3–8.

Bendroth, Margaret Lamberts. "Fundamentalism and the Mass Media, 1930–1990." In *Religion and the Mass Media: Audiences and Adaptations,* edited by Daniel A. Stout and Judith M. Buddenbaum, 74–84. Thousand Oaks, CA: Sage, 1996.

Berger, Peter. "The Desecularization of the World: A Global Overview." In *The Desecularization of the World: Resurgent Religion and World Politics,* edited by Peter Berger, 2–18. Grand Rapids: Eerdmans, 1999.

———. "From the Crisis of Religion to the Crisis of Secularity." In *Religion and America: Spiritual Life in a Secular Age,* edited by Mary Douglas and Steven Tipton, 14–24. Boston: Beacon, 1983.

———. "A Sociological View of the Secularization of Theology." *Journal of the Scientific Study of Religion* 8, no. 1 (1967) 11–12.

Berkman, Dave. "Long Before Falwell: Early Radio and Religion—As Reported by the Nation's Periodical Press." *Journal of Popular Culture* 21 (Spring 1988) 1–11.

Bertermann, Eugene R. "Plea for More Time for Gospel Broadcasts." *United Evangelical Action,* August 15, 1947.

Biery, Ruth. "Starring McPherson Semple McPherson: The Priestess Is Going in the Talkies; Will She Some Day Tell Her Love-Life?" *Motion Picture,* April 1929.

"Big Churches Learn Radio 'Savvy' to Counter Revivalist Air Racket." *Newsweek,* January 22, 1945.

Blackmore, Glenwood. "Shall the NCC Control Religious Broadcasting?" *United Evangelical Action,* July 1, 1956, 5–6.

Blau, Judith R., et al. "The Expansion of Religious Affiliation: An Explanation of the Growth of Church Participation in the United States, 1850–1930." *Social Science Research* 21 (December 1992) 329–52.

Bliven, Bruce. "Sister McPherson." *New Republic,* November 3, 1926.

Boris, Thomas A. "When WKBW Came Home." *United Evangelical Action,* February 1, 1946.

Brown, James A. "Selling Airtime for Controversy: NAB Self-Regulation and Father Coughlin." *Journal of Broadcasting* 24 (Spring 1980) 199–224.

Browning, Tamara N. "Christian Radio at 65." *Journal of Religious Broadcasting* 18 (June 1986) 14–16.
"Cadle of Indianapolis Streamlines Evangelism with Radio, Airplane, Glass-Fronted Baptismal Tank." *Life,* March 27, 1939.
Carpenter, Joel A. "From Fundamentalism to the New Evangelical Coalition." In *Evangelicalism and Modern America,* edited by George M. Marsden, 3–16. Grand Rapids: Eerdmans, 1984.
———. "Fundamentalists Institutions and the Rise of Evangelical Protestantism: 1929–1942." *Church History* 49 (1980) 62–75.
Carter, Guy C. "Walter A. Maier." In *Twentieth-Century Shapers of American Popular Religion,* edited by Charles H. Lippy, 270–77. New York: Greenwood, 1989.
"Cash and Cadle." *Time,* March 11, 1939.
"Catholics Chided on Coughlin Stand." *New York Times,* August 2, 1936.
Clark, David L. "Miracles for a Dime: From Chautauqua Tent to Radio Station with Sister McPherson." *California History* 57 (Winter 1978/79) 354–63.
Clements, William M. "The Rhetoric of the Radio Ministry." *Journal of American Folklore* 87 (October–December 1974) 318–27.
Comstock, Sarah. "McPherson Semple McPherson; Prima Donna of Revivalism." *Harper's Monthly,* December 1927.
Cox, Kenneth. "The FCC, the Constitution, and Religious Broadcast Programming." *George Washington Law Review* 34 (December 1965) 196–218.
Crowe, Charles M. "Religion on the Air." *Christian Century,* August 23, 1944.
Dacre, Douglas. "McPherson Semple McPherson: High Priestess of the Jazz Age." *Macleans,* November 1951.
Daves, Michael. "Bible Belt Broadcasting." *Christian Century,* June 28, 1961.
Davis, Richard A. "Radio Priest: The Public Career of Father Charles Edward Coughlin." PhD diss., University of North Carolina, 1974.
Doherty, Thomas. "Return with Us Now to Those Thrilling Days of Yesteryear: Radio Studies Rise Again." *Chronicle of Higher Education,* May 21, 2004.
Douglas, Mary. "The Effects of Modernization on Religious Change." In *Religion and America: Spiritual Life in a Secular Age,* edited by Mary Douglas and Steven Tipton, 25–42. Boston: Beacon, 1983.
"Dr. W.A. Maier Assails 'Subversive' Trends in Schools." *New York Times,* August 20, 1933.
DuBordieu, W. J. "Religious Broadcasting in the United States." PhD diss., Northwestern University, Evanston, IL, 1933.
Eberstadt, Mary. "How the West Really Lost God: A New Look at Secularization." *Policy Review,* June/July 2007. http://www.hoover.org./publications/policyreview/7827212.html.
"Echoes from Our Radio Audience." *Christian Beacon,* February 13, 1936.
"'Editorializing' is New Radio Issue." *United Evangelical Action,* October 1, 1947.
Edwards, Vincent. "The First Church Broadcast." *Christian Advocate,* November 14, 1968.
Eskridge, Larry K. "Evangelical Broadcasting: Its Meaning for Evangelicals." In *Transforming Faith: The Sacred and Secular in Modern American History,* edited by M. L. Bradbury and James B. Gilbert, 127–39. Westport, CT: Greenwood, 1989.
———. "Only Believe: Paul Rader and the Chicago Gospel Tabernacle." MA thesis, University of Maryland, 1985.

"Evangelical Action! A Report of the Organization of the National Association of Evangelicals for United Action" (1942). In *A New Evangelical Coalition: Early Documents of the National Association of Evangelicals*, edited by Joel A. Carpenter. Fundamentalism in American Religion, 1880–1950. New York: Garland, 1988.

"Extracts from Radio Letters." *World Wide Christian Courier*, September 1926.

"FCC Says Stations May Deny Time to Atheists." *United Evangelical Action*, October 1, 1948.

"FCC Upholds Atheists' Rights to Time on Air." *Broadcasting and Telecasting*, July 22, 1946.

Ferrin, W. H. "Greater Providence: A Great Opportunity." *Radio Caroller Announcer*, April 1929.

Fiske, Edward B. "Harry Emerson Fosdick Dies; Liberal Led Riverside Church." *New York Times*, October 6, 1969.

Fishwick, Marshall W. "Father Coughlin Time: The Radio and Redemption." *Journal of Popular Culture* 22 (1988) 33–47.

Fortner, Robert S. "The Church and the Debate over Radio: 1919–1949." In *Media and Religion in American History*, edited by William David Sloan. Northport, AL: Vision, 2000.

"Free Air for Atheists." *Newsweek*, August 12, 1946.

Gaustad, Edwin Scott. "*Did* the Fundamentalists Win?" In *Religion and America: Spiritual Life in a Secular Age*, edited by Mary Douglas and Steven Tipton, 169–78. Boston: Beacon, 1983.

Goff, Phillip K. "'We Have Heard the Joyful Sound': Charles E. Fuller's Radio Broadcast and the Rise of Modern Evangelicalism." *Religion and American Culture* 9, no. 1 (1999) 67–96.

"The Great Temple Is Dedicated." *Los Angeles Times*, January 2, 1923.

Hangen, Tona. "Fundamentalism's Unseen Victory in the Twenties." In *History in Dispute*, vol. 3, *American Political and Social Movements, 1900–1945: Pursuit of Progress*, edited by Robert Allison, 36–39. Detroit: St. James, 2000.

———. "Man of the Hour: Walter A. Maier and Religion by Radio on the *Lutheran Hour*." In *Radio Reader: Essays in the Cultural History of Radio*, edited Michelle Hilmes and Jason Loviglio, 113–34. New York: Routledge, 2001.

Harding, Susan. "Representing Fundamentalism: The Problem of the Repugnant Cultural Other." *Social Research* 58 (Summer 1991) 373–93.

Hatch, Nathan O. "Evangelicalism as a Democratic Movement." In *Evangelicalism and Modern America*, edited by George M. Marsden, 71–93. Grand Rapids: Eerdmans, 1984.

Hawkins, Karen M. "Diamond Days: Facets from the First 75 Years." *Religious Broadcasting* 28 (January 1996) 12–26.

"Hearing on Senate Bill." *Christian Beacon*, July 3, 1947.

Hood, John L. "The New Old-Time Religion: McPherson Semple McPherson and the Original Electric Church." MA thesis, Wheaton College, 1981.

Hoover, Stewart M., and Douglas K. Warner. "History and Policy in American Broadcast Treatment of Religion." *Media, Culture and Society* 19 (January 1997) 7–27.

"How Big Is Gospel Radio?" *Christian Life*, January 1954.

Hunt, Bill. "Church Big Biz for Radio." *Variety*, December 1, 1943. Reprint: BNM.

Jennings, Ralph M. "Policies and Practices of Selected National Religious Bodies as Related to Broadcasting in the Public Interest, 1920–1950." PhD diss., New York University, 1968.
Johnson, Willard. "Intolerance by Radio." In *Education on the Air: Thirteenth Yearbook of the Institute for Education by Radio*, edited Josephine H. MacLatchy, 233–36. Columbus: Ohio State University Press, 1942.
Kramer, William A. "The Walter A. Maier Study Dedicatory Address, Concordia Historical Institute, May 17, 1981." *Concordia Historical Institute Quarterly* 54 (1981) 98–101.
Lacey, Linda-Jo. "The Electric Church: An FCC 'Established' Institution?" *Federal Communications Law Journal* 31, no. 2 (1978) 252–62.
Lester, Toby. "Oh Gods!" *Atlantic*, February 2002. https://www.theatlantic.com/magazine/archive/2002/02/oh-gods/302412/.
Lewis, Peter M. "Private Passion, Public Neglect: The Cultural Status of Radio." *International Journal of Cultural Studies* 3, no. 2 (2000) 160–67.
Loevinger, Lee. "Religious Liberty and Broadcasting." *George Washington Law Review* 33 (March 1965) 631–59.
Long, Elizabeth. "Textual Interpretation as Collective Action." In *Viewing, Reading, Listening: Audiences and Cultural Reception*, edited by Jon Cruz and Justin Lewis, 181–211. Boulder, CO: Westview, 1994.
Lothrop, Gloria R. "West of Eden: Pioneer Media Evangelist Aimee Semple McPherson in Los Angeles." *Journal of the West* 27 (April 1988) 50–59.
"Lutherans." *Time*, October 18, 1943.
"Maier v. Council." *Time*, April 11, 1938.
Maier, Walter A. "Radio—What Does It Profit?" *The Gospel Voice*, March 1930.
———. "Why Not a Lutheran Broadcasting Station?" *Walther League Messenger* 30–31 (March 1923) 314.
Mander, Mary S. "The Public Debate about Broadcasting in the Twenties: An Interpretive History." *Journal of Broadcasting* 28 (Spring 1984) 167–85.
Marquis, Alice G. "Written on the Wind: The Impact of Radio During the 1930s." *Journal of Contemporary History* 19 (July 1984) 388–405.
Marsden, George M. "Preachers of Paradox: The Religious New Right in Historical Perspective." In *Religion and America: Spiritual Life in a Secular Age*, edited by Mary Douglas and Steven Tipton, 150–68. Boston: Beacon, 1983.
Martin, William. "The God-Hucksters of Radio." *Atlantic*, June 1970.
———. "Mass Communications." In *Experience of the American Religious Experience*, vol. 3, edited by Charles Lippy and Peter W. Williams, 1711–26. New York: Scribner's, 1988.
Marty, Martin E. "The Sacred and Secular in American History." In *Transforming Faith: The Sacred and Secular in Modern American History*, edited by M. L. Bradbury and James B. Gilbert, 1–10. Westport, CT: Greenwood, 1989.
McIntire, Carl. "Radio's New Code." *Christian Beacon*, September 25, 1947.
McLoughlin, William G. "McPherson Semple McPherson: 'Your Sister in the King's Glad Service.'" *Journal of Popular Culture* 1 (Winter 1967) 193–217.
McQuail, Denis. "Mass Media." In *The Social Science Encyclopedia*, 2nd ed., edited by Adam Kuper and Jessica Kuper, 511–12. New York: Routledge, 1996.
McPherson, Aimee Semple. "The Cathedral of the Air: A Radio Fantasy Built about the Angelus Temple, Radio KFSG." *The Bridal Call Foursquare* (June 1924) 2–3.

———. "Premillennial Signal Towers." *The Bridal Call Foursquare* (October 1924) 29.

"McPherson Assails Keyes in Pulpit Talk." *Los Angeles Times*, September 27, 1926.

McWilliams, Carey. "McPherson Semple McPherson: 'Sunlight in My Soul.'" In *The Aspirin Age, 1919–1941*, edited by Isabel Leighton, 50–80. New York: Simon and Schuster, 1949.

Meister, J. W. G. "Presbyterians and Mass Media: A Case of Blurred Vision and Missed Mission." In *The Diversity of Discipleship: The Presbyterians and Twentieth-Century Christian Witness*, edited Milton J. Coalter et al., 170–86. Louisville: Westminster, 1991.

Mencken, Henry L. "Two Enterprising Ladies." *American Mercury*, April 1928.

Miller, Spencer. "Radio and Religion." *Annals of the American Academy of Political and Social Science* 177 (January 1935) 27–39.

"Minneapolis Pastors Protesting Radio Ban." *United Evangelical Action*, July 1, 1946.

Minsky, Louis. "Religious Broadcasts: Report of a Work-Study Group." In *Education on the Air: Thirteenth Yearbook of the Institute for Education by Radio*, edited by Josephine H. MacLatchy, 243–56. Columbus: Ohio State University Press, 1942.

Mitchell, Jolyon. "Radio Religion: Radio Preachers in the USA: An Analysis of the Pictorial Language Used by Selected American Radio Preachers Broadcasting in a Visual Culture." Paper presented at the Conference on Media, Religion, and Culture, University of Colorado, Boulder, Colorado, 1996.

Monaghan, Peter. "Exploring Radio's Sociocultural Legacy." *Chronicle of Higher Education*, February 19, 1999.

Moores, Sean. "The Box on the Dresser: Memories of Early Radio and Everyday Life." *Media, Culture and Society* 1 (1988) 23–40.

Morley, David. "Changing Paradigms in Audience Research." In *Remote Control: Television, Audiences, and Cultural Power*, edited by Ellen Seiter et al., 16–43. London: Routledge, 1989.

"Move Toward FCCCA Super Radio Control." *United Evangelical Action*, April 1, 1948, 14.

"Mr. Bennet's Brief Presented to Senate Committee." *Christian Beacon*, July 3, 1947.

"Mr. McIntire's Testimony before the Senate Committee." *Christian Beacon*, July 3, 1947.

"Mrs. Roosevelt Attacks Lutheran Hour Preacher." *United Evangelical Action* 8 (October 1, 1949) 12.

"NAB Adopts Religious Broadcasting Standards." *United Evangelical Action*, April 1, 1948, 14.

Neeb, Martin J. "An Historical Study of American Non-commercial AM Broadcast Stations Owned and Operated by Religious Groups, 1920–1966." PhD diss., Northwestern University, 1967.

"New NAB Code Bars Attacks on Religion." *United Evangelical Action*, October 1, 1947, 9.

"New Organization in Religious Radio." *United Evangelical Action*, June 1, 1946.

Orbison, Charley. "Fighting Bob Shuler: Early Radio Crusader." *Journal of Broadcasting* 21 (Fall 1977) 459–72.

Parker, Everett C. "Big Business in Religious Radio." *Chicago Theological Seminary Register*, Winter 1944.

Parker, Everett C. and Fred Eastman. "Religion on the Air in Chicago: A Study of Religious Programs on the Commercial Radio Stations of Chicago." *Chicago Theological Seminary Registrar* 22, no. 1 (January 1942) 12–22.

"Presbyterians Move against Dr. Fosdick: Philadelphia Churchmen Complain of His Sermons in the First Church Here." *New York Times*, October 18, 1922.

"Professor Maier Sees War on Faith Like That in Russia." *New York Times*, August 6, 1930.

"Pulpit Assails Dr. Fosdick: Accuses Presbyterian of Deserting the Bible and Rejecting Vital Doctrines." *New York Times*, September 25, 1922.

Rader, Paul. "What About a Radio Church?" *World-Wide Christian Courier* (July 1926) 14–15.

"Radio Disciple Angers Wife." *Los Angeles Times*, July 14, 1926.

"Radio Ranger Watch Tower." *National Radio Chapel Announcer*, December 1925.

"Religious Radio: 1921–1971." *Christianity Today*, January 1, 1971.

"Religious Showmanship Feud: Sermons 'Waste of Good Time.'" *Variety*, August 20, 1947.

Saunders, Lowell S. "The National Religious Broadcasters and the Availability of Commercial Radio Time." PhD diss., University of Illinois, 1968.

Schneider, Robert A. "Voice of Many Waters: Church Federation in the Twentieth Century." In *Between the Times: The Travail of the Protestant Establishment, 1900–1960*, edited by William R. Hutchinson, 95–121. New York: Cambridge University Press, 1989.

Schultze, Quentin J. "Evangelical Radio and the Rise of the Electronic Church, 1921–1948." *Journal of Broadcasting and Electronic Media* 32 (Summer 1988) 289–306.

———. "The Invisible Medium: Evangelical Radio." In *American Evangelicals and the Mass Media: Perspectives on the Relationship between American Evangelicals and the Mass Media*, edited by Quentin J. Schultze, 171–95. Grand Rapids: Academie, 1990.

———. "The Mythos of the Electronic Church." *Critical Studies in Mass Communication* 4 (1987) 245–61.

Schwarzlose, Richard A. "Technology and the Individual: The Impact of Innovation on Communication." In *Mass Media between the Wars: Perceptions of Cultural Tensions, 1918–1941*, edited by Catherine L. Covert and John D. Stevens, 87–106. Syracuse, NY: Syracuse University Press, 1984.

"The Scramble for Radio-TV." *Christianity Today*, February 18, 1957.

Shanks, Kenneth H. "An Historical and Critical Study of the Preaching Career of Aimee Semple McPherson." PhD diss., University of Southern California, 1960.

Singleton, Gregory H. "Popular Culture or the Culture of the Populace?" *Journal of Popular Culture* 2 (Summer 1977) 254–65.

Smythe, Dallas W. "The Meaning of the Communications Revolution." *Social Action* 23 (April 1958) 16–23.

Stegner, Wallace. "The Radio Priest and His Flock." In *The Aspirin Age, 1919–1941*, edited by Isabel Leighton, 232–57. New York: Simon and Schuster, 1949.

Stevens, John D. "Small Town Editors and the 'Modernized' Agrarian Myth." In *Mass Media between the Wars: Perceptions of Cultural Tensions, 1918–1941*, edited by Catherine L. Covert and John D. Stevens, 21–38. Syracuse, NY: Syracuse University Press, 1984.

Susman, Warren. "Communication and Culture: Keynote Essay." In *Mass Media between the Wars: Perceptions of Cultural Tensions, 1918–1941*, edited by Catherine L. Covert and John D. Stevens, xvii–xxxii. Syracuse, NY: Syracuse University Press, 1984.

Sweet, Leonard I. "Communication and Change in American Religious History: A Historiographical Probe." In *Communication and Change in American Religious History*, edited by Leonard I. Sweet, 1–90. Grand Rapids: Eerdmans, 1993.

"Tabernacle Fights for Its Broadcasting Rights." *United Evangelical Action*, April 15, 1946.

"Thousands at Aimee Rites: Evangelist Laid to Rest After Temple Services Attended by Throngs." *Los Angeles Times*, October 10, 1944.

"Throngs Hear Fast Plea." *Los Angeles Times*, September 23, 1926.

"Time for Atheism." *Time*, December 2, 1946.

Tomaselli, Keyan G., and Arnold Shepperson. "Resistance through Mediated Orality." In *Rethinking Media, Religion and Culture*, edited by Stewart M. Hoover and Knut Lundby, 209-26. Thousand Oaks, CA: Sage, 1997.

"Tuning In: The Story of a Convalescent Girl Who 'Tuned In' and Found Happiness." *National Radio Chapel Announcer*, December 1925.

"Twisting the Devil's Tail." *Time*, March 16, 1953.

"United We Stand: A Report of the Constitutional Convention of the National Association of Evangelicals, May 3-6, 1943" (1943). In *A New Evangelical Coalition: Early Documents of the National Association of Evangelicals*, edited by Joel A. Carpenter. New York: Garland, 1988.

Van Kirk, Walter W. "The Duty of Religious Radio in Time of War." In *Education on the Air: Thirteenth Yearbook of the Institute for Education by Radio*, edited by Josephine H. MacLatchy, 223-28. Columbus: Ohio State University Press, 1942.

Voskuil, Dennis N. "The Power of the Air: Evangelicals and the Rise of Religious Broadcasting." In *American Evangelicals and the Mass Media*, edited by Quentin J. Schultze, 69-95. Grand Rapids: Zondervan, 1990.

———. "Reaching Out: Mainline Protestantism and the Media." In *Between the Times: The Travail of the Protestant Establishment in America, 1900-1960*, edited by William R. Hutchison, 72-92. Cambridge: Cambridge University Press, 1989.

Wacker, Grant. "Travail of a Broken Family: Evangelical Responses to Pentecostalism." *Journal of Ecclesiastical History* 47 (July 1996) 505-28.

Walton, Alfred G. "Reconsider Religious Radio!" *Christian Century*, September 10, 1947.

Warner, R. Stephen. "Work in Progress toward a New Paradigm for the Sociological Study of Religion in the United States." *American Journal of Sociology* 98 (1993) 1044-93.

"White Asks Shelving for His Radio Bill." *New York Times*, June 28, 1947.

"Witnesses Score White's Radio Bill." *New York Times*, June 26, 1947.

Wright, J. Elwin. "Radio Freedom of Speech." *United Evangelical Action*, September 1, 1946.

———. "Radio Problems Reviewed." *United Evangelical Action*, August 1, 1942.

Yamane, David. "Secularization on Trial: In Defense of a Neosecularization Paradigm." *Journal of the Scientific Study of Religion* 36, no. 1 (1997) 109-22.

Young, Lloyd E. "Gospel Broadcasters and Frequency Modulation." *United Evangelical Action*, March 1, 1947.

Archives

Billy Graham Center. Archives. Wheaton, IL: Wheaton College.
Charles Coughlin Collection. South Bend, IN: University of Notre Dame Archives.
Charles Coughlin Papers. Royal Oak, MI: Archdiocese of Detroit.

Charles Coughlin Papers. Shrine of the Little Flower. Royal Oak, MI: University of Detroit Mercy.
Charles E. Fuller and Grace Payton Fuller Papers. DuPlessis Center Archives. Pasadena, CA: Fuller Theological Seminary.
Collection of the National Religious Broadcasters. Manassas, VA.
Collection of the Ockenga Institute. Hamilton, MA: Gordon-Conwell Theological Seminary.
Federal Radio Commission Records. Suitland, MD: Federal Records Center.
The Foursquare Heritage Center. Aimee Semple McPherson Papers. Los Angeles, CA.
The Harry Emerson Fosdick Collection. Burke Theological Library. New York: Union Theological Seminary.
Institute for Education by Radio/TV Collection. Columbus: Ohio State University.
Presbyterian Church USA, Department of History. Records of the National Council of Churches and Federal Council of Churches. Philadelphia: Presbyterian Church USA.
The Walter A. Maier Papers. St. Louis: Concordia Historical Institute.

Index

absolute right and wrong, Maier's belief in, 102
African American church, relationship to radio, 12n40
Alexander, Charles, 113
"Almost" radio sermon, by Fosdick, 30–31
almosts of life, power to overcome, 31
"altered landscape," American thinking about the Bible as, 8
Amara, Roy, 142n8
"America, Return to God!" sermon (Maier), 92
American culture. *See also* culture
    American Protestantism as a creature of, 22n21
    McPherson tapping into the populist impulse in, 58
    Old Fashioned Revival Hour maintained religion in, 108
    populist ethos in, 10
    secularization of, 1–2, 14–15, 139
    uncritical acceptance of technology, 141
American family, Maier on the state of, 101
American Presbyterian Church, fundamentalist-modernist controversy, 17–19
American Protestantism
    as a creature of American culture, 22n21
    Lutherans ready to compromise with, 79
American Protestantism (Hudson), 21n21
Angelus Temple
    completion of, 58
    denominational composition of, 62
    hearers came along to, 68
    McPherson at dedication services for, 58n51
    McPherson extended her ministry far beyond, 63
    McPherson pastor of, 42
antimodernist dispensationalist, Fuller as, 131
antiwar position, of Fosdick, 33–36
Apostles' Creed, second article of, 91
applause, McPherson's love for, 46
appreciation
    for Fosdick, 37–38
    for Fuller, 132–35
Asbury, Francis, 61
atheism
    Maier's warnings about, 92
    of McPherson as temporary, 47
Atwood, Rudy, 121, 126

164 INDEX

audience
  of Charles Fuller around the world, 107
  difficult to gather on the internet, 141
  direct hold of Maier on, 103
  of Fosdick's radio ministry, 39
  giving to the *Old Fashioned Revival Hour*, 134
  of the *Lutheran Hour*, 96
audience-centered preaching, of Fosdick, 12
Augsburg Confession, 85
Azusa Street Revival, 48n25, 56–57, 71

Baessler, Rose, 132n80
baptismal services, on KFSG, 67
Baptist heritage, of Fosdick, 20
Baptizer with the Holy Spirit, Jesus as, 70–71
Barnhouse, Donald Grey, 3
Barnouw, Erik, 2, 4, 115n25
battlefield songs, 124, 125
Beecher, Henry Ward, 8
Berger, Peter, 3, 6, 139
Bible
  centrality of to Maier, 102
  clear affirmation of as the word of God, 80
  as definitive revelation from God, 8
  Fosdick not believing everything in, 22
  Maier's understanding of the uniqueness of, 87–88
  "simple truths" of, 107
Bible Institute of Los Angeles (Biola), 3, 111, 117, 117n37
Bible institutes, listing of fundamentalist, 111
Bible Study Hour weekly, 3
biblical Christianity, Maier's support of, 83
biblical interpretation methods, used by Fuller, 128
biblical prophecy, Fuller's interest in, 113
biographies, orienting cultural history around, 11n38

birth narrative, of McPherson, 44
"Blessed Holy Spirit, the Comforter," McPherson's experience of, 50
blood of Christ, McPherson's experience of, 49
Blumhofer, Edith, 13, 43, 60, 62
Bonnell, John Sutherland, 38–39
Book of Concord, 78, 80
The Bridal Call, program guide for KFSG, 67–68
Bridal Call Foursquare newsletter, 41–42, 42n3, 63
Briggs, Charles, 25
"Bringing Christ to the Nations-and the Nations to the Church," of the Lutheran Layman's League, 81, 81n9
broadcast media, constraints of, 139
Brown, Francis, 25
Bruce, Steve, 5
Bryan, William Jennings, 18n5

Cadman, S. Parkes, began the *National Radio Pulpit*, 9
call to decision, McPherson focused her energies on, 54
Calvary Church, Fuller and, 113, 116, 118
"Calvary Church Radio Bible Class" program, from the KGER studios, 118
Carpenter, Joel, 111, 112, 122
Carter, Guy, 82
"Cathedral of the Air," 64, 76
"The Cathedral of the Air" poem (McPherson), 63
CBS. *See* Columbia Broadcasting System (CBS)
celebrity
  Fuller as, 136, 138
  McPherson as, 53, 69, 70
  religious radio movement toward, 9–10
Chafer, Lewis Sperry, 129n71
character, 29, 30, 31
charisma, successful radio required, 140

INDEX 165

charismatic ecumenism, of
    McPherson, 58, 72
Chicago Stadium, Maier filling, 99–100
Chicago Tabernacle radio broadcasts,
    music of, 14n44
childhood home, Fosdick's memory of
    his, 20
childhood sings, of Fuller, 114
children
    Christ-centered home as the best
        hope for, 91–92
    Maier singled out as forsaking
        their mothers, 101–2
"chosen one," McPherson as, 44
Christ. *See also* Jesus Christ
    coming to for salvation, 127
    deity of, 89–90
    Fuller mentioning the cross of,
        127–28
    human substituting for the divine
        Savior, 90
    imminent return of, 72
    liberal theologians on, 89
    McPherson's experience of the
        blood of, 49
    return of as near, 131–32
    second coming of, 17, 66
Christ-centered experience,
    McPherson emphasizing, 62
"Christ-conscious family," Maier
    commended, 91
Christian gospel, McPherson's
    packaging of, 54
Christian ministry, Fosdick entering,
    24
Christian programming, McPherson's
    station as the first dedicated
    to, 64
Christian superstar, making of
    McPherson as, 43–50
Christianity
    addressing the breakdown of
        morality, 91
    classic, 78
    conservative, 130
    creedal, 18
    evangelism as for Fuller, 127, 128
    Fosdick's efforts to reform, 20
    Fuller's interpretation of, 108,
        112–13
    Lutheranism as authentic, 94
    McPherson's early exposure to,
        45n12
    nostalgic, 125
    packaging in simple revivalist
        themes, 70
    producing living above the average,
        29
    progressive, 21, 23
    relationship with modernity, 17
    salvation in Fosdick's moralistic
        version of, 30
    simple, 104
    "superior type of living" as the
        central task of, 29
    theological modernism making
        less accessible, 62
    thinking of in terms of a "mood"
        or "feeling," 62
Christology, songs not including any
    clear, 123–24
the church, in a digital age, 139–42,
    142n8
church attendance, broadcast sermons
    increasing, 83
church leaders, embraced radio during
    the 1920s, 2
"The Church Must Go Beyond
    Modernism" sermon, by
    Fosdick, 39
Church of the Open Door, in Los
    Angeles, 110
church service, first regular radio
    broadcast of a, 2
churches, moral decline of, 129
city of strangers, Los Angeles as, 55
City upon a Hill (Witham), 140n2
Clarke, William Newton, 23, 24
classic Christianity, reassertion of, 78
"classic nonconformist," McPherson
    as, 55
"closed religion," 31
Colgate University, attended by
    Fosdick, 21
Columbia Broadcasting Company
    (CBS), 3

166 INDEX

Columbia Broadcasting System (CBS), 84, 85, 117
"Come Just As You Are" song, 123
coming to Jesus, for salvation, 130
commitment to service, Fosdick's life as, 16n1
commoditization of the faith, radio contributed to, 10
common decency, without conscious recognition of God, 30
communism, Maier's warnings about, 92
competition, McPherson always strove to outdo, 42
Concordia Collegiate Institute, Maier began serious study of Latin and Greek and German, 81
"conditions of belief," understanding secularization in terms of, 6n18
conservative audience, attracted by Maier, 82
conservative Christianity, defined by the evangelistic task, 130
conservative radio preachers, transformed American religion, 9
conservative religion, on television, 14
conversion
    conservative Protestantism's concern for, 126
    experiences of listeners, 74, 132n80–33n80
    letters telling stories of, 132, 132n80–33n80, 133
    of McPherson, 47–48, 47n24, 49
correspondence. *See also* letters
    commending Maier's orthodoxy in primary sources, 98n64
    estimating audience size of the *Lutheran Hour*, 96
    flooded the *Lutheran Hour* with testimonials, 96–98
    sent to the *Old Fashioned Revival Hour*, 132
Coughlin, Father Charles, 33n57, 35, 85n24, 86n25, 86n26
creedal Christianity, Fosdick and, 16n1, 18
critical responses, to the *Old Fashioned Revival Hour*, 135–36
cross of Christ, 90, 127–28
Crusaders for Christ, young people as, 67
culture, 129, 131. *See also* American culture; religious culture; world cliché culture

Darwinism, McPherson's opposition to, 46–47
"the dean of all ministers of the air," Fosdick as, 27
death of God, coming with modernization, 6
Defenders of the Christian Faith Conference, Fuller's broadcast at, 115–16
deity of Christ, Maier defended, 89–90
delivery, of Fuller, 136
democracy, war as the greatest single enemy of, 34
democratization, of religion, 9–10
Democratization of American Christianity (Hatch), 10n34
Dennis, Mrs. Anna, 127n67
devil. *See also* Satan
    using radio for his own purposes, 66
digital age, the church in, 139–42
dispensational premillennialism, theological system of, 129
dispensationalism, 108n6, 111, 112, 130
Divine Healing service, on KFSG, 67–68
divine power, message of, 61
doctrinal differences, ignored by Fuller, 121
doctrinal formation, songs and, 123–24
doctrinal minimalism
    of Fuller exceeded Maier's, 120
    of McPherson, 41, 75
doctrinal orthodoxy, of the Missouri Synod, 80
doctrinal system, of McPherson as "unitive," 59

domestic terms, McPherson's appeal
    described in, 59
domesticity, McPherson's mother
    "caught in the devil's net" of, 43
donations, *Lutheran Hour* depended
    on, 78
Douglas, Susan, 4, 4n7
dramatic gospel presentations, of
    McPherson, 46
Durham, William, 48n25

Eade, Thomas, 69
earthquake, in Long Beach in 1933,
    118
"The Eastern Gate" song, 124
economic reconstruction, Fosdick
    emphasized, 34–35
ecumenism, of McPherson, 53
education, modern philosophy of for
    Maier, 93
electric technology, Fuller's childhood
    interest in, 114
electronic media, retribalizing
    mankind, 9
"elemental human problems," Fosdick
    focusing on, 29
"emotional disillusionment," 30
"Empty Pitchers" (McPherson), 73
Englehart, Ronald, 6
Enlightenment, "secularization theory"
    traced to, 5
entertainment
    combined with Bible teaching
        employed by Fuller, 119
    McPherson helped transform
        religion into, 13, 69, 70
    McPherson's revival meetings as
        spectacles of, 69
entertainment arts, McPherson
    experimenting with as a
    teenager, 46
essential truths, remaining constant for
    Maier, 93–94
Evangelical Lutheran Church, 80
evangelical Protestantism, 7, 14, 137,
    140
evangelical religion, *Lutheran Hour*
    and, 105

evangelical scholarship, on the relation
    between technology and
    religion, 141–42
evangelicalism, 14, 106, 108, 123
evangelicals, 121, 132, 141
evangelism
    Charles Fuller's ministry defining
        American religion in terms
        of, 106
    Fuller became deeply committed to
        at Biola, 112
    Fuller came of age when radio was
        beginning, 115
    Fuller defining Christianity in
        terms of, 128
    Fuller's emphasis on, 126–27
    Fuller's growing zeal for, 112n19
    Fuller's ministry defining
        American religion in terms
        of, 137
    as priority for Fuller, 107n2
evangelist, making of Fuller as, 108–10
evangelistic ministry, McPherson's
    sense of call to, 51
evangelistic skills, McPherson honing,
    52
everyman's preacher, Fosdick as, 37
evil forces of darkness, McPherson
    depicting, 67
evils, of modernism, 93
evolutionary biology, McPherson
    confronting, 46–47
exceptionalism, McPherson's personal
    lens of, 46
excommunication, used by Fosdick, 36
experience, Christian thinking starting
    with, 26
experience of God, McPherson's, 50
experience of the divine, as
    confirmation of McPherson's
    birth, 44
experiential approach to religion, 25,
    54
experiential moralism, 30
experiential religion, 43, 50
experientialist faith, of McPherson, 52
Ezekiel, vision of, 59–60

168 INDEX

faces, perceived by Ezekiel, 60
facets, of McPherson's theology, 59
fame, of McPherson, 65, 74–75
families, Maier's emphasis on
  strengthening, 13
family devotions, held in Fuller's
  family, 109
Federal Council of the Churches of
  Christ in America, 2–3, 12, 26,
  36–37
fellowship, granting to other
  Christians, 80
Fessenden, Reginald A., 1
"The Fight Is On" song, 124–25
"Fighting Rebel," Fosdick as, 16n1
"The Finished Work" doctrine, of
  Durham, 48n25
Finke, Roger, 7–8
First Presbyterian Church, Fosdick
  resigned from, 18
Fiske, Edward, 39
"Five Sectors of the Peace Movement,"
  sermon by Fosdick, 33
"flamboyant oratory," of Maier, 102
folk geniuses, American religious
  leaders as, 10n34
"For God so loved the world, that He
  gave His only begotten Son,"
  first words on radio station
  KFSG, 64
Fosdick, Amie Weaver, 20
Fosdick, Harry Emerson, 16–40
  birth and death of, 19
  compared to Maier, 91
  death of, 39
  declined invitation to become a
    Presbyterian minister, 18
  given sustaining (i.e., free) airtime,
    26
  "gloried in ambiguity and
    sentiment," 8
  listener imploring Maier to be
    more like, 98
  movement away from Protestant
    orthodoxy, 12
  on *National Vespers*, 9
  possible link to Maier, 85n24
  preached simple virtues, 4, 140
  retirement of, 38–39
  ways to view the life of, 16n1
*Founding Fathers and the Place of
  Religion in America* (Lambert),
  10n35
foursquare fundamentalism, of
  McPherson, 78
Foursquare Gospel, 42, 58–62, 70, 76
Foursquare Gospel (McPherson), 61n65
Frame, James Everett, 25
"free marketplace of religion,"
  emergence of, 10n35
"From Nineveh to Tarshish and Back,"
  as the period of McPherson's
  marriage to Harold, 52
"full gospel evangelism," of Angelus
  Temple, 62
Fuller, Charles E., 106–38
  began broadcasting in 1924, 115
  birth of, 108
  compared to Maier, 13
  decided to serve God, 110
  decision to pursue a regular radio
    ministry, 116
  defined American religion in terms
    of evangelism, 13–14, 106
  described what was obvious to
    millions, 131
  distanced himself from militant
    fundamentalism, 4, 140
  evoked nostalgic religious feelings, 9
  interpretation of Christianity, 108
  simple songs chosen by, 73
  simplified the Christian message,
    140
  trained young people to be
    preachers, 107n2
Fuller, Daniel
  to attend Dallas Theological
    Seminary, 129n71
  on Charles Fuller being at odds with
    Placentia Presbyterian, 113
  on Charles Fuller never content to
    simply be a pastor, 118
  on Charles Fuller studying debate
    and Grace training at the
    Cumnock School, 110

INDEX 169

on childhood sings of Charles
    Fuller, 114
Fuller, Grace, 110, 110n10, 121
Fuller, Henry and Helen Day, 108
Fuller Theological Seminary, 106–7,
    129n71
Fuller's Fancy Oranges, 108
"fundamental Christian," Fuller as, 124
fundamentalism
    Charles Fuller distanced himself
        from militant, 4, 140
    concerns of promoted by Maier, 82
    foursquare of Aimee Semple
        McPherson compared to
        Maier's accessible orthodoxy, 78
    listener bemoaned Maier's, 99
    Maier's identification with, 83
    popularity of Bible institutes
        within, 112
    radio served Fosdick's campaign
        against, 26
fundamentalist Christianity, of Fuller,
    112–13
fundamentalist radio, flourishing of, 3
fundamentalist response, to Fosdick, 17
fundamentalist-modernist controversy,
    11, 17–19, 62, 85, 126
fundamentalists
    on the Bible, 88
    debates between separatist and
        constructive, 120–21
    dispensationalism's appeal among,
        130n76
    Fosdick strove against, 19, 27–28, 39
    Maier as, 101
    McPherson, Maier, and Fuller seen
        as, 17
    reactions to Fosdick, 28
    transforming the religious
        landscape, 107–8
funeral, of McPherson, 74–75

Gaebelein, Arno C., 111
"gift of tongues," at Azusa Street, 57
global reach
    Maier's desire for, 82
    of McPherson's broadcasts, 74
    of radio, 63

God
    affirmation of as Trinity for Maier,
        89
    of Glory, Jesus Christ as, 90
    goodness without, 29–30
    McPherson as the chosen
        instrument of, 60
    rejection of as most fatal weakness,
        102
    as still on the throne for Fuller, 130
Goff, Philip, 109n7, 120–21, 134n88
Golden Age of Crackpotism, in Los
    Angeles, 55
Golden Age of radio, 40, 140
"good old Gospel" radio, of Fuller, 107
"good old religion," people hungry
    for, 94
Goodman, Frank C., 27
goodness, without God, 29–30
gospel broadcasting, McPherson's
    description of, 66
Gospel Broadcasting Association,
    107n3, 119
"Gospel Car," of McPherson, 52
gospel of Jesus Christ, as the issue for
    Maier, 86
gospel songs, 14n44, 73, 113, 122
gospel temple, McPherson began
    planning, 54
Gough, Betty, 27, 37
Great Tribulation, 112
Green, H. Leland, 121, 126

Hangen, Tona, 52, 69, 115n25
Hannah, McPherson's mother reading
    the story of, 44
"Happy Hour," of special music,
    117n35
Harkness, Robert, 113
Harnack, Adolf von, 25
Harry Emerson Fosdick (Miller), 16n1
Hart, Darryl G., 130n76, 131–32
Harvard University, Maier as a student
    and professor, 100–101
Hatch, Nathan, 10
healer, Jesus as for McPherson, 71
healing, role in McPherson's ministry,
    53–54

Heart to Heart Talk newsletter, 127, 129–30, 134
"Heavenly Sunshine" (song), 122–23
Hebrews 13:8, as a key text for McPherson, 61
hell-fire-and-brimstone preaching, effect upon Fosdick as a child, 21
here and now, Fosdick emphasizing, 30, 31
History of Broadcasting in the United States (Barnouw), 4
Hitler, Fosdick depicting, 34
holiness, Christians attaining, 61
holiness movement, Seymour advocated, 57
Hollywood, McPherson employed methods of, 43
Hollywood morality, Maier's warnings about, 92–93
"Holy Ghost Revival," led by Robert Semple, 48
Hoover, Herbert, as Secretary of Commerce, 66–67
Horton, Thomas, 113
"the house that God built," for McPherson, 53
human achievement, Fosdick's emphasis on, 31
human Christ, substituting for the divine Savior, 90
Hutchinson, Anne, 9

identity, American Protestantism's loss of, 22n21
"illustrated sermons," performed by McPherson, 69
"I'm a Pilgrim" song, 124
Immanuel Missionary Fund, of Henry Fuller, 109
immigration, impact on America, 20
individualism, transforming into collectivism, 9
inerrancy, 17, 88
inspiration, of the Bible, 88
intellectual credibility of Christian faith, Fosdick's struggle with, 22, 23–24

"international collective security," Fosdick on, 35–36
internet, 14, 141

Jesse James of the theological world, Fosdick as, 16n1
Jesus Christ. *See also* Christ
  forgiveness found in, 95
  as God of glory, 90
  gospel of for Maier, 86
  and a Holy Spirit as reality, 48
  imminent return of, 129
  phases of His ministry, 59
  as the same yesterday and today and forever, 61
  as Son of the living God, 90
  songs portraying, 123
  starting with life itself, 32–33
  as the ultimate example, 30
Jesus Is Coming (Blackstone), 111
"Jesus Saves" theme song, of the *Old Fashioned Revival Hour*, 121, 122
Jonah, in the Old Testament, 51

KDKA radio station, in Pittsburg, Pennsylvania, 2
Kennedy, James and Mildred "Minnie," 44
KFSG (Kall Foursquare Gospel) radio station, 63–75
  at the center of a failing marriage, 74n98
  as "the first totally religious station," 42
  number of listeners turning in to, 74n99
  operational costs annually, 42n3
  supported by its listeners, 64n73
  variety of Christian programming, 67
KFUO radio station, on the campus of Concordia Seminary, 85
KGER radio station, population covered, 117
"kingdom of God," promoting the expansion of, 80
Knox, George William, 25

INDEX   171

Kramer, William, 104
KREG radio station, 116, 117
Kyng, Morten, 142n8

"latter rain," 60
legalistic and terrifying religion,
    Fosdick against, 21
letters. *See also* correspondence
    to the Gospel Broadcasting
        Association offices, 132
    sent to Fosdick, 27, 37–38
    sent to Maier, 91
liberal, progressive Christianity, 21
liberal faith, of Fosdick, 40
liberal theologians, acknowledging
    only Christ's humanity, 89
liberalism, 24n28, 108
"Life Begins at Foursquare," sermon
    broadcast in 1939, 70
liquor, drinking of increasing, 129–30
listeners
    appreciated Fuller's old-time
        religion, 133
    instant gratification from, 117n35
    Maier replying to critical, 99n65
    Maier's practical advice to, 91
*Listening In: Radio and the American
    Imagination* (Douglas), 4
living
    above the average, 29
    religion about for Fosdick, 33
Long Beach Municipal Auditorium,
    14, 136n95, 138
"Look Away to Heaven" song, 124
"Lord, I'm Coming Home" song, 124
Los Angeles
    Church of the Open Door in, 110
    McPherson decided to put down
        roots in, 54–55
Luther, Martin, 90–91
Lutheran Church-Missouri Synod,
    79, 80
Lutheran Hour
    on America's supreme need, 86
    broadcasting "the infallible truths
        of Scripture," 88
    commitment to a simple Protestant
        orthodoxy, 78, 93

    global reach of, 120
    as a great missionary offensive,
        77–78
    growth of under Maier's leadership,
        96, 97
    keeping financially viable, 104
    listeners responding with criticism,
        98–99
    positioned firmly against
        modernism, 87
    premiere broadcast of, 85
    range of subjects covered on, 94
    story of Maier and, 13
Lutheran Laymen's League, 81n9,
    84–85, 104
Lutheranism
    as "authentic Christianity," 94
    Maier's audience transcending,
        94–104
    Maier's broadcast did not promote,
        79, 82
    Maier's reach beyond as
        intentional, 94
    as orthodoxy for Maier, 13, 77,
        87, 91

Macartney, Clarence Edward, 18, 18n5
Machen, J. Gresham, 17, 18n5
Madness of Crowds (Murray), 142n8
Maier, Anna, 80–81
Maier, Emil William, 80
Maier, Paul, 78
Maier, Walter, 77–105
    birth of, 80
    combination of Protestant
        orthodoxy and evangelical
        appeal, 78–79
    education of, 81
    forsook Lutheran particulars, 4,
        140
    like a Fourth of July orator of the
        old school, 102
    movement toward a simple
        orthodoxy, 13
    as radio preacher in the 1920s, 3
    uniqueness of, 96–97
    wanted to help people fare better in
        this life, 91

INDEX

mainline denominations, disdained fundamentalist radio preachers, 135
Mainline Protestants
   McPherson tapped into popular piety in, 57
   secured free time (sustaining time), 2–3
Marconi, Guglielmo, 1
marriage, Christ-conscious family esteeming, 91
Marsden, George, 129, 129n71
mass marketing tools, McPherson using, 52
mass media, McPherson's adoption of, 47
masses, reaching, 136, 140
Matthews, Mark A., 18n5
McGiffert, Arthur Cushman, 25
McLuhan, Marshall, 9
McPherson, Aimee Semple
   accused of having an affair and staging a kidnapping, 68
   adult ministry of, 43, 45
   agreed to reenter vocational ministry on her deathbed, 51
   compared to Fuller, 136
   compared to Maier, 13, 91
   compassion for the lost souls of the world, 63
   conducted her own Salvation Army meetings as a child, 45–46
   created an entire radio station, Kall Foursquare Gospel (KFSG), 42
   credited her early exposure to Christianity to her mother, 45n12
   death of, 74
   equated efforts to abandon her call with the disobedience of Jonah, 51
   evoked nostalgic religious feelings, 9
   "finished work" view of sanctification, 48n25
   left her husband Harold, 52
   may have found television success, 140n2
   ministry of, 41–76
   movement toward an experiential religion, 12
   promoted charismatic ecumenism, 4, 140
   as radio preacher in the 1920s, 3
   redefining herself in the face of relentless hostility, 68
   return to classic Pentecostalism, 48n25
   sensationalism of, 10
   set apart for sacred purposes, 44n9
   spiritual experience by the deathbed of Robert Semple, 50
McPherson, Harold, 51–52
McPherson, Rolf, 52, 74
media, Walter Maier's radio ministry not lost on, 99
medium of print, launching the medium of radio, 42n3
Mencken, Henry L., 135
Messenger, monthly publication of the Walther League, 81, 83
Methodism, McPherson's childhood exposure to, 44–45
methodology, of this book, 11–15
Meyer, Carl, 79
Miller, Robert Moats, 19, 27
Milligan, Don, 118
ministerial work, Fosdick's commitment to, 24
ministry
   example of his parents led Maier to pursue, 80–81
   McPherson's call to, 51–54
ministry career, of Maier, 81
Missouri Synod, 79, 80
modern life, secular assumptions as axiomatic, 9
modern thinking, categories of, 23
modernism
   as an enemy for Maier, 87
   evils of, 93
   Maier's stance against, 84
   making Christianity less accessible, 62
   simple Protestant orthodoxy as an alternative to, 78
Modernism's Moses, Fosdick as, 17, 38

INDEX 173

modernist, making of Fosdick as a, 19–26
modernist gospel, doing battle against the enemies of, 39
modernity
    Christianity's relationship with, 17
    Lutheran Hour against any compromise with, 85
    Maier and McPherson decrying aspects of, 13
    McPherson exposed to as a teenager, 46
    not as antagonistic to religion as had previously been asserted, 6–7
    undermining the old certainties, 7
modernization, causing society to become less religious, 5
money, solicited by McPherson during broadcasts, 68
mood, of McPherson's ministry, 62
Moody Bible Institute, established a radio station, 3
the moral, as much more than the doctrinal, 25–26
moral decline, as the norm, 131
moral foundation, technology creating a culture without, 141
moral looseness, increasing, 130
moral standards, Maier perceived as crumbling, 101
morality, addressing the breakdown of, 91
Morse code, Charles Fuller learning as a boy, 114
mother, of McPherson served as Junior Sergeant-Major in the Salvation Army, 45
movement leader, Fuller as, 14
moving pictures, captured by Satan according to McPherson, 66
Murch, James DeForest, 108
music. *See also* songs
    broadcast over KFSG, 72–73
    designed to evoke feelings of nostalgia, 122
    of the *Old Fashioned Revival Hour*, 14

Mutual Broadcasting System, 119, 120, 134n88
"My Home, Sweet Home" song, 124

nation, prosperity of for Maier, 92
National Association of Evangelicals, 3, 14, 121
National Broadcasting Company (NBC), 3, 26, 84
national periodicals, commemorated McPherson's death, 75
National Radio Pulpit, 9
National Religious Broadcasters, 14, 121
National Vespers Hour, 16–40
    broadcast of, 12
    described, 26–39
    Fosdick's radio career on, 9, 16n1
natural man, 131
neglect of God, as the reason for sins, 102
"new" evangelicalism, Fuller epitomized, 137
New Testament, 61n66, 128
"new theology," Fosdick championing, 21
newspapers, coverage of, 75, 99, 137
Noll, Mark, 8
non-Christian listener, letter to Fosdick by a, 38
nonconformity, of Fosdick, 19
nonsectarian approach, of radio preachers, 4, 139–40
Norris, Pipa, 6
North Americans, as spiritually starved, 57
nostalgic Christianity, songs tapping into, 14, 125

offerings, Fuller depended on, 135n90
"Oh Gods!" (Lester), 7n22
Old and New Testaments, as the written Word of God, 80
Old Fashioned Revival Hour
    advancing the old-time gospel with religious sentimentalism, 114
    broadcast by Fuller live each week in front of three to six thousand people, 14, 117n35, 136

Old Fashioned Revival Hour (continued)
  estimated number of listeners during peak years, 137
  format for, 119, 121
  helped maintain religion in American culture, 108
  mailing list of, 127
  music of, 14n44
  name of the program, 119–20
  opened with "Jesus Saves," 122
  promoted secularization of the American church, 132
  as simple, entertaining, and easily accessible, 122
  united disparate fundamentalists and various conservative Protestants, 120
  united disparate fundamentalists and various conservative Protestants throughout the nation, 121
  world-renowned host of radio's, 106
old Gospel, giving only, 119
old orthodoxy, McPherson's traditional religion accelerated trend away from, 56
Old Testament, containing shadows of things to come, 128
"The Old-Fashioned Meeting" song, 125
old-time religion
  Americans reaching out for, 62
  of Charles Fuller, 78, 108, 108n6
  Fosdick's disdain for, 28
  loved by listeners, 73–74
  McPherson's preaching promoted, 53
  music of, 122–26
  preaching of, 126–32
  radio reaffirming for McPherson, Maier, and Fuller, 40
  responding to, 132–37
  restoring to the church, 72
"Old-Time Religion" song, 125–26
oneness of God, Maier proclaimed, 88–89
open religion, 31
Ormiston, Kenneth Gladstone, 68

Orthodox Presbyterian Church in America, 17
orthodoxy, 20, 22–23, 36, 77–105

pacifism, of Fosdick, 33–36
parents, 20, 102
Parham, Charles F., 57
Park Avenue Baptist Church, WJZ broadcast the morning service of, 27
Saint Paul, calling Christ "God, blessed forever," 90
Payton, Grace, 110
peace, 35–36, 36n61
"Peace, Peace, When There Is No Peace" antiwar sermon by Fosdick, 36n61
Pentecostal revolution, in the holiness movement, 56
Pentecostalism
  as God's voice, 60
  of McPherson, 53, 75
  spread of helping explain McPherson's success, 57
  as too restrictive for McPherson, 60n62
personal ethical theories, Fosdick and Coughlin united by, 35
personal morality, Fosdick's sermons emphasizing, 29
personalities, of radio preachers as larger than life, 140
Pieper, Franz, 82
"pilgrim" status in this world, songs reminding listeners of their, 124
"The Pilgrim's Hour," 117, 117n37
Pittsburgh Calvary Episcopal Church, KDKA remote broadcast from in 1925, 2
Placentia Bible Class, Fuller advertised, 113
Placentia Presbyterian Church, 112, 112n20–13n20
"Plain Account of Christian Perfection" (Wesley), 61
political peace, "gospel" of, 35–36

INDEX   175

Pomona College, Charles Fuller graduated cum laude with a degree in chemistry, 110
popularity, 10, 140, 141
popularizer, McPherson as a great, 58
populist ethos, in American culture, 10
possibilities, potential of, 31
Postman, Neil, 141
postmillennialism, compared to dispensational premillennialism, 129
poverty, listeners giving from, 135
power
    of the gospel, 61
    of overcoming the world, 31
pragmatism, of the *Old Fashioned Revival Hour*, 121
prayers, on the *Lutheran Hour*, 94–95
preachers, gathered a massive radio audience, 11
preaching, 107, 126–32
"predatory economic imperialism," 35
preemptive action, against the old orthodoxy, 28
Presbyterian Church, in the 1920s, 17n5–18n5
Presbytery of Philadelphia, 18
press, radio evangelists and, 135, 137
profits, economic order motivated by, 35
progressive Christianity, producing a genuine piety, 23
Protestant orthodoxy, 12, 16n1, 82
Protestant religious radio, development of, 11–12
Protestantism, 21n21–22n21. *See also* American Protestantism; evangelical Protestantism
public office, honor and honesty in, 130
"Putting Religion into the Thick of Daily Life" (Fosdick), 32

Rader, Paul, 3, 110, 113
radio. *See also* religious radio
    for Fosdick, 21, 26, 28
    ideally suited for McPherson, 41–42, 63
    Maier's campaign for, 83
    as a platform for fame and notoriety, 43, 140
    unifying Christians, 42n3
Radio Act of 1927, 2
"The Radio Bible Class," 118n38
radio broadcasting
    of Maier advanced simple Protestant orthodoxy, 103
    McPherson's first encounter with, 65
    as a medium of religious communication, 1
    as a ministry tool, 63
"Radio Fantasy," of McPherson, 76
radio fund, establishment of Fuller's first, 117
radio industry, growth of, 2
radio licensing law, in 1912, 2
radio ministry
    of Fosdick contributed to secularization, 16
    Fuller's decision to pursue, 116
    mass appeal of Maier's, 103
    McPherson's first experience with, 64
radio preachers, 2, 3, 139
"radio rallies," conducted by Fuller, 137
"The Radio Revival Hour," 119
radio sound engineers, Maier's voice and, 103
radio stations
    KDKA, 2
    KFSG (Kall Foursquare Gospel), 42, 42n3, 63–75, 64n73, 74n98, 74n99
    KFUO, 85
    KGER, 117
    KREG, 116, 117
    Rockridge Radio Station of Oakland, 64–65
    WJZ, 27
radio technology, 115, 138
radio work, Fosdick never accepted compensation, 26
"raging of great events," for Fosdick, 19
Redeeming the Dial (Hangen), 42n3

religion
- faded most in affluent and secure nations, 6n18
- Fosdick transforming emphasis from God to man, 31–32
- Fosdick's negative experience of, 20–21
- framing in the language of commerce, 10
- Fuller adapting to radio, 108
- interrelationship with radio, 1
- reshaped by religious radio, 8

religious broadcasters, altered religion, 2
religious celebrity and democratization, movement toward, 9–10
religious culture, wide-open in Los Angeles, 55
religious demand, shaped by perceived security, 6n18
religious empire, founding of, 54–58
religious leaders, using radio to extend religious faith, 2
religious radio, 1–2, 4, 8, 139. *See also* radio
religious sentimentalism, 9, 109, 125
religious transformation, 8–10
religious-radio stars, McPherson as one, 12–13
repentance, from sins violating family happiness, 92
reshaped religion, as a form of secularization, 8
resistance movement, 3, 7, 8, 139
revival, as a "sign of the times," 60
revivalist evangelicalism, 59
revivalist themes, packaging Christianity, 70
revolt against Calvinist ethos, Fosdick's life as, 16n1
Rimpaw, Jim, 114
The Rise of Radio (Balk), 4n7
Rockridge Radio Station of Oakland, 64–65
Roosevelt, Franklin, closed all the banks, 118
Rosell, Garth, 107

Sacred and Secular (Norris and Inglehart), 6n18
sacrificial givers, to the *Old Fashioned Revival Hour*, 135–36
salvation, 30, 50, 123, 130
Salvation Army, McPherson and, 13, 44–45
salvation of souls, working and praying for, 131
Samson, stories of as Hebrew folklore, 22
Satan, 66, 129, 130, 131. *See also* devil
Saturday Evening Post, profile of Walter Maier and the *Lutheran Hour*, 100–101
Schricker, Henry F., 99
Schultze, Quentin, 10
Scripture, 87, 88, 108
"second blessing," of the Holy Spirit, 57
second coming of Christ, belief in as folly, 17
sectarianism, McPherson avoiding strict, 76
Secular Age (Taylor), 6n18
secularism, 39
secularization
- of the American church, 43
- of American culture, 1–2, 14–15
- explaining quality or content of belief, 8
- in a society when belief in God is an "embattled option," 6n18

secularization theory, 5–8
self-conscious exceptionalism, of McPherson, 44, 60, 75
Semple, Robert, 48, 48n25, 49, 50
sentimental evangelicalism, American religion and, 121
sentimentalism, move toward, 14
Seymour, William J., 57
"Shall the Fundamentalists Win?" sermon, 17, 18, 18n7
Sheldon, Frank, 20
shut-ins, welcoming the spoken word, 84
sickness, as Satan's work, 71
simple Christianity, Maier's reaffirmation of, 104

simple evangelism, Fuller transformed gospel into, 138
simple orthodoxy, of Maier, 77, 85, 91, 95, 140
simple songs
 creating a feeling about religion, 126
 not advancing doctrinal understanding, 124
"simple truths" of the Bible, preached by Fuller, 107
sin, old-time religion's emphasis on, 136
singing, the old-time religion, 122–26
Small Catechism, of Martin Luther, 91
social networking channels, tempting preachers to excel at self-promotion, 141
social significance, religion losing, 6
soldiers, *Old Fashioned Revival Hour* brought comfort to, 134
Son of the living God, Jesus Christ as, 90
songs, 73, 119, 123. *See also* music
speaking in tongues, 49, 57
Spence, Hartzell, 100–101, 102, 103
spiritual change, revival service sparked in Fuller, 110
spiritual contribution, Fosdick's desire to make, 24
spiritual warfare, Christians engaged in, 124
spotlight, Fuller reveling in, 136
Stark, Rodney, 7–8, 7n22
Straton, John Roach, 3, 17–18
studios, for KFSG located within Angelus Temple, 64
subjective emotion, displacing objective doctrine, 62
subjective religious experience, McPherson's emphasis on, 44
substitutionary death, belief in as unnecessary, 17
Sunday, William A. (Billy), 18n5, 102–3
Sunday School Times, editor of, 107
Sunshine Hour, on KFSG, 67
"superior type of living," as Christianity's' "central task," 29

superstar status, of McPherson, 75
support, McPherson using radio to rally, 68–69
Sutton, Matthew, 43, 47, 61
"Sweet By and By" song, 124

"The Tabernacle in the Wilderness," sermons on, 128
Tabernacle music, radio-tailored, 14n44, 122
Taft, President, 2
"technical religionists," 32
technology, 141, 141n3, 142n8
television, 140, 141
television ministry, Fosdick's radio ministry augmented by, 40
"temple," planned by McPherson to rival King Solomon's, 54
testimonials, flooded the *Lutheran Hour*, 96–98
theological content, Fuller eschewing substantive, 114
theological discourse, radio preachers eschewed, 140
theological foundation, of Fuller, 111
theological liberalism
 of Fosdick, 19, 22, 23
 popularized by Henry Ward Beecher, 8
 radio exposure facilitated the spread of, 8
 reasonable and practical piety of, 38
theological minimalism
 effect of leaving Christians more vulnerable, 132
 fostered by the *Old Fashioned Revival Hour*, 122
 McPherson's shift toward, 70
 promised an experience with God, 72
 promoted secularization of the American church, 126
 religious radio contributed to, 9
theological modernism, making Christianity less accessible, 62
theological substance, aversion to, 124
theologically liberal programs, Maier distancing himself from, 85

theology
    facets of McPherson's, 59
    hybrid pentecostal-fundamentalist, 43
    Lutheran, 79
    new championed by Fosdick, 21
    no longer viewed as a fixed body of eternally bound truths, 8
    Old Fashioned Revival Hour and American, 113–22
    Semple instructed in pentecostal, 48n25
"There's An Open Heaven Tonight" song, 123
Third World, upsurge of religious movements in, 7
This Is That (McPherson), 43
Time magazine, Maier as the "Chrysostom of American Lutheranism," 99
"A Time to Stress Unity" sermon, 27, 37
Times of the Gentiles, 131
Torrey, Reuben, 112, 113, 127
Towner, Daniel B., 113
"tried and true" gospel, 58
trinitarianism, Maier and, 88
Trumball, Charles, 121
Trumbull, Charles, 107, 113
truth, as an open field for Fosdick, 22
typology interpretation method, 127–28

"Under His Wings" (McPherson), 73
Understanding Media (McLuhan), 9
Union Theological Seminary, 25, 26
"The Use and Misuse of Religion," Fosdick's inaugural *National Vespers* sermon, 28–29

Van Etten, Jan, 2
Vatican, Coughlin's silencing by, 86n26
Victoria Hall Pentecostal Mission, 53
Victorious Life movement, Fuller influenced by, 113
video sharing services, tempting preachers to self-promotion, 141
virgin birth, belief in as unnecessary, 17
"virtual communities," radio and, 42n3
virtuous living, 30, 33
"The Vision of Ezekiel," 59–60
voice of her Lord, came to McPherson on her deathbed, 51
Voskuil, Dennis, 120

Wacker, Grant, 75
Walther, Carl F., 79
Walther League, 81
Walther League Messenger, 81, 83
Wanamaker, John, 18n5
war, 33–34, 36n61
Wells, David, 9
Wesley, John, 61
Wesleyan-Holiness tradition, McPherson's theological system and, 61
Westminster Confession of Faith, 18, 18n5
What the Bible Teaches (Torrey), 112
Whitefield, George, 10
"Who is Jesus?" as the question for Maier, 90
"whole gospel," Angelus Temple stood for, 62
Winrod, Gerald, 135, 136
wireless telegraph receiver, Fuller set up as a teenager, 114
Witham, Larry, 140n2
WJZ radio station, Fosdick preaching on, 27
world cliché culture, leaving no place for God, 9
world evangelism, Henry Fuller supporting, 109
world evangelization, Charles Fuller's longing for, 14
"world tours," of Henry Fuller, 109
World War I, Fosdick as a staunch supporter of, 33

Zionist movement, Charles Fuller's interest in, 113

www.ingramcontent.com/pod-product-compliance
Lightning Source LLC
Chambersburg PA
CBHW071231170426
43191CB00032B/1313